THINKING ABOUT HISTORY

HIS

THINKING ABOUT

TORY

SARAH MAZA

The

University of

Chicago Press

Chicago and London

The University of Chicago Press, Chicago 60637
The University of Chicago Press, Ltd., London

Published 2017

Printed in the United States of America

26 25 24 23 22 21 20 19   2 3 4 5

ISBN-13: 978-0-226-10916-9 (cloth)
ISBN-13: 978-0-226-10933-6 (paper)
ISBN-13: 978-0-226-10947-3 (e-book)
DOI: 10.7208/chicago/9780226109473.001.0001

Library of Congress Cataloging-in-Publication Data

Names: Maza, Sarah C., 1953– author.
Title: Thinking about history / Sarah Maza.
Description: Chicago : The University of Chicago Press, 2017. |
    Includes index.
Identifiers: LCCN 2016054305 | ISBN 9780226109169 (cloth : alk. paper) |
    ISBN 9780226109336 (pbk. : alk. paper) | ISBN 9780226109473 (e-book)
Subjects: LCSH: History. | History—Methodology. | Historiography.
Classification: LCC D16 .M417 2017 | DDC 900—dc23
LC record available at https://lccn.loc.gov/2016054305

♾ This paper meets the requirements of ANSI/NISO Z39.48-1992
(Permanence of Paper).

CONTENTS

INTRODUCTION

What historians do, while it may seem obvious, proves surprisingly hard to define once you start thinking about it. Most people would describe the discipline of history as "the study of the past." But "the past" is a huge category that includes the time since you started reading this sentence. What we mean by "the past" in this context is "past enough that we have some perspective on it," which in practice takes us back at least one or two generations. But most academic disciplines outside of the sciences concern "the past" in that sense. Most research in the humanities—in departments of literature, art history, and philosophy, for instance—concerns the human past. Many sociologists, anthropologists, and political scientists also work on material that goes back decades or even centuries. What is special, then, about history as a discipline?

While it does concern itself uniquely with the past, history as a field of study is unusual in its lack of overarching structure or definition—a trait that paradoxically accounts for its wide and enduring appeal beyond academia. Other fields in the humanities and social sciences are more tightly bound to canons or bodies of knowledge, to technical methods, or both. People who teach in literature departments are expected to have read a list of great works of fiction, drama, and poetry, even if over the decades some authors fade away while others settle in. Sociologists are required, among other things, to be conversant with major figures such as Karl Marx, Emile Durkheim, and Max Weber, philosophers with a core pantheon of authors stretching from Plato to John Rawls. Literary and art-historical studies have developed very specific methods for analyzing texts and deciphering images. Other fields require mathematical or quantitative expertise. These commonalities give other disciplines coherence, but they often have a problematic side-effect, the emergence of "insider-speak" and in some cases technical jargon. A history department, by contrast, might include a specialist in Tokugawa Japan, another working on the Ottoman Empire, and a third studying the Reagan presidency. They may never encounter any of the same books, since there exists no historical "canon," yet they need to evaluate the work of colleagues with other historical focuses and to present their own research to them. This is one reason why history written by academics is, compared to work in other fields, low in jargon and technicalities and more accessible to general readers. Ideally (though, alas, this is far from true in practice) anyone should be able to pick up any history book, even an academic one, and understand its contents without the benefit of prior training.

This is not to say that researching and writing history requires no specific skills; on the contrary, depending on one's period and place of concentration, the technical requirements can be steep. You may need to master a difficult language—Aramaic, say, or Mandarin—or in some cases more than one. Some subfields, such as medieval history, require advanced paleographic training just to read the documents; for others you need expertise in archaeology, macroeconomics, or linguistics. (And while it might seem easier to work on a recent period in your native language, specialists working on quasi-contemporary history will tell you that an infinite amount of potential source material can be its own kind of curse.) History does not have a governing technical "method" precisely because it can accommodate so many of them, from sifting through dirt to reading philosophy. But once the research is done, a historian is expected to put forward a narrative and argument that any well-educated person can understand. History, one is tempted to say, is written by specialists for nonspecialists, but even that is not entirely true: witness how often people with no disciplinary credentials produce superior works of history. In just the last fifteen years, the most prestigious history award in America, the Pulitzer Prize, has gone to an English professor (in 2002), to journalists (in 2003 and 2007), and to a banker (in 2010). Imagine, by way of contrast, the Nobel Prize in physics or economics being awarded to someone with no formal training in those fields!

Eclecticism is what makes the discipline of history so vibrant and broadly appealing: the skills required to do it are those both of the specialist and of the nonspecialist. To define cutting-edge questions, academic historians must immerse themselves in a large body of scholarship that defines topics and debates: planning a project on some aspect of American slavery, the British Empire, or the Vietnam War requires finding your way around a vast literature so that you can be sure of contributing something new and worthwhile. On the other hand, the research process itself is something most historians learn about on the fly, just by doing it: aside from technicalities such as language and paleography, "historical research" is mostly impossible to teach. It requires ingenuity (where do I start looking for evidence about same-sex relationships in the seventeenth century?); initiative to figure out how to begin, whom to talk to, where to go; and persistence to sift through many boxes of archival material or pages of online documents to find the elusive evidence one is tracking. How do you teach researchers to cope with the letdown of finding that the archive they've traveled to doesn't have what they want, and the imagination to turn the situation around by figuring out what the disappointing documents might actually contain that they had not anticipated? The skills and temperaments of good research historians are very similar to those of successful journalists: curiosity, ingenuity, patience, and doggedness. And like journalists, good historians know how to put a story together and make it understandable to a wide range of readers.

It is much easier, then, to define history by contrasting it with other disciplines than to describe a historical "method." People in fields like art history, literature, or philosophy usually work on an existing "object": they exercise interpretive skills on a set of texts or images that serves as a point of departure for their research—the novels of Toni Morrison, Romanesque murals in Catalan churches, the collected works of Hegel.[1] Historians begin with no such object; their task consists in creating, through research, the thing that they work on. Social scientists usually begin their projects with a research design and a hypothesis they will attempt to confirm or disprove using questionnaires, experiments, or calculations. Historians also start out with a question or a tentative thesis but typically have no direct access to their subjects; most often the chaotic evidence produced by historical research ends up reframing the initial question, which is never answered with any degree of certainty.

The work of historians, then, is less theory-driven than that of just about anyone else in the academy, but that does not mean that theory is not there. As William H. Sewell has argued, historians' distinctive contribution to the

1. For the point about existing versus constructed objects, see Gabrielle Spiegel, "History, Historicism and the Social Logic of the Text in the Middle Ages," *Speculum* 65 (January 1990): 75. Scholars in literary and art-historical fields have extended their purview beyond traditional works of art and literature to a wide range of "texts" and the infinite corpus of "visual culture"; I would argue, however, that their disciplinary habits endure even as the objects change.

social sciences is their analysis of how human action unfolds over time.[2] The work of any given historian is deeply rooted in the specifics of a certain time and place, incommensurable with any other: in that sense, historians are the ultimate empiricists. But historians, Sewell argues, also reconstruct sequences of "events" and their consequences, tracing complicated patterns of causality and attending to a complex of contextual factors that render the outcome of any given situation contingent. This practice of detailed description, attentive to the interplay between event and context, evinces a theory of "social temporality" that governs historians' work. Historical temporality, Sewell writes, "is lumpy, uneven, unpredictable, discontinuous," speeded up by events like wars and revolutions.[3]

Historians, that is, operate according to distinct theories of temporality and causality, even if those are most often left implicit. Theory is rarely foregrounded in historical work, in part because of the discipline's strong empirical bent, and in part because of a traditional commitment to narrative and to an ideal of evocative writing. Most historians would probably agree that their task is ideally twofold: to explain the unfolding of change in the past, and to make the people and places of the time come alive for their readers. To be a great historian you need not just the skills of a journalist but those of a novelist. (Many people are drawn to study a specific period in history not because of an intellectual problem or a political agenda but because novels or movies about it set their imagination on fire.) In some languages the words for "history" and "story" are the same, as if chroniclers of the past have always been their society's best spinners of tales.

History is not only the ultimate hybrid field, borrowing its languages and methods from both the social sciences and the humanities; it is also the discipline that most frequently crosses over from the academic world into the public sphere. Works of popularized psychology, sociology, or economics sometimes pop up on the best-seller lists, but history books camp out there continuously. Therein lies another distinctive feature of history, its conspicuousness in public life—in school curricula from the earliest grades; in museums and war memorials, heritage sites and theme parks; as a constant reference point in the speeches of politicians. Unlike sociology, history has its own television channel, unlike economics, its own book club. It

2. William H. Sewell Jr., *Logics of History: Social Theory and Social Transformation* (Chicago: University of Chicago Press, 2005), 1–21.
3. Ibid., 9.

is precisely because history looms so large in public life that controversies about the content and nature of historical inquiry flare up so frequently both inside and outside of academia.

Disputes over heritage sites and museums are described in chapter 4, but the quintessential fights over history concern school curricula: what should children learn about their country's past, and how should they learn it? In the United States the biggest dustup of this sort occurred in the early 1990s in the context of efforts to establish national standards for primary and secondary education. The 1994 National History Standards were drafted by a committee of academics, schoolteachers, and administrators, incorporating new scholarship on the history of women and minorities and recommending that courses in global history replace the traditional "Western civilization" survey.[4] Even before the document was published, Lynne Cheney, the conservative former director of the National Endowment for the Humanities (who, ironically, had been involved in setting up the original drafting council), delivered a strident attack on it in the *Wall Street Journal* entitled "The End of History." She charged that the proposed curriculum foregrounded historical actors like the escaped slave Harriet Tubman at the expense of more important figures like George Washington, Ulysses S. Grant, and Alexander Graham Bell, and that it offered a "grim and gloomy" portrayal of American history focused on such subjects as the Ku Klux Klan and McCarthyism. Letters to the *Journal* chimed in, accusing drafters of using the National History Standards as a ploy to "indoctrinate" children with liberal "hatred of America" and to advance the multicultural "balkanization" of the nation.[5] The ruckus broke out at a charged moment of political transition: a Democrat, Bill Clinton, had taken office in 1993, and the right fretted that liberals would now have free rein to pursue this supposed agenda.

Similar "history wars" over curricula in schools have broken out in Britain and Australia, and other countries—Russia, South Africa, France—have faced the complex process of balancing patriotic pride with accounting for the darker aspects of their past.[6] While English departments were also

4. Gary B. Nash, Charlotte Crabtree, and Ross E. Dunn, *History on Trial: Culture Wars and the Teaching of the Past*, 2nd ed. (New York: Vintage, 2000), chapters 1, 7–10.

5. Ibid., 1–6, 189.

6. Ibid., chapter 6; Steven L. Kaplan, *Farewell Revolution: Disputed Legacies, France 1789/1989* (Ithaca, NY: Cornell University Press, 1995); Stuart Macintyre

rocked in the 1990s by "culture wars" over who should be included in the literary canon (or whether there should be a canon at all), history is the discipline most regularly embroiled in public controversy.[7] The reason for this is evident. Historians construct narratives that provide social groups—national, regional, ethnic, and other—with a collective identity, in the same way that we construct our personal identity by telling ourselves the story of our life. We can, of course, gain a new sense of ourselves by achieving a new perspective that transforms the narrative: many forms of psychotherapy aim at helping patients do just that. Changing the story of a collective entity such as a nation can be liberating, but is almost inevitably fraught and usually meets with enormous resistance.

"History" changes all the time because it is driven by the concerns of the present—it is often described as "what the present needs to know about the past." In archaic and hierarchical societies, the "useful" past is that of monarchs, military leaders, and great dynasties; in a democracy, citizens want to hear about the history of "the people." Since the end of the eighteenth century, in the West and elsewhere, the story that elites wanted to tell, and people wanted to hear, was that of their nation's unique destiny. Groups of people who felt excluded from the nationalist script—workers, women, ethnic and racial minorities—later felt the need for research that captured experiences at odds with the master narrative. In recent years, as our experience of globalization has led us to realize how interconnected the planet's people are and have been in the past, global histories are beginning to edge out national narratives. At the same time, historians are nothing if not respectful of the past, and the discipline is more eclectic and less trend-sensitive than most others, especially since many substantive, research-intensive books can take ten or fifteen years to research and write. Such traditional genres as military history and biography, buoyed by the reading public's appetite, continue to flourish alongside relative newcomers like global and environmental history. While the discipline usually identifies a "cutting edge"—cultural approaches yesterday, global and transnational

---

and Anna Clark, *The History Wars* (Carlton, Australia: Melbourne University Press, 2003).

7. For an excellent discussion of the historical context for the "canon wars" and "history wars," see Daniel T. Rodgers, *Age of Fracture* (Cambridge, MA: Harvard University Press, 2011), especially chapter 6.

ones today—much of the best work proceeds by way of layering and combining topics and methods.

Thinking About History evokes the capaciousness and diversity of history but also highlights the inherent tensions and regular controversies that shape the discipline. Each chapter is structured around a central question, to which it brings elements for discussion but no definitive answer. The first half of the book considers ways in which history has changed in recent decades as historians have turned to new actors, new spaces, and new objects. Whose history do we write, and how does writing about different people affect what stories get told and how they are told (chapter 1)? How did people come to think of the nation as the inevitable context for history, and what happens when we think of history outside of national spaces, as stories that happen before, between, and beyond those arbitrary national entities (chapter 2)? And what has happened to various subfields of history since a traditional hierarchy of historical topics—knowledge at the top, nature and things at the bottom—has been shaken up by new approaches (chapter 3)?

The second half of the book revolves around three ways in which the historical enterprise gives rise to internal or external controversy—the discipline's productive tensions. "How Is History Produced?" asks about the differences and overlaps between academic, public, and popular history and the elusive and sometimes problematic nature of historians' sources (chapter 4). "Causes or Meanings?" follows another fault line, this one within historical analysis, between description and what can be loosely termed interpretation. Finally, "Facts or Fictions?" concerns perennially tricky questions about objectivity and invention in historical research, via the storm over postmodernism that shook the profession in the 1990s. While that crisis has abated, it has, I suggest here, shaped our thinking about historians' practices in enduring ways.

This book is about how we think about history, not why we should study it. Many attempts to explain the importance of reading and writing history drift into platitudes of the "those who don't study the past are condemned to repeat it" variety. History doesn't teach lessons, and trying to fit a scenario from the past onto one in the present can be disastrous: "We will liberate Iraq, as we did Europe!" "Don't go for a diplomatic solution—remember Munich!" On the other hand, most people agree that attempts to ignore, distort, or erase the past can have catastrophic effects for societies.

There are lots of reasons for learning about history—political passion, the quest for identity, intellectual curiosity, a taste for the exotic—and most people are drawn to the study of the past for a combination of reasons. As Peter Mandler has argued, history's ethical value does not reside in neatly packaged "lessons" from the past but in the mind-expanding experience of sorting out complex questions within settings very different from our own.[8] The aim of this book is not to justify to readers the importance of history for themselves and their communities. Rather, taking for granted the importance of studying the past, its aim is to describe the ways in which innovations and controversies have shaped this field of inquiry in the last few decades.

In the chapters that follow, I have done my best to describe evenhandedly the questions and controversies that shaped the writing of history in the recent past. But as the book makes clear, especially in the final chapter, the vast majority of historians working today reject the view that any scholar can be truly "objective," and the point applies to this author as much as any other. While I draw on a wide variety of examples, the fact that I work on social and cultural, rather than military or political, history has surely influenced my choice of questions and books. My perspective is even more profoundly shaped by my specialization in French (and more broadly European and Western) history: most of the examples I offer and the authors I discuss are drawn from the fields of European and United States history. To a large extent, this was inevitable: whether or not we like it, the questions and concepts that have shaken up the discipline of history in the last half century—labor and social history, agency and resistance, gender, cultural analysis, material culture, and social practices, to name but a few—were initially formulated by historians of Europe and the United States. Although there have been significant changes in recent years, the conspicuousness of Euro-American history in the following pages reflects in part the much larger story of several centuries of Western dominance over the rest of the world, which has shaped global intellectual life as well as much else. But invoking world historical patterns does not, in the end, get me off the hook: while I have tried to correct for my limitations by getting help from colleagues in African and Asian history, I have surely not escaped the blinders of my training and field. A volume on this subject written by a

8. Peter Mandler, *History and National Life* (London: Profile Books, 2002), 145–47.

historian of Africa, Asia, Australia, or Latin America would likely be quite different.

If this book has a thesis, it is the one implicit in its design. Its chapters are organized around six questions with no set answers, describing decades' worth of conversations and controversies. *Thinking About History* offers, not answers or prescriptions, but an invitation to continue the conversation. We need our collective pasts for all the familiar reasons: to gain wisdom and inspiration from the successes and failures of our forebears, to find out who we were and are, to nourish our imaginations. But the past would surely die if we merely memorialized it, if we did not argue about it. Based on the premise that much of the excitement about history comes from the controversies, substantive and methodological, that it ignites, this book is intended as a contribution to the urgent task of keeping those arguments alive.

THE HISTORY OF WHOM?

I

"GREAT MEN" AND A FEW WOMEN

Who are the actors of history? Until a few generations ago, the answer seemed self-evident. The "makers of history" were men with the power to affect the course of events in the world around them. The rulers, military commanders, and other leaders of past societies mattered more than anyone else because they made the decisions that shaped the experience of thousands or millions of their contemporaries. When individuals hold that sort of sway, their lives can seem indistinguishable from the history of their times. People write and read the stories of Alexander the Great, Napoleon Bonaparte, Abraham Lincoln, Adolf Hitler, or Mao Zedong as organizing principles for the history of their times.

Widespread interest in the history of "great men" (and sometimes women) is very much alive today: best-seller lists in the United States nearly always include biographies of American Founding Fathers and presidents, or of admired or controversial figures like Winston Churchill or Marie-Antoinette. The success of this type of historical writing is due to the very genre of biography. To the general reader, history books can sometimes seem abstract or confusingly detailed. Connecting the events of a period to the life of a prominent individual gives both shape and color to the past. Readers who might otherwise be intimidated by the history of the Russian Revolution are drawn in by the dramatic destiny of the last tsar, Nicholas II, brutally executed in a basement room along with his wife and five children by the Bolshevik authorities.[1] Historical biography thrives not just because it makes for great reading, but because the actions and personalities

---

1. Robert K. Massie, *Nicholas and Alexandra: An Intimate Account of the Last of the Romanovs and the Fall of Imperial Russia* (New York: Atheneum, 1967), was a best-seller for several years after its publication and was adapted as a movie in 1971.

of some individuals did have a defining impact on their contemporaries. This is especially true for all-powerful rulers in political systems characterized by a porous boundary between private and public life: who would deny the impact on English history of Henry VIII's erotic and dynastic obsessions? Henry's decision to divorce Catherine of Aragon and marry Ann Boleyn, thereby precipitating the English Church's break from Rome and unleashing generations of confessional violence, is a classic instance of a deliberate choice by a single individual that unquestionably shaped the religious, social, political, and diplomatic life of his contemporaries and of later generations.

The oldest histories, in most world cultures, center on political and military leadership. In the West, from classical antiquity to the comparatively recent past, the "who" that mattered most to historians was a nation's leader, and the most important activity of that leader was the waging of war: classic political history has overlapped considerably with military and diplomatic history. From Herodotus to last week's crop of books about Abraham Lincoln, the extraordinary leader enjoys a loyal following of scholars and readers for whom his deeds offer history's most thrilling episodes. Implicit in the "great man" genre (which includes a sprinkling of "great women" like Cleopatra, Elizabeth I, and Indira Gandhi) is often the view that the actions of a single individual can shape an era, and the corollary that without them events would have unfolded in a completely different manner.

It is of course possible to take the view that "great men" are mostly the products of circumstance. In the late 1790s the French had just lived through a revolution that left the country bitterly divided and the political class mostly discredited and ineffective. The only thing going well for France was a European war in which a mass of fervently patriotic citizen-soldiers regularly routed their opponents. Generals enjoyed far more prestige than politicians, and the latter came to rely on the former for political support. Under these circumstances, was it not extremely likely that someone *like* Napoleon Bonaparte would seize control of the nation, even had it been a military leader less brilliant and charismatic than the diminutive Corsican officer? Was it a stroke of extraordinary good luck that Nelson Mandela, a shrewd, widely revered, and generous leader, was at hand to oversee South Africa's transition out of apartheid in the early 1990s, or was the historical moment just right for such a figure to emerge? "Personality or circumstance?" is a traditional topic for classroom debate, an ultimately unanswerable question that is good for getting students to line up social and political conditions on one side and personal traits on the other, and to think about the connections between them.

While most people would acknowledge that circumstances play at least some role in the emergence of remarkable figures, many of us are still beholden to an idea of individual "genius" inherited from eighteenth- and nineteenth-century Western culture.[2] Even the most committed social determinists are easily mesmerized by individuals as obviously exceptional as Martin Luther, Mohandas Gandhi, or, in a different register, Adolf Hitler. As the example of Luther suggests, the "great man" approach to the past has not been limited solely to rulers and political leaders. While political and military matters are the oldest subjects of historical writing (think of the book of Kings in the Old Testament, or Homer's stories of the Trojan War), the history of ideas, broadly defined, runs a close second. Here too, major historical changes in the way we think and believe are commonly chalked up to the genius of individuals like Confucius, Copernicus, Karl Marx, or Simone de Beauvoir. Elements of change may have been in the air, but it took that exceptional individual—the Adam Smith, Harriet Beecher Stowe, or Steve Jobs—to formulate the "idea that changed the world." Intellectual "geniuses" have been the objects of traditional history for the same reason as political and military leaders: the assumption that the most interesting or most significant lives in our past are those of exceptionally gifted and influential people.

Asking "whose history?" amounts to pondering what sphere of human activity matters. For a very long time the answer to that question seemed obvious: the history that counted was about politics, and "politics" was defined as the exercise of, or struggles over, public power. In the West until the eighteenth century, the only conceivable political history was that of legitimate dynasties, princes, monarchs, and established ruling families like the Medici in Florence. The family trees of rulers might get trimmed, pruned, staked, or even cloned by struggles between family branches or the claims of upstart pretenders, but roughly the same horticultural entity remained in place. In the late 1700s the American and French Revolutions inaugurated a tree-chopping tradition that expanded the canon of "great national leaders" to include individuals who fundamentally challenged and sometimes

2. Darrin McMahon, *Divine Fury: A History of Genius* (New York: Basic Books, 2013).

destroyed established political systems. Political histories thereafter included oppositional or revolutionary heroes like Robespierre, Ho Chi Minh, and Martin Luther King, whose leadership credentials frequently offer some combination of political, intellectual, and spiritual dimensions.

No ruler or leader exercises power in a social vacuum, and in much of traditional "top-down" history they share the limelight with a "ruling" or "political" class. The biographical enthusiasm of historians has always extended to powerful individuals like ministers, royal advisers, and leading military commanders in absolute monarchies, prime ministers and influential politicians in mixed systems like the British one, and a larger cast of characters in democracies. Even dictators have close collaborators whose actions are grist for many narrative mills. Leaders and their associates always operate within a larger group of elite political actors making up a royal or princely court, a presidential cabinet, or some form of representative assembly. Historians have for centuries chronicled the activities of men and women in those settings.

Until about half a century ago most professional historians believed that the history of leaders, political elites, and state-related activity was the one that mattered most, and indeed many people both inside and outside of academia are still of that opinion. Implicit in the traditional prioritizing of political history are a set of assumptions, all of which have been seriously challenged, if not necessarily overturned, over the last few decades: that the state and government are the most important arenas of human activity, that political leaders more than anyone drive historical change, and that "politics" is an activity that happens in the public sphere. Some champions of political history would go even further. The outspokenly conservative historian Gertrude Himmelfarb has argued, following Aristotle, that political history should matter above all else because the state is where humans pursue their highest form of rationality, "reflected in the rational ordering and organization of society by means of laws, constitutions, and political institutions." She approvingly cites Aristotle's view that politics, which ultimately distinguishes humans from animals, is an activity that takes place in "the higher sphere of the *polis* where men achieve the purest expressions of reason in pursuit of the common good and 'the good life.'"[3]

---

3. Gertrude Himmelfarb, *The New History and the Old: Critical Essays and Reappraisals*, 2nd ed. (Cambridge, MA: Harvard University Press, 2004), 39, 43.

SOCIAL HISTORY AND QUANTIFICATION

The discipline of history does not evolve through the abrupt and complete replacement of one type of history by another. Political history, with its emphasis on government and leadership, is alive and well today, and conversely, social history has appeared at various points in the past, most notably in the nineteenth century. In France from the 1820s on, historians inspired by the Revolution, like Adolphe Thiers and Jules Michelet, wrote histories in which groups like "the bourgeoisie" or "the people" were the main movers in an epic struggle against a selfish aristocracy, which led to the nation's revolutionary birth in 1789. Leading English historians wrote "social history" long before the 1960s: Thomas Babington Macaulay's 1848 *History of England from the Accession of James the Second*, a landmark chronicle of the nation's progress through political emancipation, includes a section on England in 1685 that covers everything from social classes to coffeehouses, street lighting, and newspapers.[4] Nearly a century later, in the midst of World War II, Macaulay's great-nephew, the Cambridge historian George Macaulay Trevelyan, wrote a highly successful volume entitled *English Social History*. First published in 1942, Trevelyan's book is a six-hundred-page account of social conditions in England from the Middle Ages to 1901, which like Macaulay's covers a breadth of topics, from trade routes and population trends to marriage customs and diets. Leafing through Trevelyan you may come across stories of young girls in the age of Chaucer being beaten into accepting unattractive marriage partners, reports on upper-class drinking and smoking habits in the late seventeenth century, or a vividly imagined account of what life felt like (extremely damp, among other things) in a peasant home around 1750.[5]

The type of social history written by Macaulay and Trevelyan, which has equivalents in other national traditions, was clearly subordinate and accessory to political history.[6] In Macaulay's *History of England* the lengthy

4. Thomas Babington Macaulay, *The History of England from the Accession of James the Second*, 3rd ed. (London: Longman, 1849–1861), vol. 1, chapter 3.

5. G. M. Trevelyan, *English Social History: A Survey of Six Centuries from Chaucer to Queen Victoria* (London: Longmans, Green and Co., 1946), 64–65, 314–15, 430.

6. Since the 1940s the Hachette publishing house in France has produced more than four hundred titles in the highly popular series "La Vie quotidienne," dealing with daily life in past times all over the world.

opening section on "the state of England in 1685" serves as a scenic back-drop to the significant action taking place center-stage, the political ma-neuverings of James II, William of Orange, and their associates. Trevelyan wrote his *English Social History* as a late-career outtake from his previous works of political history; it was intended to boost wartime morale in the country at large as a sort of Shakespearean paean to the land of thatched cot-tages and "stout yeomen." The volume aptly illustrates Trevelyan's much-quoted, controversial, and pithy description of social history as "the his-tory of a people with the politics left out."[7] The older "customs and living conditions" tradition of social history epitomized by Trevelyan's book is indeed notable for the assumption that "politics" is purposeful activity that happens only in the highest realm and is therefore absent from society at large. The poor and middling are presumed not to affect historical change; as a result, a book like *English Social History* reads like a series of pictur-esque descriptions rather than an argument or a story.

Ordinary people, then, have never been completely ignored by historians; before the mid-twentieth century, however, they were rarely regarded as significant actors of history.[8] When they were effective as a crowd—at the Boston Tea Party, the siege of the Bastille, or the storming of the Win-ter Palace—historians celebrated them for advancing the purpose of their forward-looking superiors, while never acknowledging them individually by name.

In the 1960s all of this began to change as "normal" (political, diplo-matic, military) history became part of a binary that academic historians re-ferred to early on as "history from above" versus "history from below," or "top-down" versus "bottom-up." Suddenly, it seemed, everyone wanted to write history from the point of view of the masses rather than the elites. The destabilizing creativity of the new historical shift in perspective is perhaps

7. Trevelyan's biographer David Cannadine argues that the famous phrase has been taken out of context and that Trevelyan adopted it only reluctantly as a de-scription of a book project designed precisely to complement his writings about politics. Cannadine, *G. M. Trevelyan: A Life in History* (London: HarperCollins 1992), 224.

8. A small number of American historians produced works on African-American, Native American, and working-class history as early as the interwar decades: see Ellen Fitzpatrick, *History's Memory: Writing America's Past, 1880–1980* (Cambridge, MA: Harvard University Press, 2002).

best illustrated by the book that in 1976 marked the advent of something called the new military history, *The Face of Battle* by John Keegan. The experience of the common foot soldier had not been absent from previous military history, but Keegan's book was the first notable work to make it the central subject of investigation and thereby to upend our views of how battles are fought, won, and lost.

In *The Face of Battle*, Keegan took issue with the dominant assumption among military historians that success or failure in warfare depends on leadership, command, and discipline. Combat, he points out, "is as complicated and multiform as any other sort of human activity, and given the stakes at issue more so than most."[9] Even courageously idealistic soldiers do not necessarily want the same outcome as do their commanders, and the most commonly cited motivations for combatants to advance in the face of great danger—training, coercion, solidarity with their brethren—often evaporate in the presence of actual danger. Battles, Keegan insists, are won and lost by armies rather than commanders, and the most significant task for a military historian is therefore to understand what battles felt like at "ground level," what circumstances might cause soldiers to stand their ground or to break rank and run.

In a brilliant reconstruction of the battle of Waterloo, which Napoleon's army lost to the Duke of Wellington's on June 18, 1815, Keegan first recreates the physical state and experiences of soldiers on both sides. Exhausted from extensive marching the previous day, sleep-deprived due to overnight damp and cold, and poorly fed, the combatants' senses were assaulted on the battlefield by the fog of smoke from black-powder weapons and the rattle of bullets on swords that sounded "like a stick being drawn across park railings."[10] Reactions of sheer terror are hardly surprising under such conditions. When the French Imperial Guard found themselves suddenly facing a British brigade that rose out of the fog at speaking distance, their column fell apart and retreated, even though they outnumbered their enemies. At Waterloo, British soldiers stood their ground much better than their opponents, owing, Keegan speculates, not to superior command but, on the one hand, to a combination of exhaustion and alcohol and, on the other, to square formations that made them feel protected by their comrades (though

9. John Keegan, *The Face of Battle: A Study of Agincourt, Waterloo, and the Somme* (New York: Vintage, 1977), 53.
10. Ibid., 134–43, quote p. 141.

in actuality such large formations were prime targets for artillery shelling).[11] Keegan's work offers a vivid example of the insights that can be gained by shifting perspectives from the officers in tents and on horses to the men groping through black smoke. His work strikingly evokes the effect that ordinary people can have—albeit in this case involuntarily—on "great events."

By the 1970s the subfield of "social history" was sweeping the historical profession in the United States (the expressions "history from below" and "bottom-up" fell out of favor for sounding judgmental or mildly salacious). In 1948 virtually no dissertations in social history had been filed in American Universities; by 1978 the proportion was one-quarter and growing. In the late 1950s the number of courses in social history offered each year at places like Harvard, Yale, Michigan, and Wisconsin ranged from zero to two; twenty years later those same institutions listed thirteen to seventeen each.[12]

Even in its heyday as the cutting edge of the discipline, however, there was little consensus as to what "social history" was or how to do it. One early popular view held that social history is the history of the social structure and that the best way to capture "society" is through the systematic gathering of the largest possible amount of comparable data about human beings in the past. History, in other words, should be approached as a social science. If one takes it for granted that numbers don't lie, and that the bigger the sample the more it can be trusted, then the most solid truths about history must be found in large numbers. The upshot of this reasoning was the advent, and prominence for a time in the 1960s and 1970s, of what was known as quantitative history.

Quantification, still practiced by many historians, was initially a way of establishing the "scientific" credentials of social history. Collecting and comparing vast amounts of data and tracking variations over time provides unarguable evidence in a way that literary or descriptive evidence, of the sort Trevelyan used, does not. A notable feature of quantitative history is that its most reliable sources cluster in predictable areas. Authorities of various sorts in centuries past have kept track over time of economic activity, such as prices and yields, and recorded the major milestones in people's lives, such

11. Ibid., 167–84.

12. Robert Darnton, "Intellectual and Cultural History," in Michael Kammen, ed., *The Past before Us: Contemporary Historical Writing in the United States* (Ithaca, NY: Cornell University Press, 1980), 336, 350–51.

as birth, marriage, and death. Governments started centuries ago drawing up censuses that allowed for more effective taxation, and modern democracies have usually kept track of the residence patterns and political choices of voters. Quantification, in short, works best for broad historical questions about population, the economy, and mass politics.

Sustained use of quantification in historical research prevails to this day in the field of economic history, long dominated by an approach known as cliometrics, "the application of economic theory and quantitative techniques to the study of history."[13] Economic history was initially almost as narrative as other subfields, consisting in descriptions of such matters as farming techniques, livestock, and trade routes. In the 1950s and 1960s a coterie of younger American scholars trained in economics departments began to posit that quantitative evidence about the material bases of life could be extracted from a wide array of historical sources reaching back as far as the Middle Ages, and subjected to analyses similar those carried out by mainstream economists for recent data: the field as it exists today was shaped by economists with an interest in history rather than vice versa.[14] Since the 1960s the "new economic history" has flourished, occasionally amid controversy, most notoriously around a 1974 book, *Time on the Cross*, which purported to demonstrate that American slavery was an effective and relatively benign system of production.[15] Since the heyday of cliometrics the field of economic history has greatly diversified to include work that covers everything from ideas and technologies to families and banks.[16] Not only does economic history remain more centrally committed to the use of quantitative methods than any other kind of history, there are signs that

13. "Cliometrics," in Joel Mokyr, ed., *The Oxford Encyclopedia of Economic History*, 5 vols. (Oxford: Oxford University Press, 2003), 1:446–47.

14. For an early description of the birth of the field, see D. N. McCloskey, "Does the Past Have Useful Economics?" *Journal of Economic Literature* 14 (June 1976): 434–61. More recently, see J. W. Drukker, *The Revolution That Bit Its Own Tail: How Economic History Changed Our Ideas on Economic Growth* (Amsterdam: Aksant, 2006), and in a more polemical mode, Francesco Boldizzoni, *The Poverty of Clio: Resurrecting Economic History* (Princeton, NJ: Princeton University Press, 2011).

15. Robert Fogel and Stanley Engerman, *Time on the Cross: The Economics of American Negro Slavery* (Boston: Little Brown, 1974).

16. A good description of the field's current capaciousness is Joel Mokyr's preface to the *Oxford Encyclopedia of Economic History*, 1:xxi–xxvii.

numbers will loom even larger in the near future. As more and more records of population, military enlistment, marriage, death, and the like become available, and the technology to link individuals across databases
grows more accessible, it will become ever easier, as Ran Abramitzky puts
it, "to convert large-scale qualitative information into quantitative data."[17]
While the computing revolution of recent decades has shored up the
status of economic history within economics departments, other historians still mostly shy away from making numbers the central focus of their
arguments.

In the mainstream of the field, enthusiasm for quantitative methods was
at its height among groups of practitioners of history in Europe and America between the end of the 1950s and the early 1970s. For historians in the
West, gathering and sorting huge amounts of data about anonymous lives
in the past dovetailed perfectly with Cold War–era commitments to both
science and democracy (see chapters 4 and 6). From 1961 to 1978 the percentage of pages containing numerical tables in leading history journals in
the United States increased fivefold, while large numbers of graduate students and younger professors signed up for summer programs at leading
institutions to learn the finer points of statistics.[18]

Quantitative history in its heyday asked big questions, which it answered
with big numbers. A distinguished example of the genre in United States
history is Stephan Thernstrom's 1973 *The Other Bostonians* (the title meant
"other than the Brahmin elite"), a study of social mobility in Boston from the
1880s through the 1960s based on a computer-assisted analysis (a novelty
at the time) of large amounts of data drawn from census manuscripts, marriage records, birth certificates, and the Boston City Directory. By tracking
samples of individual men over time, comparing their occupations to their
fathers', and following changes in residence from one neighborhood to another, Thernstrom was able to arrive at well-documented, plausible conclusions. He showed that patterns of mobility from manual to nonmanual work
occurred at roughly the same rate throughout this period, though changes
in status were typically limited in scope (the son of a factory worker was far

17. Ran Abramitzky, "Economics and the Modern Economic Historian," *Journal of Economic History* 74 (December 2015): 1248.

18. J. Morgan Kousser, "Quantitative Social-Scientific History," in Kammen,
The Past before Us, 437–39, 449–50.

more likely to become a clerk than a doctor); that some groups (Russian Jews) moved up in society faster than others (Italians); and that mobility for black Bostonians was practically nil.[19] *The Other Bostonians*, along with the work of other scholars in a similar vein, offers solid evidence in answer to the question, Was America in the last two centuries really a land of opportunity, and if so for whom?

To many professional historians in the 1960s and 1970s, work like Thernstrom's represented the quintessence of "social history." If by social history we mean "the history of society," then asking and answering questions about social mobility clearly should be central to that subfield's agenda. Quantitative sources encompass the largest possible number of individuals and, despite endless debates over methodologies, often yield persuasively solid information. Two related problems, however, have dogged quantified history since its beginnings: on the one hand, it reduces human beings to one-dimensional aggregates, and on the other, it rarely makes for exciting reading. Thernstrom, a master of the genre, is a clear thinker and elegant writer, but it still takes fortitude to make it through a whole book made up mostly of passages like "Half or more of the men from middle-class families who entered blue-collar jobs—63, 51, and 50 percent respectively—were manual workers only temporarily; they later returned to their class of origin. By comparison, only half to a third as many youths of blue-collar origins and blue-collar first jobs later climbed to a non-manual position."[20]

Numbers do have stories to tell, sometimes gripping or disturbing ones. A recent atlas of the transatlantic slave trade, for instance, offers a succession of arresting maps such as one showing the aggregate number of slaves carried off from West Africa between 1642 and 1807: the fat red arrows representing the 3.2 million black captives transported on British ships to the Caribbean and the 3 million on Portuguese vessels to Brazil can make your stomach tighten even if you are told nothing about a single person.[21]

19. Stephan Thernstrom, *The Other Bostonians: Poverty and Progress in the American Metropolis, 1880–1970* (Cambridge, MA: Harvard University Press, 1973).

20. Ibid., 95–96.

21. David Eltis and David Richardson, eds. *Atlas of the Transatlantic Slave Trade* (New Haven, CT: Yale University Press, 2010), 26. Even the most "objective" seeming quantitative evidence can provide gist for debate: see the somewhat critical review of Eltis and Richardson's *Atlas* by Stephanie Smallwood in *The William and Mary Quarterly* 58 (January 2011): 253–61.

Even at the height of its prestige, however, quantitative history left many professional historians unsatisfied, and not only methodological conservatives like the eminent Carl Bridenbaugh, who thundered in his 1962 Presidential Address to the American Historical Association that "the finest historians will not be those who worship at the shrine of the Bitch-goddess QUANTIFICATION."[22]

Statistical methods allow the historian to make claims about the largest groups of people available in the sources and to address questions of change convincingly by tracking a database over time: one can trace, fairly conclusively depending on the source, rises and declines in the price of wheat, patterns of infant mortality, or social mobility for Irish workers in Boston. But numbers do not tell you if a peasant family accepted famine as an ordeal sent by God, whether they were grief-stricken by another young child's death or inured to it because they had already lost three babies to the plague, or whether America turned out better or worse than what Joseph O'Shea had imagined back in County Clare.

As Stephanie Smallwood has argued, historians' traditional emphasis on the sheer numbers of slaves who died during the Middle Passage places them uncomfortably close to the accounting of slavers; it obscures the actual meaning of individual deaths to the slaves who remained on board, tormented by the knowledge that a soul was trapped on the ship, unable to join its ancestors.[23] Counting can describe from the outside the experience of large groups, but it can't explain what leaving one's homeland, getting married, or being transported on a slave ship meant to individuals. And this, in turn, is symptomatic of a larger problem: not only are the individuals in quantitative histories anonymous, they are also inert. Numbers provide the shocking fact that millions of slaves "were transported," in the passive voice, across the Atlantic. But what of those captives who engaged in doomed rebellions against slave traders? Quantification can show you what happened to the majorities in "society," but not what individual social actors did and what those actions meant to them. It remains a powerful means of analyzing many different kinds of data from the past, allowing for convincing claims about changes in everything from reading tastes to

22. Carl Bridenbaugh, "The Great Mutation," *American Historical Review* 68, no. 2 (January1963): 326.

23. Stephanie Smallwood, *Saltwater Slavery: A Middle Passage from Africa to American Diaspora* (Cambridge, MA: Harvard University Press, 2007), chapter 5.

the world climate. Many historians continue to resort to quantitative analysis as one of many items in their tool kit. It is much rarer nowadays, however, to encounter a historical work based primarily on numbers: most of the time these are combined with other, more descriptive evidence.

The "social" in "social history" can refer to "the whole of society" (though it should be noted that Thernstrom's studies left out fully half of society, namely women), but to many historians and social activists in the twentieth century "social" meant "the working class." This equation is a legacy from the nineteenth century, when reformers in Europe and America expressed alarm about what they called "the social question," by which they meant the devastating impact of the industrial revolution on the lives of workers. In the 1830s and 1840s, middle-class observers wrote exposés on the squalor of the lives of contemporary urban workers, the apparent result of the introduction of new machines and technologies and the exploitative labor practices they brought with them; the most famous of these, *The Condition of the Working Class in England,* was written by Karl Marx's close collaborator Friedrich Engels. The nineteenth-century development of European working-class movements inspired a first generation of labor historians, active in the decades just before and after 1900, to write the history not just of what industrialization had done to the workers, but what workers were doing in response: organizing, protesting, going on strike, spearheading revolutions. This cohort of historians—including John Lawrence, Barbara Hammond, and Sidney and Beatrice Webb in England, Eduard Bernstein in Germany, and Edouard Dolléans in France—were often not academics but journalists, writers, and politicians close to labor movements, active socialists, and sometimes union members. Theirs was an insider's view, and one predictably very sympathetic to its subjects.

Early labor history was, to flip around Trevelyan's phrase, social history with the politics back in, often to a fault. Eric Hobsbawm, an eminent British left-wing historian, once pointed out that most traditional history of the labor movement was "technically and methodologically rather orthodox," much resembling old-style political history in that it privileged the activities of the leadership rather than the experiences of ordinary workers, and often devolved into endless accounts of factional struggles within the movement.[24] The classic labor-history version of social history presup-

24. Eric Hobsbawm, "Labor History and Ideology," *Journal of Social History* 7 (1974): 374.

poses a hierarchical view of the world of the working poor in which the male union member is the dominant figure: in this view the "working classes" were identical to "the labor movement."[25] Classic labor history, mostly written in the early and middle decades of the twentieth century, showcased the efforts of working men (almost never women) to flex their collective muscle in the political arena. As such it represents an important early form of "history from below" in which the struggles of the past provided a narrative of origins for later progressive and radical traditions. For anyone at any remove from the relevant labor movement, however, these chronicles of party and union struggles heavily sprinkled with the acronyms of competing groups (TUC and STUC, SFIO, CGT and CGTU, AFL and IWW, CISL, DGB) made for seriously heavy lifting. For outsiders to the labor movement, classic labor history often seemed, in short, narrowly focused and forbidding.

E. P. THOMPSON'S HISTORICAL REVOLUTION

This background explains the radical novelty and enormous impact of one book, *The Making of the English Working Class* (1963), whose author, E. P. Thompson, has been called "the most widely cited twentieth-century historian in the world."[26] Thompson's epic-length chronicle of the effects of nascent capitalism on ordinary English people between around 1780 and 1830 rewrote the rules for labor history, and indeed for social history as a whole. In the English-speaking world at least, *Making* was without a doubt the work most widely read and most often cited by professional historians in the second half of the twentieth century. Why did this one study make such a wide and deep impression?

Some of the book's influence surely had to do with its author's persona and reputation. Articulate, charismatic, and strikingly handsome, Edward Palmer Thompson (1924–1993) came from a cosmopolitan upper-middle-class English family of missionaries and academics. A poet, literary critic, and political activist as well as historian, Thompson was known throughout his life for his defiantly principled choices: he joined the Communist Party while he was a student, then left it when the horrors of Stalinism became apparent; he spent his early career teaching adult education classes to workers

25. Ibid., 372.
26. Eric Hobsbawm, "E. P. Thompson," *Radical History Review* 58 (1994): 157.

rather than seeking a university position; he devoted much of his time, throughout his life, to social and political movements such as the world-wide campaign for nuclear disarmament.[27] The moral authority Thompson commanded in Britain and beyond on the left of the political spectrum doubtless had something to do with how the book, as well as Thompson's subsequent work, was received.

That said, Thompson was mostly famous for his writing, and especially for *The Making of the English Working Class*. Thompson was a Marxist historian, and shared with that intellectual tradition the central project of documenting and explaining the destructive effects of capitalism on the lives of the poor.[28] But where standard Marxist histories focused on the triumphs and failures of labor movements, *Making* had little to do with workers' organizations; where Marxism made claims to "scientific" rigor, Thompson's book contained not a single numerical table, focusing instead on the subjective experiences of its protagonists. *Making* was specifically *not* about the people usually considered the main victims of industrialization, factory workers. Instead, it shows the effects of early capitalism on England's traditional workers: weavers, shoemakers, blacksmiths, and other craftsmen whose patterns of work and way of life were doomed by mechanization and competition from cheap unskilled labor. The pressure they were under was cultural as much as it was economic, Thompson argued. Workers lost control of their own time, for instance; instead of working in intense bursts on specific tasks, drinking on Sunday, and taking the following day off in honor of "Saint Monday", they were subjected to modern "work discipline" to ensure regular productivity. While the children of the poor had always worked hard, they previously did so at home, under the supervision of their families; youngsters were now forced out into the mills and mines where the risk of exploitation was much higher. "The experience of immiseration came upon [workers]," Thompson wrote, "in a hundred different forms; for the field labourer the loss of his common rights and the vestiges of village democracy; for the artisan, the loss of his craftsman's status; for the weaver, the loss of livelihood and independence; for the child, the loss of

27. Harvey J. Kaye, *The British Marxist Historians: An Introductory Analysis* (Cambridge: Polity Press, 1984), chapter 6; Bryan D. Palmer, *E. P. Thompson: Objections and Oppositions* (London: Verso, 1994), chapter 1.

28. On Marxist history, see chapter 5 below.

work and play in the home; for many groups of workers whose real earnings improved, the loss of security, leisure, and the deterioration of the urban environment."[29] From these experiences, class consciousness—the awareness of common exploitation—was born.

Although *The Making of the English Working Class* is not an easy book to read today—eight hundred pages long and haphazardly organized, it takes for granted a deep background in English history—it immediately became the gold standard for what was known as the "new social history." Two of its legacies have been especially important for historical writing. First, much of Thompson's book concerns workers who were not in the vanguard organizing and making specific political demands; his "working class" includes the very poor, the marginal, the inarticulate, those on the "losing side" of history. They too, he maintained, deserve our attention. "I am seeking," he memorably wrote, "to rescue the poor stockinger, the Luddite cropper, the 'utopian' artisan . . . from the enormous condescension of posterity."[30] Second, Thompson insisted that "class" and "class consciousness" were not sociological abstractions that could be deduced from theories or numbers but particular relationships and experiences that needed to be described in a specific time and place: class consciousness was just as present in the textile workers who blackened their faces and rode out at night to smash the new mechanized gig-mills, or in the tens of thousands who assembled to hear the millenarian prophetess Joanna Southcott call God's wrath upon the "whorish" moneyed elite, as in labor unions.[31]

That such points may seem obvious to us now is a testimony to the success of Thompson and historians like him in expanding definitions of "actors" of history and what it means to make "political" demands. The vast majority of humans in the past, with no material resources or education, have had no way to register their dreams or grievances; should their stories not also be told, their gestures of anger and defiance, their puzzling beliefs, taken seriously? Thompson's work opened up the definition of who should be considered a member of the "working class" (or classes), and with it the scope of social history. But it did more than that. Thompson devoted

29. E. P. Thompson, *The Making of the English Working Class* (New York: Vintage, 1963), 445.

30. Ibid., 12.

31. Ibid., 382–93, 523–30.

serious attention to material conditions and everyday lives: workers were radicalized in this period, he argued, because of the ways early capitalist pressures affected not just their incomes but their family lives, their patterns of work and recreation, their religious beliefs, their customary ways of doing things. *The Making of the English Working Class* began a process of rescuing Trevelyan-type social history—the history of material environments, family life, folk customs, and beliefs—from its second-class status by showing how these themes might be connected to such obviously "public" matters as industrial change and radical protest. It was difficult, from then on, for anyone to denigrate social history as "apolitical."

While in theory no historical approach inherently carries a specific set of political beliefs that is not always the case in practice. From its beginnings, social history has nearly always been linked to democratic or progressive agendas, with "social" implying either "the majority of the people" or "the poor." Histories in which "the people" act out a nation's destiny first appeared in the nineteenth century in Western democracies, written by men on the liberal end of the political spectrum, such as Michelet in France, Macaulay in Britain, and George Bancroft in the United States.[32] In later generations quantification has flagged the connection between democracy and social history, since it offers a way of allowing past generations to "vote" on who they were and what they did by drawing conclusions from the experiences of majorities. In France, for instance, in the middle decades of the twentieth century, members of the cutting-edge *Annales* school of history (named after their flagship journal) dedicated themselves to recovering their nation's history by writing massive works about French regional history in the early modern period, and especially about the French peasantry. These exhaustive productions, which could take fifteen or twenty years to complete and often included hundreds of pages of tables and graphs, were powered by the belief that the true and deep history of France resided in the peasantry, which had until the twentieth century made up the overwhelming majority of the French population.[33]

32. Thomas N. Baker, "National History in the Age of Michelet, Macaulay, and Bancroft," in Lloyd Kramer and Sarah Maza, eds., *A Companion to Western Historical Thought* (London: Blackwell, 2002), 185–204.

33. See Peter Burke, *The French Historical Revolution: The* Annales *School, 1929–89* (Cambridge: Polity Press, 1990), and André Burguière, *The Annales School: An*

Does "social history" have to mean "the history of the impoverished majority"? Not necessarily. To be sure, descriptive histories of the upper classes have sometimes been regarded by professional historians as a frivolous diversion, akin to watching a BBC costume drama. But while in its beginnings social history focused mainly on the poor, even historians with solid left-wing credentials acknowledged that "the oppressors" were every bit as much a social group as "the oppressed," and that their collective behavior and fate was of serious historical import. In the 1950s and 1960s, for instance, a massive academic brawl took place in Britain among the leading specialists on the Tudor-Stuart period over the question of whether the English Revolution of the 1640s resulted from a massive realignment of status and wealth among the British elites wherein the rise of a gentry of lesser landholders undermined the preeminence of the higher aristocracy. The "war over the gentry," which one of its protagonists later described as "a kind of academic gladiatorial show in which no quarter was offered," was waged with the weapons of the new social history: exhaustive numerical compilations of landholdings, manor houses, patterns of indebtedness, and the like alongside more traditional descriptive sources.[34] Similarly heated debates among historians have concerned the role of the bourgeoisie in the origins of the French Revolution and the nature of the slave-owning class in the United States: Was the French bourgeoisie a class-conscious group intent on destroying the nobility, or did they espouse aristocratic values and aspirations? Were American slaveholders capitalist businessmen or preindustrial paternalists?[35] Even in the absence of major controversy, the social history of elites, including the middle classes, is now widely accepted

---

Intellectual History, trans. Jane Marie Todd (Ithaca, NY: Cornell University Press, 2009). Famous examples of this genre include Pierre Goubert, *Beauvais et le Beauvaisis de 1600 à 1730* (Paris: SEVPEN, 1960), and Emmanuel Le Roy Ladurie, *Les paysans de Languedoc* (Paris: Mouton, 1966). See also chapter 5 below.

34. For a summary of the controversy, see Lawrence Stone, *The Causes of the English Revolution, 1529–1642* (New York: Harper & Row, 1972), chapter 2, quote p. 31; a bibliography of the debate can be found in the endnotes to the chapter (41–43).

35. See William Doyle, *Origins of the French Revolution*, 3rd ed. (Oxford: Oxford University Press, 1999); Eugene Genovese, *Roll, Jordan, Roll: The World the Slaves Made* (New York: Pantheon, 1974); and James Oakes, *Slavery and Freedom: An Interpretation of the Old South* (New York: Knopf, 1990).

as crucial to understanding class relations and social change in any given society.[36]

RESISTANCE AND AGENCY

A central agenda of social history has always been to recover the lives, voices, and struggles of society's disempowered groups. For E. P. Thompson's peers, or the following generation that came of age in the 1960s, a natural focus was the history of protest and rebellion by the working poor. Historians of organized labor have never had trouble explaining the motives behind workers' strikes—it is easy to grasp why one might organize and act against low wages, terrible working conditions, and other forms of exploitation, especially in a context where there is good reason to believe that collective effort will bring results. The "new social historians" of the 1960s and beyond, however, were drawn to other forms of protest: the archaic, apparently fruitless and irrational rebellions of the poor. The agenda of these writers was to show the ways in which the dispossessed took action against perceived injustices, even though their specific forms of protest might be puzzling to modern observers. Thompson, again, provided a model, in an influential 1971 essay entitled "The Moral Economy of the English Crowd in the Eighteenth Century."[37] Taking issue with traditional descriptions of preindustrial mob actions as unthinking violent responses to grain shortage, Thompson noted specific patterns of behavior and of demands. Rural crowds did not storm farms, mills, or granaries in a mindless rage or to pilfer grain. They had specific demands, such as those articulated in an anonymous letter placed in a farmer's barn: "Sir, if you do not bring your Wheat into the Market and sell it at a reasonable price, your Barns shall be pulled down."[38] Crowds, sometimes headed by women, grabbed stacks

36. Recent decades have seen the publication, for instance, of major works on the middle classes or bourgeoisie. Some salient examples are Peter Gay, *The Bourgeois Experience: Victoria to Freud*, 5 vols. (New York: Oxford University Press, 1984–1998); Leonore Davidoff and Catherine Hall, *Family Fortunes: Men and Women of the English Middle Class, 1780–1850* (Chicago: University of Chicago Press, 1987); and Jerrold Seigel, *Modernity and Bourgeois Life: Society, Politics and Culture in England, France and Germany since 1750* (Cambridge: Cambridge University Press, 2012).

37. E. P. Thompson, "The Moral Economy of the English Crowd in the Eighteenth Century," *Past & Present* 50 (February 1971): 76–136.

38. Ibid., 125.

of grain and, instead of stealing them, scattered their contents along the road or dumped them in the river. In the name of their communities, they tried to intimidate merchants, farmers, and millers into selling at what they considered a "fair price," a "customary" level that would allow the poorest families to survive. In short, they countered, in word and deed, the amoral workings of the market with a "moral economy" based on community values.

With the rise of the new social history, we have learned a great deal about how people with little access to power or education protested and made demands. There have been studies of the massive agrarian uprisings in 1830s England, in which crowds destroyed threshing machines and left notes signed "Captain Swing"; of the peasants in southwestern France who, calling themselves the *demoiselles*, or "ladies," in those same years protested an aggressive new Forest Code by riding out at night with their faces painted red and black and their shirts hanging loose; of the "Rebecca" rioters in Wales a decade or so later who cross-dressed before attacking toll gates in anger at what they deemed unfair taxation.[39] Young men in sixteenth-century French towns and sailors on the eighteenth-century Atlantic organized mock courts of law that parodied established institutions.[40] In nineteenth-century Swahili villages young men marked major religious festivals such as Eid al-Hajj and Eid al-Fitr by donning finery and performing dances and satirical songs that easily turned threatening toward their social superiors and sometimes resulted in violence.[41]

Historians have explained these acts of resistance by carefully researching their socioeconomic context, accounting for what triggered them (in most cases a decision by outsiders perceived as an attack on customary

39. Eric Hobsbawm and George Rudé, *Captain Swing* (New York: Pantheon, 1968); Peter Sahlins, *Forest Rites: The War of the Demoiselles in Nineteenth-Century France* (Cambridge, MA: Harvard University Press, 1994); David J. V. Jones, *Rebecca's Children: A Study of Rural Society, Crime, and Protest* (Oxford: Clarendon Press, 1989).

40. Natalie Zemon Davis, *Society and Culture in Early Modern France* (Stanford, CA: Stanford University Press, 1975), chapter 4; Marcus Rediker, *Between the Devil and the Deep Blue Sea: Merchant Seamen, Pirates, and the Anglo-American World, 1700–1750* (Cambridge: Cambridge University Press, 1987), 245.

41. Jonathon Glassman, *Feasts and Riot: Revelry, Rebellion, and Popular Consciousness on the Swahili Coast, 1856–1888* (Portsmouth, NH: Heinemann, 1995), 170–74.

livelihoods and values), and interpreting their symbolic dimensions. For preindustrial workers, for instance, there were many overlapping reasons to cross-dress for a riot: women's clothing was the most easily and cheaply available disguise; actual women frequently participated in grain riots and were traditionally spared prosecution if caught; gender-bending belonged to the symbolic repertoire of Carnival, a time when switching identities and taunting one's "betters" was tolerated; and, as Alfred Hitchcock intuited, a large man dressed as a woman can be just plain scary, especially if he is masked or wearing face paint. Inspired by E. P. Thompson's work, historians began in the 1960s and 1970s to demonstrate that popular resistance to the laws of the masters or the marketplace was no less important or worthy of attention when it happened outside of institutions like labor unions and took on seemingly bizarre, irrational, or self-defeating guises.

Social historians have shown that even in circumstances of extreme deprivation and powerlessness, men and women in the past have carved out areas of freedom by finding strategies to challenge, circumvent, or psychologically rise above oppressive power. One of the richest and most controversial fields for testing this proposition is the history of American slavery. Debates about North American slave culture and resistance were triggered long ago by the publication of Stanley Elkins's *Slavery: A Problem in American Institutional and Intellectual Life* (1959). At once sympathetic to the plight of slaves and deeply influenced by the horrors of World War II, Elkins argued that North American slavery had been a "total institution," akin to the world of concentration camps, that stripped its "inmates" of their original African culture and violently deprived them of all human connection, leaving slaves with warped psyches and no cultural resources, unable to push back against their brutal circumstances. In subsequent decades, magnificent works of scholarship by Eugene Genovese, Lawrence Levine, Ira Berlin, Philip Morgan, and other historians have thoroughly refuted the Elkins thesis. Levine and Sterling Stuckey, for instance, have shown the vitality of folk culture among Americans of African descent.[42]

It was virtually impossible for slaves in North America to challenge openly the system that brutalized them. In contrast to slaves in the Caribbean, who by the nineteenth century had carried out several successful revolts, Ameri-

42. For a convenient summary of the controversies and conclusions, see Peter Kolchin, *American Slavery, 1619–1877* (New York: Hill and Wang, 1993), especially chapter 5.

can slaves typically worked on smaller farms and plantations, closely super-
vised by masters who knew them individually, and were vastly outnumbered
by whites. In his classic study, *Roll, Jordan, Roll: The World The Slaves Made*
(1974), Eugene Genovese described what he saw as the irony at the heart
of the cultural dynamic between masters and slaves in the Old South, one
that resulted from precisely the small-scale and personalized nature of American slavery. Slave-owners degraded and exploited their bondsmen on a daily
basis. But they also saw themselves as benevolent paternalists looking out for
the welfare of "their people," and as such promoted precisely those institutions and values—family and church—that allowed the slaves to survive and
resist, at least psychically and spiritually. Masters encouraged reproduction
and family structures, ostensibly for moral reasons; slaves in turn depended
on their families for material and psychological resources and to resist the
rigors of slavery, for instance, through patterns of naming that reinforced
distance from the masters' culture and allowed family members to find each
other if they were separated. Similarly, owners discouraged the practice
of African religions and instead favored Christianity, which they believed
would promote resignation and docility; but slaves adapted Christian traditions and texts to their own ends, finding in them a means to reinforce community and celebrate ideals of redemption and liberation.[43] As one former
slave put it, "Dat ole white preacher jest was telling us slaves to be good to
our marsters. We aint keer'd a bit 'bout dat stuff he was telling us 'cause we
wanted to sing, pray, and serve God in our own way."[44] In short, Genovese
argued, slaves seized upon their masters' self-serving paternalism to create
their own forms of "under the radar" resistance.

Over the years Genovese's book has come in for its share of criticism
from fellow historians, who have objected that he exaggerated the extent of
slaveholder benevolence and understated the degree to which slaves were
autonomously active and creative, and in fact outright insubordinate.[45]
The book was a landmark however, in that it invited historians to think

43. Genovese, *Roll, Jordan, Roll*; the opening section, "On Paternalism" (3–7),
lays out the book's analytical framework.

44. Quoted in Kolchin, *American Slavery*, 144.

45. See, for instance, Peter H. Wood's review in the *Journal of Interdisciplinary
History* (Autumn 1975): 289–97, and James P. Anderson, "Aunt Jemima in Dia-
lectics: Genovese on Slave Culture," *Journal of Negro History* 61 (January 1976):
99–114.

about ways in which people can engage in covert, everyday forms of resistance, even within the most tightly controlled environments. In order to identify and interpret such strategies, historians often borrowed insights from other disciplines. In the 1990s many of them were influenced by the writings of James C. Scott, a political scientist and anthropologist who coined the phrase "hidden transcript" to describe the "offstage" speech and behavior of those without power. Forced into a "public transcript of deference," subordinates use a different code with one another behind their masters' backs: not only do they express their real feelings about their "betters," but they might agree among themselves, for instance, not to work too hard or sell below a certain price. Slaves and others without power also develop what Scott calls an "infrapolitics," behaviors such as wasting time, damaging tools, disappearing from the workplace, or pretending to misunderstand orders, and so on—which help explain stereotypes of certain groups as lazy or incompetent. The oppressed can also cultivate emotional strategies, such as training themselves not to respond to insults, as African-American boys do when exchanging "dozens": learning to be "cool" is, for certain groups, a crucial means of self-protection.[46] Concepts such as infrapolitics have greatly expanded our understanding of the ways in which the mundane activities of daily life can be reconceived as a framework for resistance to oppressive power.

Much social history, then, has been concerned with questions about the many forms resistance has taken for groups with little or no power, from well-organized strikes and protests to subtle acts of sabotage to simply finding the emotional and spiritual resources to avoid despair. The greater the power imbalance, the more urgently historians have felt the need to recapture the ways in which the powerless pushed back against their oppressors. In his landmark book about the American domestic slave trade, for instance, Walter Johnson was able to document ways in which some men and women reduced to mere commodities were able to shape their own sale so as to avoid undesirable masters: they adjusted their tone of voice and posture, cooked terrible food, lied or told the truth about illnesses, all

46. James C. Scott, *Domination and the Arts of Resistance: Hidden Transcripts* (New Haven, CT: Yale University Press, 1990). Similar ideas with a more specific focus are developed in Scott's earlier *Weapons of the Weak: Everyday Forms of Peasant Resistance* (New Haven, CT: Yale University Press, 1985).

the while walking a dangerously fine line between buyer and seller, either of whom could exact terrible retribution. As the former slave John Parker remembered it, "I made up my mind I was going to select my owner so when anyone came to inspect me I did not like, I answered all questions with a 'yes' and made myself disagreeable."[47]

What is at stake in demonstrating that certain groups—preindustrial or industrial workers, colonized peoples, illiterate peasants, slaves, and others—engaged in overt or covert, effective or symbolic, acts of resistance? Why is it imperative to establish such histories? Is the historical record of resistance by the downtrodden important as a form of inspiration, as a lesson to those who might oppress others, as ammunition in today's political debates, as a component of a group's present-day identity? Do we assume that the "we" who read and write history are the descendants or allies of the oppressed? Do these histories add up to a more general assertion that the dynamic between unequal groups is the most significant feature of our common human past? Or does any "nation" with which we identify, be it Korean or Spanish, Queer or Cherokee, need a story that includes oppression, resistance, and victory?

Many historians of oppressed groups in the last few decades have stated that their aim is to award or restore "agency" to the people they study—to show that slaves, laborers, peasants, inmates, or members of marginalized minorities did not suffer passively but took purposeful action against their circumstances. Walter Johnson, whose book on the slave trade is mentioned above, has written a series of incisive essays asking why this has become a central project for social historians, particularly in the United States. Who are we, Johnson asks, to "give back" agency or anything else to people long dead? (And, he points out, "agency," which includes crime, betrayal, and collaboration with oppressors, is not always what right-thinking historians would like it to be.) More importantly, he cautions, we should keep in mind that "agency," roughly equivalent to "self-directed action," usually refers back to an implicit ideal of liberal individualism. The assumption that a central purpose of life—and therefore a natural focus of historical inquiry—is to take action and alter one's circumstances for the better is one that has few counterparts outside of modern Anglo-American ideals of

47. Walter Johnson, *Soul by Soul: Life inside the Antebellum Slave Market* (Cambridge, MA: Harvard University Press, 1999), 176–88, quote p. 179.

self-improvement.[48] This is not to say—and Johnson does not imply—that the concept of agency should be tossed out; but if we are going to give it such importance, we should be willing to explain exactly what it means and why it matters.

POWER AND THE PRIVATE SPHERE

Women are one of the groups whose "agency" has been energetically re-covered in the last few decades. As the previous pages may suggest, wom-en's history was a relative latecomer in the new social history. Thompson's workers, Thernstrom's Bostonians, and the various peasants and artisans whose activities were chronicled in the famous early works were almost all men. The presence of women was, of necessity, acknowledged: one can-not responsibly study peasant households, artisanal shops, grain riots, or factories without noting female presence and activity. But women never seemed to make any difference to the story; they remained in the shadows, the spotlight trained elsewhere.

"Women's history," like "social history," has been around for a long time, spawning classics like Alice Clark's *Working Life of Women in the Sev-enteenth Century* (1919) and Ivy Pinchbeck's *Women Workers and the In-dustrial Revolution* (1930). Before the 1970s, however, women's history was considered a niche specialty, an appropriate focus for the tiny number of women who entered academia, or the occasional eccentric man like the French scholar Léon Abensour, author of a 1921 general history of femi-nism. That women have always made up half or more of the population never seemed to matter—certainly not to old-style political historians, ex-cept when an Elizabeth Tudor or a Catherine the Great happened to hog the limelight, and neither, for a long time, to the postwar new social his-torians. Even among the radical young historians of the 1960s and 1970s, busily recovering the history of the working man, the assumption lingered that women in the past had lived outside of history: helpful auxiliaries at best, they inhabited a politics-free private sphere, they reproduced instead

48. The most developed statement is Walter Johnson, "On Agency," *Journal of Social History* 37 (Fall 2003):113–24. See also Johnson, "OAH State of the Field: Slavery," http://156.56.25.5/meetings/2004/johnson.html (accessed February 3, 2016), and Johnson, "A Nettlesome Classic Turns Twenty-Five," *Common-Place* 1, no. 4 (July 2001), http://www.common-place-archives.org/vol-01/no-04/reviews/johnson.shtml (accessed February 3, 2016).

of producing, and with rare and brief exceptions like suffrage movements, they never drove historical change. The lives of women could therefore be consigned to the social-history-as-local-color genre: marriage, the family, child-rearing, food and cooking, servants, actresses, prostitutes—these topics might be of interest to curious amateurs but not to serious chroniclers of power, conflict, and change.

The notion that the family is an arena free of power struggles may strike anyone who has ever been a child, parent, or spouse as, at best, darkly hilarious. Indeed, this assumption provoked rage in an early generation of feminist historians whose work revolved around uncovering the origins of "patriarchy." Inspired by theorists like Shulamith Firestone and Mary O'Brien, who argued that the exploitation of women's work and sexuality in family structures was analogous to (and in fact prior to) relations of class domination, feminist historians set about analyzing the origins and development of the oppression of women by men.[49] Books like Sheila Rowbotham's *Hidden from History: Three Hundred Years of Women's Oppression and the Fight against It* (1973) and Gerda Lerner's *The Creation of Patriarchy* (1986) may now seem heavy-handed in their relentless focus on the subordination and exploitation of women, but this initial work was crucial in making historians pay attention to the relationship between the private and the public spheres and acknowledge the existence of exploitation and violence in the former.[50]

As late as the 1980s, young women were warned away from women's history when choosing their dissertation topics. At best it was viewed as a scholarly ghetto with little relevance to the important questions about the past; at worst choosing the field might mark you as an "angry feminist." "Save it for your second book, after you get tenure," was the usual advice.

49. Shulamith Firestone, *The Dialectic of Sex: The Case for Feminist Revolution* (New York: Morrow, 1970); Mary O'Brien, *The Politics of Reproduction* (Boston: Routledge and Kegan Paul, 1981).

50. Sheila Rowbotham, *Hidden from History: Three Hundred Years of Women's Oppression and the Fight against It* (London: Pluto Press, 1973). (Rowbotham's book was published the following year in the United States with the watered-down subtitle *Rediscovering Women in History from the Seventeenth Century to the Present.*) Gerda Lerner, *The Creation of Patriarchy* (New York: Oxford University Press, 1986). See also Judith M. Bennett, "Feminism and History," *Gender and History* 1 (Autumn 1989): 251–72, which makes a case for retaining this general approach.

Some of the earliest and hardest-hitting women's historians had no interest in "mainstreaming" their field: just as radical feminist philosophers of the 1970s and 1980s like Andrea Dworkin maintained that all heterosexual intercourse amounts to rape, some proponents of "herstory" believed the only possible relationship between men and women in the past was that of oppressor and oppressed. But even to the most ideologically committed feminist, a strict analogy between men/women and bosses/workers or masters/slaves has always been problematic, for obvious reasons: most workers, peasants, and slaves had little or no direct contact with their bosses, lords, or masters, whereas nearly all men are raised by women, sleep with them, father them, or otherwise encounter them in intimate ways every day. It is infinitely harder for a historian of women to ignore men than for a labor historian to study workers separately from bosses, and it should conversely be impossible for mainstream historians to overlook women.

Some of the early, important work in women's history was dismissed by the historical mainstream as "compensatory," or merely additive, amounting to the message: "Yes, and women were there too." We learned, for instance, that women were active in the French Revolution: some wrote pamphlets, many participated in marches and demonstrations, a few like the famous Madame (Marie-Jeanne) Roland were influential in high political circles, many more took part in the radical activities of the plebeian *sans-culottes*, while a few middle-class women opened political clubs.[51] Skeptics were unimpressed: this information might make for an interesting lecture or an additional textbook chapter, but did it in any way alter our fundamental understanding of the French Revolution?

In some cases, women's history challenged the very definition of "big events" in history. A famous 1977 article by Joan Kelly, for instance, asked the question "Did Women Have a Renaissance?" The Renaissance, everyone knew, was the crucible in which "modern man" appeared in the West: early modern Italy saw the appearance of new forms of statehood and advanced commercial economies, and with them the wealth of cultural expression known as "humanism," which celebrated the individual and sang the praises of humankind. But if for elite men "the Renaissance" brought new forms of freedom and creativity, for their female counterparts, Kelly argued, the story was just the reverse. Prior to the Renaissance, in agrarian-

51. Dominique Godineau, *The Women of Paris and Their French Revolution*, trans. Katherine Steip (Berkeley: University of California Press, 1998).

based feudal societies, elite women often wielded considerable authority: in-heritance laws could work in their favor, and there were long periods when their husbands were absent, gone to war. The literature of courtly love, which in some cases endorsed adultery, suggests the emotional and erotic freedom some women may have enjoyed. The rise of commercial societies, and with it a stricter division between personal and public life, introduced a different relation between the sexes, one that sharply curtailed upper-class female freedom and expression. "There was no renaissance for women," Kelly bluntly concluded, "at least, not during the Renaissance."[52] Work in a similar vein has argued that the French Revolution, with its cult of Greek and Roman manhood and its enshrining of military "fraternity" as a cultural ideal, was actually a step backward for women. Such readings imply that women had more of a French Reaction than a French Revolution.[53]

Much of the pioneering feminist work in women's history, then, stressed either the oppression women suffered in the past or the difference of their experience from men's. "Excuse me: we were there too, and it did not hap-pen like that for us," was a necessary initial statement. But despite a con-tinued emphasis on separate female experiences, almost from the start his-torians of women recognized that the real power of women's history lay in the demonstration that women's story was inseparable from that of men, that crucial aspects of *any* history would be overlooked, incomprehensible, or impoverished absent careful consideration of gender relations.

One reason for women's long-standing historical invisibility was the as-sumption that they did not work, or that the work they did was not crea-tive, productive, or significant since it was not recognized, hence made "real," by monetary compensation. In fact, in nearly every known society, the ma-jority of women have engaged in lifelong labor, paid or unpaid, and their work has been a central component of most economies. One of the main tasks of women's history has been to make this simple fact visible and to assess its consequences in any given society. The point is not that taking

---

52. Joan Kelly, *Women, History and Theory: The Essays of Joan Kelly* (Chicago: University of Chicago Press, 1984), 19. The essay was originally published in 1977 under the name Joan Kelly-Gadol. For a good overview of the development of the field, see Laura Lee Downs, *Writing Gender History* (London: Bloomsbury, 2004).

53. Joan Landes, *Women and the Public Sphere in the Age of the French Revolu-tion* (Ithaca, NY: Cornell University Press, 1988); Lynn Hunt, *The Family Ro-mance of the French Revolution* (Berkeley: University of California Press, 1992).

care of babies and growing garden vegetables are activities that deserve (historical) recognition but that, for all but the wealthy, making ends meet has always been a family strategy involving women and children as well as men. In colonial Kenya, daughters sent the money they earned as sex workers in Nairobi back home to rescue family farms from the effects of drought and disease, and to pay for their brothers' bridewealth.[54] In Europe well into the nineteenth century, women did much more than housework: besides planting, harvesting, and tending livestock alongside men, they spun, wove, and sewed at home for wages, wet-nursed other people's children, and left home for stretches in their teens to earn money as servants or factory hands.[55]

Female work was obscured, to contemporaries as well as to later historians, because families have traditionally been defined by the identity and status of the men who headed the households. Thernstrom, like many historians, studied social mobility by tracking the careers of men, with no mention of the *other* "other Bostonians." But, as some notable studies have shown, male status has often been achieved and maintained via household hierarchy and exploitation. Tessie Liu's study of textile workers in western France in the nineteenth century depicts a world in which male weavers struggled, much like E. P. Thompson's embattled English artisans, to maintain their economic independence and dignity as traditional producers in the face of threats to the craft. To the extent they succeeded, she shows, it was because their wives and daughters worked long, poorly paid hours in the low-status "sweated" trades, mass-producing garments and shoes. The price paid for a worker's dignity was an exploitative family hierarchy.[56] Similarly, yeomen farmers (small landowners) in the antebellum South Carolina low country prided themselves on their self-reliance and on the theoretical equality they claimed with their neighbors, the great planter-aristocrats.

54. Luise White, *The Comforts of Home: Prostitution in Colonial Nairobi* (Chicago: University of Chicago Press, 1990).

55. See, for instance, Louise Tilly and Joan Scott, *Women, Work and Family* (New York: Holt, Rinehart and Winston, 1978); Olwen Hufton, *The Prospect before Her: A History of Women in Western Europe, 1500–1800* (New York: Knopf, 1996), chapters 2–6.

56. Tessie P. Liu, *The Weaver's Knot: The Contradictions of Class Struggle and Family Solidarity in Western France, 1750–1914* (Ithaca, NY: Cornell University Press, 1994), especially chapter 9.

But these "masters of small worlds" could lay claim to independent status only because their wives produced goods for market and worked the fields, sometimes alongside the family's few slaves. Southern yeomen enthusiastically espoused the secessionist cause to uphold not just slavery but also a divinely sanctioned family and gender hierarchy that obeyed, in their eyes, the same principles.[57]

In short, a central task of women's history has been to show how the relationship between women and men has shaped every society in the past, even when the presence of women as actors is concealed by dominant ideologies. Some historians of women prefer the expression "gender history," which captures the ways in which women's and men's histories are intertwined as well as the ideological dimensions of that relationship. As the historian Joan Scott explained, in what remains the single most famous article on the subject, "gender," a term derived from linguistics, serves to express the idea that masculinity and femininity are socially constructed categories that vary according to time and place and cannot be reduced to stable biological sex differences. Gender is also, she points out, "a primary way of signifying relationships of power."[58] Gender ideologies structure most human activities, including dynamics between members of the same sex. In the American South during the Jim Crow era, for instance, lynching, the unofficially sanctioned murder of black men, was justified by those who engaged in it as a form of "chivalry": the fears and resentments of white men in the face of black emancipation were expressed as an imperative to protect preemptively the virtue of their womenfolk.[59]

Gender analysis vastly extends the reach of women's history by showing how even the most traditionally male pursuits and preserves—and specifically, those relating to public power—have been profoundly shaped either by the activities of women or in symbolic opposition to an imagined femininity. "Total wars" such as the twentieth-century world wars, for instance,

57. Stephanie McCurry, *Masters of Small Worlds: Yeoman Households, Gender Relations and the Political Culture of the Antebellum South Carolina Low Country* (New York: Oxford University Press, 1995), especially chapter 2.

58. Joan Wallach Scott, "Gender: A Useful Category of Historical Analysis," in *Gender and the Politics of History* (New York: Columbia University Press, 1988), 42. The essay was originally published in the *American Historical Review* in 1986.

59. Nancy Maclean, *Behind the Mask of Chivalry: The Making of the Second Ku Klux Klan* (Oxford: Oxford University Press, 1994).

are events that "ritually mark the gender of all members of society, whether or not they are combatants." Even as women on the home front step, willingly or not, into roles and activities opened up by male absence, they are idealized in the most traditional of guises—nurse, mother, patiently longing wife—while masculine activity on the battlefront "takes economic and cultural priority."[60] To take another example, the fact that eighteenth- and nineteenth-century political bodies were emphatically and completely male derives from the gendering of modern notions of citizenship and contractual government. The necessary attributes of citizens and their representatives—independence, rationality, dedication to the wider polity—were imagined as inevitably male, in opposition to woman's characteristic state of dependency and devotion to the narrow interests of family and home.

Thus, gender history can encompass the most traditional realms of historical writing—war and politics—precisely because such domains are "male" in the sense of "explicitly not female," and press male and female actors into sharply defined roles. Men, such arguments go, make claims to power by asserting their masculinity, which is itself predicated on a continual process of rejecting and repressing femaleness. At the same time, language about women has always served as a way of describing and understanding power relations between men. Gender historians have shown that in imperial China, for instance, the private behavior of elite women provided a model for political loyalty: a wife who committed ritual suicide after a husband's death, or remained alive to serve his family for the remainder of her life embodied the ideal relationship between a virtuous man and his ruler. Conversely, in the early twentieth century, Chinese intellectuals rejected traditional femininity and such rituals as foot-binding as symbols of "ignorance, economic parasitism, and China's humiliation at the hands of more virile powers."[61]

Not only did gender analysis expand the reach of women's history, it also helped open up other fields, especially gay and lesbian history. The latter presents especially interesting problems to historians in that gays and lesbians are not just people who were neglected in the historical record, like

60. Margaret Higonnet, Jane Jenson, Sonya Michel, and Margaret Weitz, eds., *Behind the Lines: Gender and the Two World Wars* (New Haven, CT: Yale University Press, 1987), 4, 7.

61. Gail Herschatter and Wang Zheng, "Chinese History: A Useful Category of Gender Analysis," *American Historical Review* 113 (December 2008): 1407–9.

women and the poor; most were, and still are in most cultures, invisible to those around them and in many cases even to each other. Gay and lesbian history followed the same course as women's history, from early documentary efforts to interpretive insights that have had implications for all fields of historical research. Even more than women's history, the field was greeted with initial scorn and disbelief, dismissed as the narrow and somewhat trivial preoccupation of a small interest group. Choosing to work on this topic had even more significant consequences for scholars, since in most cases it amounted to coming out at a time when homophobia remained widespread in the academy. Much of the early scholarship recovered worlds ignored by historians up to then: passionate friendships between medieval male clerics, sodomy in Renaissance courts, male prostitution in the eighteenth century, intimate relationships at same-sex boarding schools, and so on. The best and most ambitious gay history, however, has forced us to reevaluate, through history, everything we have believed about sexual identities and relationships.

In the 1980s and 1990s classic works in the field upended a simplistic view of past and present attitudes, which held that, except in ancient Greece, homosexuality was everywhere reviled and persecuted until more enlightened attitudes began to emerge in the later twentieth century. The medievalist John Boswell's magisterial tome *Christianity, Social Tolerance, and Homosexuality* (1980) sought to show that neither the Bible nor the early Christian church were much concerned with homosexuality per se, as opposed to excessive lust in general. In the early Middle Ages, Boswell argued, homosexual acts were neither criminalized nor persecuted, and gay relationships took place openly, for instance among segments of the twelfth-century aristocracy. Only starting in the thirteenth century was homosexuality singled out for violent censure and punished by torture or death.[62] In Japan, as Gregory Pflugfelder shows, sexual relations between men and adolescent boys—codified as "the way of youth" and valued as an endeavor requiring specific knowledge and skills—posed no major problem in a culture that did not proscribe nonreproductive sex. It was not until the Meiji period (1868–1921) that male-male sexuality was outlawed,

62. John Boswell, *Christianity, Social Tolerance, and Homosexuality: Gay People in Western Europe from the Beginning of Christianity to the Fourteenth Century* (Chicago: University of Chicago Press, 1980).

in an effort to align with Western social codes, and only after 1900 did Japanese doctors begin to frame homosexuality as pathological.[63]

Since the 1980s major works in gay and lesbian history have challenged everything we thought we knew about sexual and social identities, even in the recent past. Until the publication of George Chauncey's *Gay New York* in 1994, it was generally assumed that gay male life in American cities was swathed in secrecy and shame until the 1970s, after the 1969 Stonewall riots, a watershed event that triggered both individual comings-out and collective expressions of defiance and pride that gelled into an open and activist gay community. In a book now recognized as a classic in social and cultural history, Chauncey demonstrated that the homosexual world of New York from the 1890s to the 1930s was infinitely more complicated and surprising, and more implicated with the straight world, than anyone could have imagined.[64] Chauncey's research uncovered a complex landscape of identities—"fairies," "pansies," "sissys," "nances," "gays," "trade," "faggots," "queers"—at odds with any simple binary of hetero- and homosexuality. In the 1910s and 1920s, for instance, Irish and Italian working men, as well as sailors on shore leave, just as easily picked up effeminate "fairies" as they did female prostitutes, and the latter in fact complained of the unfair competition. Men who had sex with "fairies" (who were thought of as a sort of third sex) considered themselves quite normal, as long as they took the sexually active role in the encounter. Meanwhile, middle-class "confirmed bachelors" did not think of themselves as shamefully closeted but as living a double life, playing two roles, sometimes with great ease and satisfaction. Only with the advent of postwar ideals of personal "authenticity" did such double lives become a source of confusion and self-loathing. Prewar gay life was relatively open, culminating in huge drag balls that drew straight New Yorkers into what was known at the time as the "pansy craze." The expression "coming out," coined at the time, was an explicitly campy reference to the tradition of upper-class female debutante balls. The term's origin, as Chauncey incisively remarks, is revealing: gay

63. Gregory M. Pflugfelder, *Cartographies of Desire: Male-Male Sexuality in Japanese Discourse, 1600–1950* (Berkeley: University of California Press, 1999).

64. George Chauncey, *Gay New York: Gender, Urban Culture, and the Making of the Gay Male World, 1890–1940* (New York: Basic Books, 1994).

people in the 1920s and 1930s did not imagine themselves to be coming *out of* a closet but to be coming *into* "homosexual society."[65]

The point was not to paint a rosy picture of gay life in interwar New York, where homosexuals were usually mocked and despised, and frequently harassed, beaten up, and arrested. Like Boswell, Chauncey sought to historicize the sexual identities and practices we call "gay" by showing that they have varied greatly across time, place, and social class, and that their history confounds any simple narrative of progress from the bad old days of the past to the liberated present. As Chauncey's work suggests, histories of sexuality challenge us to question categories and labels we take for granted. Other historians, for instance, have documented intense same-sex relationships in the past that were not considered in the least deviant: in nineteenth-century America, women friends wrote passionately longing letters to each other, showered one another with kisses, spent nights cuddling in bed. Around 1870 Molly Hallock Foote wrote to her dear friend Helena: "Imagine yourself kissed a dozen times my darling. Perhaps it is well for you that we are far apart. You might find my thanks so expressed rather overpowering."[66] Contemporaries found intimate, fervent relationships between female friends like Molly and Helena perfectly appropriate. Does that bond fall under the rubric of "gay history"? What matters, as the author of this article points out, is not whether these young women engaged in sexual acts together (which raises the question of what we count as "sexual") but why female friendships were so emotionally and sensually intense in this place and time, and why the society around these young women not only condoned but encouraged such relationships.[67] Gay and lesbian history invites us to think about the very definition of the groups we study in the past by presenting us with an extreme example of mostly hidden and fluid identities elusive to all but the most imaginative and tenacious historians.

This chapter by no means catalogs all of the groups of people historians have singled out for study—others, though far from all, will appear in later

65. Ibid., 7.

66. Carroll Smith-Rosenberg, "The Female World of Love and Ritual: Relationships between Women in Nineteenth-Century America," *Signs* 1 (Autumn 1975): 6–7.

67. Ibid., 27–29.

chapters. Merely listing additions to the historical canon—occupational groups, ethnicities, religious majorities and minorities, and so on—is not the point. What does emerge from the preceding pages is a sense of how the practice of history itself and the questions historians ask are transformed and renewed every time a new set of actors lays claim to its past. For instance, quantification arose out of a deep commitment to a democratic history of the ordinary individual and, whatever its limitations, constituted a sharp departure from the narrative mode of traditional political history. Social history in its various guises taught us to decipher patterns of behavior that give us access to the beliefs and aspirations of the powerless and illiterate. In the process, historians had to come up with new ways of interpreting actions—like staging a grain riot only to dump the grain—that make no sense to the "rational" mind.

The history of American slavery brought entirely new agendas to the table, as scholars tried to understand how generations of bondsmen and women not only endured but asserted themselves and developed rich cultures while living deprived of freedom and in constant jeopardy. The resulting questions—about culture, resistance, and agency—have shaped fields far beyond African-American history. Women's history made historians realize that what they thought of as "normal" history was in fact male history, that it is impossible to disentangle the lives of men from those of women, and that every expression of a society's ideals and values takes the form of implicit or explicit statements about masculinity and femininity. Women's history trained us all to look for those aspects of the past that are unspoken, interstitial, and repressed, but constantly and insistently present. Gay history, and the history of sexuality more generally, forced its practitioners and readers to come to terms with the inadequacy of our modern categories to make sense of intimate behaviors and identities in the past. In short, every time we reframe part of the historical picture to take account of another set of people, the whole image changes. As the next chapter will show, the same is true of the "where" of history: how we understand the past depends not only on how we look at people but how we carve out space.

2

THE HISTORY OF WHERE?

HOW NATIONAL HISTORY BECAME UNNATURAL

The "where" of history is, by default, the nation. Despite increasing attempts to break away from national frameworks, "normal" history remains grounded in discrete political-cultural-geographical units. Schools and universities have dramatically increased their offerings in "world" or "global" history, as well as courses on thematic, comparative, and transnational subjects, but faculty members continue, in most cases, to be classified as "United States," "Chinese," or "German" historians. Practical and logistical issues make it extremely difficult to depart from this tradition: in order to become a reputable historian of Mexico or South Africa you have not only to absorb the essential scholarship in the field—stacks of books and articles—but to learn where to find what in the archives and libraries, to gain complete command of one or more languages, and to spend a lot of time in the relevant places at home or abroad. It is exceedingly difficult—usually downright impossible—for a historian of the United States, for instance, to decide in midcareer to switch gears because of sudden curiosity about a topic in Brazilian or Japanese history: the start-up cost is just too steep. Until recently, it was rare for academic historians to work in more than one national context.

Historians are trained to self-identify as specialists in one country, and if they have graduate students they will usually pass on that focus to them. For most of the twentieth century, furthermore, some national histories decisively trumped others: no respectable American history department of a certain size could get on without at least one historian each (and often more) of Britain, France, and Germany, alongside its phalanx of Americanists, while it was acceptable to have one staff member teach all of Latin American or African history. Scholars who worked on places outside of North America or Western Europe were often attached to interdisciplinary "area studies" clusters set up during the Cold War and funded by foundations and government agencies. Such arrangements signaled that the histories of places like Eastern Europe, Indonesia, or Egypt did not matter for their own sake but as part of a bundle of regional expertise to be deployed as needed in the nation's interest.[1]

Until recently, a national focus for history writing seemed an entirely unproblematic state of affairs because most people imagined—and indeed, most still do—different "histories" unfolding inside specific landmasses with sharply defined contours, areas easily visible on a map: the African continent, the French hexagon, the diamond shape of India, the British Isles.[2] So deeply ingrained is this way thinking that it seems commonsensical to imagine national histories as the accomplishment of geographical destiny. It was long taken for granted that France was "unified" by a succession of early modern kings, just as Germany was by Bismarck in the nineteenth century, as if the pieces of a jigsaw puzzle were being popped into place. In the same way, the anticolonial struggles of the twentieth century "liberated" countries like Algeria, Indonesia, and Angola that did not exist as such before becoming nineteenth-century colonized units. Did the populations of Italy and Germany really think of themselves as "scattered" before they were brought together? Who decreed that the United States had to stretch from sea to shining sea or that Italy had to look like a thigh-high boot? The large island we call Great Britain seems like an inevitable national unit, but only starting in the later eighteenth century did most of its inhabitants, including the Scots and Welsh, start to think of themselves as "British."[3]

Both the nations and the national histories we now take for granted are very recent creations. Most of the countries on today's world maps did not exist a hundred years ago: they secured independence within boundaries initially drawn by Western imperialists whose own nations resulted from eighteenth- and nineteenth-century revolutionary movements. Before the

1. Masao Miyoshi and H. D. Harootunian, eds., *Learning Places: The Afterlives of Area Studies* (Durham, NC: Duke University Press, 2002); see especially Bruce Cumings, "Boundary Displacement: The State, the Foundations, and Area Studies during and after the Cold War," 261–302.

2. On the history of geographical imagination, see Martin W. Lewis and Kären E. Wigen, *The Myth of Continents: A Critique of Metageography* (Berkeley: University of California Press, 1997).

3. Linda Colley, *Britons: Forging the Nation, 1707–1837* (New Haven, CT: Yale University Press, 1992).

nineteenth century, "the nation" was not usually the context or object of Western historical writing. Chronicles of the past might focus on smaller units, such as city-states in Greece, Rome, and Renaissance Europe, or much larger ones, such as Christendom or the Roman Empire. European histories were framed around the destinies of patriarchs, popes, rulers, and dynasties, not the stories of larger chunks of territory.[4] All of this changed starting in the later eighteenth century, the era of the American and French Revolutions. National sentiment certainly existed prior to the eighteenth century, usually expressed in opposition to some other national or religious group: you knew you were Dutch in the sixteenth century because you loathed the Spaniards, British in the eighteenth century because you despised the French.[5] But the "age of revolutions" saw the coupling of nationalism with democracy, the belief, in the words of one historian, "that state power should represent the collective will of a particular population or 'citizenry' that lived within the borders of a large, well-defined territory."[6]

In the nineteenth century, leading historians in various parts of the West published classic works of national history built around the premise that their country's past illustrated the advent of admirable values and ideals embodied in its people. Jules Michelet's *History of the French Revolution* (1853) shows the great Revolution of 1789 laying the groundwork for the people of France to come together around its central core, the peasantry, and begin its exceptional journey toward ever more perfect liberty and equality. Thomas Babington Macauley's *History of England* (1848) showcases the British people and state as models of restraint and moderation, achieving progress wisely through gradual reform. George Bancroft's *History of the United States*, written from the 1850s to the 1870s, combines democratic and religious themes in a narrative that celebrates Americans' devotion to the spirit of freedom and their debt to the guiding hand of

4. Lloyd Kramer and Sarah Maza, eds., *A Companion to Western Historical Thought* (London: Blackwell, 2002), chapters 1–6.

5. See, for instance, David Bell, *The Cult of the Nation in France: Inventing Nationalism, 1680–1800* (Cambridge, MA: Harvard University Press, 2003); Colley, *Britons.*

6. Lloyd Kramer, *Nationalism in Europe and America: Politics, Cultures and Identities since 1775* (Chapel Hill: University of North Carolina Press, 2011), 29.

Providence. In each case the fate of the writer's nation was both unique to itself and a shining example to others.[7]

Nineteenth-century nationalism was also closely entangled with racial assumptions, such as the English myth of a deep-rooted Anglo-Saxon identity or the "blood and soil" beliefs common among continental conservatives.[8] The racial thought of that era left its imprint as well on other sorts of tenacious imagined geographies. Why do people today casually describe someone from Senegal or Botswana as "an African" when they would never similarly refer to someone from Italy or Switzerland as "a European"? The collapsing of multiple histories and cultures into a single, continental identity is partly the effect of long-standing Western prejudice and ignorance. But it also stems from the efforts of progressive black American Pan-Africanists like Alexander Crummell and W. E. B. Du Bois in the nineteenth century, and of twentieth-century proponents of the Afrocentric movement called *négritude*, who held that all Africans share a common destiny, not because of a shared ecology or history, for instance, because they had all experienced Western colonialism, but because they all belong to one race.[9] Many strands of racial belief, including those of African-American and African intellectuals, thus contributed to the naturalizing of "Africa" as a unit, obscuring the continent's vast linguistic, religious, and cultural differences.

Where Europe was concerned, the way in which history was organized as a profession in the later nineteenth century further reinforced the rise of national and nationalist specialties. Universities, which grew and flourished in the 1870s and after, were state institutions in most of continental Europe. The prestigious private institutions of higher learning in Britain and the United States overlapped with government in other ways, since professors were members of the same small upper class as politicians. It was natu-

7. Thomas N. Baker, "National History in the Age of Michelet, Macauley, and Bancroft," in Kramer and Maza, *Companion to Western Historical Thought*, 185.

8. Hugh B. MacDougall, *Racial Myth in English History: Trojans, Teutons, and Anglo-Saxons* (Hanover, NH: University Press of New England, 1982); Zeev Sternhell, *Neither Right nor Left: Fascist Ideology in France* (Princeton, NJ: Princeton University Press, 1996).

9. Kwame Anthony Appiah, *In My Father's House: Africa in the Philosophy of Culture* (London: Methuen, 1992), especially chapters 1–2.

ral, if not inevitable, for the first generations of "professional" historians to focus on, and usually celebrate, the history of their respective nations.[10]

Of course, most history books are not general surveys of a country's past; they deal with more focused topics—a person or group of people, a town, an event, a specific theme. For professional historians the scale that makes things manageable and allows for in-depth research is regional; in order to say something significant about prostitution, labor disputes, religious practice, consumer culture, or the effects of war it is usually best to focus on a specific area. Take, for instance, a book that is considered a classic in its field, *Family Fortunes: Men and Women of the English Middle Class, 1780–1850* by Lenore Davidoff and Catherine Hall (1987), which opens thus: "*Family Fortunes* is a book about the ideologies, institutions, and practices of the English middle class from the end of the eighteenth to the mid nineteenth centuries."[11] In fact, the book focuses on a very specific place, the manufacturing city of Birmingham and two rural counties adjacent to it, Essex and Suffolk. Yet the authors apply their conclusions to "England" as a whole, arguing that the middle classes made claims to moral superiority over both the aristocracy and the working classes based on the practice of evangelical Protestantism, that women were central to this process, and that their religion-centered culture "had lasting effects not only on relations between the sexes but also in definitions of who was part of the English nation."[12]

Family Fortunes is just one example—thousands more could be easily found—of the paradox at the heart of most academic historical practice: in order to do serious work, your focus must be local; in order to be taken seriously, your questions and arguments must be national.[13] You may work on Kentucky, Chiapas, or Hubei Province, but you are entering a conversation

10. Georg Iggers and Q. Edward Wang, *A Global History of Modern Historiography* (New York: Routledge, 2013), chapter 2.

11. Leonore Davidoff and Catherine Hall, *Family Fortunes: Men and Women of the English Middle Class, 1780–1850* (Chicago: University of Chicago Press, 1987), 13.

12. Ibid., 450.

13. This local/national pattern applies especially to social history. The strategy of close scrutiny in the service of larger-gauge arguments, the typical approach of academic historians, gets applied in other ways to different subfields, as when a study of a circle of a dozen scientists is the basis for a book subtitled "Scientific Thought in the Sixteenth Century."

among professional historians about the United States, Mexico, or China. Graduate students writing masters' theses or dissertations, even undergraduates writing papers or theses, are routinely badgered by their professors to explain how their work contributes to the debate about a Big Question. And that question is nearly always national in scope.

Why should we not continue—as indeed, to a large extent we do—writing history as a conversation about national events and national destinies? The answer is essentially twofold: first, overlapping developments over many decades have led scholars to emphasize how recent, artificial, fragile, and culturally limited is the very concept of the nation-state; second, in recent years scholars, especially historians, have become increasingly aware of the many aspects of the past that are either neglected or distorted if we confine ourselves to national contexts. As we saw in the last chapter, the nature of historical inquiry is significantly altered when we look to different kinds of people in the past. Similarly, the questions and answers change significantly depending on how you carve up space.

A century ago nationalism was at its height. When a Europe-wide war broke out in 1914 for obscure reasons of international diplomacy, political parties in each country put aside their differences, soldiers marched off in a haze of patriotic fervor, and almost nobody questioned the need to slaughter fellow Europeans or the glory of a battlefield death. Since then, multiple and overlapping historical developments have made such unquestioning nationalist zeal a thing of the past. Over the last century, for every morally defensible conflict, such as World War II, there have been many more, from World War I to the conflicts in Vietnam, Afghanistan, and Iraq, that have left people wondering why so many must perish in the name of "national interest." Even the archetypal "good war" delivered the horrors of Hiroshima and Nagasaki. Extreme nationalism was tainted in the mid-twentieth century by its association with murderously repressive regimes in Spain, Italy, Japan, and especially Germany. And in subsequent decades, critics of the West began to point out that standard concepts of the nation and nationalism were Euro-American inventions arbitrarily imposed upon colonized peoples. With nationalist enterprises increasingly subject to question, many people, the young especially, sought the selfless idealism once associated with national spirit in international institutions like the United Nations or the International Criminal Court, and especially in nongovernmental organizations such as Amnesty International or Doctors without Borders. Finally, in recent decades cheaper air travel and telecommunications, and above all the internet, have brought national barriers down at an increasing pace—especially for the sorts of people who read, write, teach, and learn history.

These developments in the public world have been mirrored in the academic world by scholarly trends toward "denaturalizing" nationhood, that is, exposing its artificiality by looking at how and why this particular way of conceiving of human communities came about. The book that ignited this approach, and remains highly influential, is *Imagined Communities: Reflections on the Origin and Spread of Nationalism* (1983) by the political scientist Benedict Anderson.[14] At a time when most people thought of "the nation" as a natural and inevitable unit, Anderson proposed a far different definition: the nation "is an imagined political community—and imagined as both inherently limited and sovereign." Nations are *imagined*, he argues, because unlike a parish, a village, or a city-state they are made up predominantly of people who will never meet: they exist, not "out there," but in people's heads. Unlike potentially universal entities such as empires or religions, a nation is imagined as *limited*, with finite physical boundaries that separate them from other states; as *sovereign*, independent from any supranational body, as in "one nation under God indivisible"; and as a *community*, a horizontal "fraternity" of beings bound together by emotional ties and beliefs so vivid that men—citizens were long imagined as only male—are willing to kill and die for them.[15] Nationalism might be visceral and idealistic, Anderson argues, but it grew out of eighteenth- and nineteenth-century technological and commercial developments such as the "print capitalism" that gave us the daily national newspaper. Readers who consume the same information, the same day, in a language particular to their country, are constantly made aware of the existence of others to whom they are virtually connected by such time- and space-bound rituals.[16] In the nineteenth-century West, faith remained a powerful guide and consolation for individuals, but with the decline of religion as a way of explaining broader public and historical forces, membership in a "nation," with a particular, redemptive destiny, became a way of linking random individual fates to a larger purpose, of "creating links between the dead and

14. Benedict Anderson, *Imagined Communities: Reflections on the Origin and Spread of Nationalism*, 1st rev. ed. (London: Verso, 1991).

15. Ibid., 6–7.

16. Ibid., 22–46.

the yet unborn."[17] While scholars following Anderson have stressed that modern countries are neither natural nor "timeless," they also recognize that nations take concrete forms leading to tangible effects. "Imagined communities" spawn bureaucracies, armies, schools, laws, police forces, censuses, passports—in short, multiple forms of instruction and control that affect, sometimes tragically, the real lives of millions of people.

Around the same time Anderson's book appeared, historians were beginning to draw attention to the various ways fictions of the modern nation's deep historical roots had been constructed.[18] In Europe and America most of the major symbols of national belonging—flags, national capitals, anthems, monuments, and commemorative holidays—date from the last quarter of the nineteenth century: Bastille Day did not become a national holiday in France until 1880, royal jubilees in England began under Queen Victoria, and as we are reminded every time a controversy erupts, the American Pledge of Allegiance dates from 1892 and only received federal endorsement in 1942. Republics are not the only regimes to work at fabricating the illusion of deep roots. The most creative architects of national "tradition" have been the British, who began in the latter part of Queen Victoria's reign to fabricate and market royal ceremonies and trappings that were quickly enshrined as customs preserved from a distant past: royal weddings, coronations, jubilees, and funerals, the opening of Parliament, horse-drawn carriages, and flashy regalia—all of which would have been unrecognizable to the British two centuries ago.[19] (The most egregious case of the "invention of tradition" in the British Isles, however, took place a century earlier, in the 1760s, when enthusiasts for the Scottish past, some of them enterprising British businessmen, created the Scottish Highland tradition from whole cloth, concocting kilts, tartans, and an entirely fake ancient bard named Ossian.)[20] It was also in the late nineteenth century that Japanese political elites, inspired by Western developments, constructed the "centuries-old" cult of the emperor as avatar of the nation, building an imperial palace in 1889, instituting numerous ceremonies centered on the monarch, and sending

17. Ibid., 10–11.

18. The book that opened this line of inquiry, published the same year as *Imagined Communities*, was Eric Hobsbawm and Terence Ranger, eds., *The Invention of Tradition* (Cambridge: Cambridge University Press, 1983).

19. Ibid., chapters 1, 4, 7.

20. Ibid., chapter 2.

him on imperial tours that would expose him to the eyes of as many subjects as possible. Prior to the Meiji period, popular impressions of the emperor were vague, nonexistent, or enmeshed with folk beliefs that had little to do with politics or national consciousness.[21]

Nations, then, for all their political, cultural, and emotional power, are relatively recent historical developments for which the illusion of deep historical roots was created over time by historians, politicians, and others. Their creation stems from international as well as domestic developments: the earliest forms of modern nationalism were forged in North and South America in opposition to British and Spanish metropolitan power, and the latest, in twentieth-century Africa and Southeast Asia as part of a complicated dynamic of imitation and repudiation of foreign colonizers.[22] For all that it is comparatively recent, national identity has loomed large in people's self-understanding, and historians have long been interested in exploring how people come to view themselves as "Korean," "Irish," or "Australian," and how the specific components of that identity may change over time.

For communities as for individuals, what we choose to do (agency) is inseparable from who we think we are (identity), and the latter in turn depends on the selection and management of memories from our individual and collective pasts. As cognitive psychologists remind us, "remembering" is a slippery process that has as much to do with our vision of the future as with our ideas about the past.[23] When historians began in the 1980s to approach the modern nation as an "imagined community," a new field of historical study emerged, devoted to the study of memory in history, and specifically to the ways in which the leaders and populations of modern nations have chosen to remember, but also, crucially, to forget, elements of their collective past. As the nineteenth-century French writer Ernest Renan famously put it, "The essence of a nation is that all individuals have many things in common, but also that they have forgotten many things."[24]

---

21. Takashi Fujitani, *Splendid Monarchy: Power and Pageantry in Modern Japan* (Berkeley: University of California Press, 1996).

22. Anderson, *Imagined Communities*, chapters 4 and 7.

23. Jay Winter, *Remembering War: The Great War between Memory and History in the Twentieth Century* (New Haven, CT: Yale University Press, 2006), 3–4.

24. Cited in Kramer, *Nationalism in Europe and America*, 73. See also John Gillis, ed., *Commemorations: The Politics of National Identity* (Princeton, NJ: Princeton University Press, 1994), 7.

Most modern nations were born through a twin process of repudiation and commemoration. In France, for instance, the revolutionaries of 1789 quickly started calling the past from which they distanced themselves the "Old Regime" and introduced a new calendar that took as its year one the establishment of the Republic in 1792. The leaders of the French Revolution obliterated the past by organizing large festivals to celebrate what one historian has called the "mythic present": on the first anniversary of the fall of the Bastille, hundreds of thousands gathered from across the nation in a giant "Festival of Federation," the first of many such celebrations of the new order.[25] The United States dates its birth from the rejection of colonial rule, as later would many nations in the Americas, Africa, and Asia. The celebrations that accompany the commemoration of revolutionary origins—fireworks, speeches, military parades—have interested historians as the most obvious expressions of the construction and reinforcement of national identity. Mostly, though, histories of national memory have gravitated to the ways in which nations organize the remembrance of war: in the wake of murderous conflict, what gets remembered, how, and why?

Before the twentieth century, military heroics were commemorated—in histories, paintings, tapestries, and sculptures—as the exploits of rulers and commanders: it was Alexander, Mehmed II, or Frederick the Great who "won" the battles, not the anonymous cannon fodder hastily thrown into burial pits before the army lumbered on. Before the twentieth century obscure men who died in violent circumstances were occasionally listed on monuments—English insurgents in the 1819 Peterloo Massacre, Parisians who perished in the Revolution of 1830—but the Great War of 1914–1918 was a watershed in the democratization of national remembrance. For the first time, governments in Europe and America started recording the names and identifying the bodies of the hundreds of thousands of ordinary soldiers who died in battle. As early as 1916 the British government set about collecting the corpses and marking the graves of as many fallen men as possible, and as soon as the war was over its major battlefields were marked by huge cemeteries and monuments bearing the names of the dead. In hundreds of French villages statues were erected in the central town square

---

25. Lynn Hunt, *Politics, Culture and Class in the French Revolution* (Berkeley: University of California Press, 1984); Mona Ozouf, *Festivals and the French Revolution*, trans. Alan Sheridan (Cambridge, MA: Harvard University Press, 1991).

depicting a *poilu*—the hairy-faced trench-fighter—atop a pedestal listing fallen locals, and to honor those whose bodies or names were lost in the carnage governments created and solemnly honored a tomb of the "unknown soldier."[26] Modern practices of war remembrance, from World War I to Vietnam and beyond, thus assert the link between democracy and nationalism: the sheer number of the dead, the names that rise above you or surround you at Menin Gate or the Vietnam War Memorial, provide a visceral demonstration that the ultimate proof of the nation's existence is the purposeful mass sacrifice of "ordinary heroes" on the battlefield.

Nations exist, then, through what they choose to remember, and how. But nation-making and nurturing also usually involves, as Renan noted, forms of collective amnesia, and this is especially the case in the wake of traumatically divisive events. Take, for instance, the American Civil War: how would the United States come to grips, after it ended, with the deaths of some 620,000 soldiers in a conflict that tore the nation apart? How could one possibly commemorate such deeply divisive carnage? As David Blight argues in a landmark book, *Race and Reunion*, North and South came together after the war by conveniently "forgetting" the cause of the fighting, slavery, and its outcome, black emancipation. In the decades after the war, a "reconciliationist" theme dominated official commemorations such as "Decoration Days" and the newly minted Memorial Day, which emphasized the commonalities between fallen "blues" and "grays." Poets, politicians, and veterans themselves stressed the similarity between Northern and Southern soldiers who, it was said, gave their lives gallantly for what they believed to be a just cause. Meanwhile, a white-supremacist version of past events, which found its most famous expression in D. W. Griffith's blockbuster movie *Birth of a Nation* (1915), proposed that blacks themselves had somehow caused the war by coming between "Aryan" brothers and sexually threatening their womenfolk. At the fiftieth-anniversary commemoration of the battle of Gettysburg in early July 1913, attended by over fifty thousand surviving combatants as well as President Woodrow Wilson, not a word was said about slavery and emancipation, and black veterans were specifically excluded from the ceremony. The civil and political rights

26. Thomas W. Laqueur, "Memory and Naming in the Great War," and Daniel Sherman, "Art, Commerce, and the Production of Memory in France after World War I," in Gillis, *Commemorations*, 150–67, 186–211; Winter, *Remembering War*.

of African-Americans, Blight concludes, became "sacrificial offerings on the altar of reunion."[27]

Reunion and reconciliation were similarly burning issues for the French in the wake of World War II. After their country fell in 1940, the French were jointly governed by the German authorities and by Marshal Pétain's collaborationist government based in Vichy, while General Charles de Gaulle fled to London, where he proclaimed himself the head of the Free French. The "dark years," 1941–1945, were a messy period of compromise and betrayal; most notoriously, French officials actively participated in, and in some instances initiated, the deportation from their country of around 77,000 Jews, most of whom were killed by the Nazis. Segments of the French population joined, sometimes belatedly, the many anti-German resistance groups; after the liberation, resisters took violent revenge against known or suspected collaborators. Coming to power in the 1950s, De Gaulle and his associates brought the country together by promoting a narrative of the recent past in which the Vichy government had no popular support and a majority of the French either belonged to or supported the Resistance. The new leaders consciously orchestrated the cult of Jean Moulin, the head of the Free French Resistance; tortured and executed by the Germans, Moulin became the official face of the war years. While Oradour-sur-Glane in central France, where in 1944 over six hundred villagers were massacred by the Germans, became a pilgrimage site as early as 1946, its torched ruins carefully preserved for visitors, it took decades for the French authorities to acknowledge their role in sending hundreds of Jewish children to their deaths.[28] As in the case of the American Civil War, national cohesion was predicated on willful amnesia, in this case concerning France's active collaboration with the Germans and its role in the Holocaust.[29] In both the American and the French cases, historians working on the construction of national identity have uncovered ways in which leaders and populations cre-

27. David W. Blight, *Race and Reunion: The Civil War in American Memory* (Cambridge, MA: Harvard University Press, 2001), 139.

28. Sarah Farmer, *Martyred Village: Commemorating the 1944 Massacre at Oradour-sur-Glane* (Berkeley: University of California Press, 1999).

29. Henry Rousso, *The Vichy Syndrome: History and Memory in France since 1944*, trans. Arthur Goldhammer (Cambridge, MA: Harvard University Press, 1991).

ate stories and ceremonies that enshrine some memories and seek to bury others, sometimes at the expense of whole categories of the population.

The nation as "imagined community," the "invention of tradition," the cultivation and manipulation of "national memory"—all of these areas of inquiry have produced research and writing by historians in support of the proposition that "national identity" is not typically deep-rooted, inevitable, or eternal. Even as most historians continue to focus on entities like Japan, Germany, or Brazil, a couple of decades' worth of work on the "cultural construction" of nationhood has made for much more intellectual skepticism about the once self-evident link between history and the national context. Alongside this denaturalizing of the nation has developed a growing awareness that many aspects of humanity's past, and extremely important ones at that, simply cannot be studied within the confines of a nation.

OCEANS, MIDDLE GROUNDS, BORDERLANDS

Probably the best-known instance of a history that transcends not only national borders but continental divides is the story of the Atlantic slave trade, which from the sixteenth to the nineteenth century involved the forced transportation of about eleven million Africans (the exact number is disputed, the order of magnitude is not) from their native continent to the Americas. The "triangular trade" was long regarded as a morally reprehensible but marginal feature of early modern European history that took place mostly in the eighteenth century: British and French merchants brought "trinkets" to gullible African chiefs, exchanged these for slaves, swapped their human cargo for colonial products, and returned to enrich themselves and their countries of origin. For many decades now, historians have gone far beyond that simplistic, Europe-centered scenario to demonstrate that the Atlantic slave trade has a long, deep, and complicated multinational history, with controversial causes and immense consequences—a story that can be studied in one part of the world but whose ultimate explanation requires knowledge of many populations, economies, and cultures.[30] The capture and enslavement of significant

30. The literature on this subject is enormous; the portion in English includes the works of Philip Curtin, David Eltis, Stanley Engerman, David Galenson, Herbert S. Klein, Joseph Miller, David Richardson, and John Thornton, among many others. For a striking visual overview of the subject, see Eltis and Richardson, eds., *Atlas of the Transatlantic Slave Trade* (New Haven, CT: Yale University Press, 2010).

numbers of Africans goes back at least to the sixteenth century, when the Portuguese put them to work on sugar plantations in Atlantic locales such as the Azores, Canary Islands, and Cape Verde. It involved all of the countries on the western end of Europe—Portugal, Spain, France, Holland, and Britain principally—and resulted not just in the sort of plantation slavery familiar to students of United States history but in forced labor in occupations ranging from gold, silver, and diamond mining in Mexico and Brazil to domestic service in New England.

Explaining the Atlantic slave trade involves stripping away facile assumptions ("Africans were destined for slavery," "slave traders were evil racists") and posing questions whose answers require a deep knowledge of the economies and cultures of three continents. Why didn't Europeans just transport the very poor from their own cultures? Why didn't they enslave populations that were native to the Americas? And most controversially, to what extent and why were Africans themselves active agents in the trade, capturing their countrymen for the slave market? The answers to these and other questions involve knowledge about demography and labor markets in Europe, landholding and political structures in preconquest Latin America, epidemiology, the history of African warfare, and business institutions and attitudes toward religious and racial "others" in premodern Europe, to name but a few of a long list of topics. Just as the causes of this huge history exceed one national or even continental context, so do the consequences. Understanding why many Africans, both in the New World and in Africa itself, embraced Christianity necessitates a deep understanding of both African and European religious traditions: the commonalities mattered (both traditions revolved around the interpretation of revelation), as did the differences (African spiritual life, less susceptible than its European counterpart to rigid orthodoxies, was more open to outside influence).[31] Understanding the massive slave rebellion that broke out in what is now Haiti in August 1791 and resulted in the Haitian Revolution requires knowing about the African spiritual traditions of Voodoo and Santería, about work and social relations on the island's sugar plantations, and about the political his-

---

For a narrative overview, see Klein's *The Atlantic Slave Trade* (Cambridge: Cambridge University Press 2010), which includes a helpful bibliographic essay.

31. John Thornton, *Africa and Africans in the Making of the Atlantic World, 1400–1680* (Cambridge: Cambridge University Press, 1992), chapter 9.

tory of the French Revolution.[32] In short, the Atlantic slave trade, a centuries-long process whose consequences still shape much of the western hemisphere, is an episode of humanity's past that transcends the familiar national frameworks of history.

What happens when you put bodies of water instead of landmasses at the center of historical inquiry? Scholarship on the Atlantic slave trade is probably the best-known example of a distinct and increasingly popular form of historical research centered on oceanic expanses rather than countries or continents. The template for this genre is Mediterranean history, which has for a very long time been the context for the study of Western antiquity, but recent decades have seen the flowering of Atlantic, Pacific, and Indian Ocean histories as well.[33] The current popularity of these "oceanic" histories clearly reflects the preoccupations of the late twentieth and early twenty-first centuries, our fixation on cultural encounters and hybridity, and on human movement—commerce, migration, travel—rather than tradition and stasis.

Practitioners of, for instance, Atlantic history acknowledge that the label covers a vast array of different questions and approaches.[34] Despite the label, very little Atlantic history concerns the ocean itself: while some scholars point out that currents, trade winds, and tributary rivers (Rhine, Amazon, Saint Lawrence, Mississippi) have shaped the history of this part of the globe, others counter that climatological differences between the North

---

32. Laurent Dubois, *Avengers of the New World: The Story of the Haitian Revolution* (Cambridge, MA: Harvard University Press, 2004).

33. For useful introductions to this mode of inquiry, see the forum "Oceans of History," *American Historical Review* 111 (June 2006): 717–80, which includes an overview and helpful articles on Mediterranean, Atlantic, and Pacific history. See also Jerry H. Bentley, Renathe Bridenthal, and Kären Wigen, eds. *Seascapes: Maritime Histories, Littoral Cultures, and Transoceanic Exchanges* (Honolulu: History of Hawaii Press, 2007).

34. Alison Games, "Atlantic History: Definitions, Challenges, and Opportunities," *American Historical Review* 111 (June 2006): 741–57; Bernard Bailyn, *Atlantic History: Concepts and Contours* (Cambridge, MA: Harvard University Press, 2005); Jack P. Greene and Philip Morgan, eds., *Atlantic History: A Critical Appraisal* (Oxford: Oxford University Press, 2009); David Armitage, "Three Concepts of Atlantic History," in Armitage and Michael J. Braddick, eds., *The British Atlantic World, 1500–1800* (London: Palgrave Macmillan, 2002).

and South Atlantic define two different natural worlds.[35] In any event, "the Atlantic" is every bit as much a cultural construction as any land-based nation; it was only identified as a single body of water once Europeans began to sail and chart its waters. Atlantic history in the most literal sense might be taken as the story of life upon the ocean, much of which has been chronicled over the years with great skill: histories of merchants and explorers, of sailors, pirates and convicts, of war at sea, and most tragically, of the ordeal of slaves during the notorious "middle passage." All of these topics, now folded into Atlantic history, once made up the canon of what is more traditionally known as "maritime history."[36]

In its more broadly accepted sense, Atlantic history is less concerned specifically with these water-bound experiences than with charting the interaction between populations across the ocean's vast expanse: the transport of African slaves, the emigration of Europeans to North and South America, the movement of goods in both directions, the interlocking of economies, the exchange of ideas and culture. The field has sometimes invited criticism or suspicion that it is rooted in Cold War ideology: in 1945 the president of the American Historical Association, Carleton Hayes, delivered a famous address inviting scholars to focus on the Atlantic, and especially on the Anglo-American nexus, as they once had on the Mediterranean, as the new "inland sea of Western civilization," now under threat from forces in the East.[37]

We may have moved away from the notion that Columbus and others "discovered" something called "the New World," but there is no denying the initial centrality of European history to the Atlantic field, which usually starts with Portuguese and Spanish seafarers sailing west in the fifteenth century, culminates in the age of "Atlantic revolutions," and tapers off with the growth of a more global world system in the nineteenth century. Renais-

35. Bailyn, *Atlantic History*, 83; Greene and Morgan, *Atlantic History*, 6.

36. For examples of this approach, see Marcus Rediker, *Between the Devil and the Deep Blue Sea: Merchant Seamen, Pirates, and the Anglo-American Maritime World, 1700–1750* (Cambridge: Cambridge University Press, 1987); Peter Linebaugh and Marcus Rediker, *The Many-Headed Hydra: Sailors, Slaves, Commoners and the Hidden History of the Revolutionary Atlantic* (Boston: Beacon Press, 2013).

37. Bailyn, *Atlantic History*, 12–13. Armitage and Braddick, *British Atlantic World*, 13–14.

sance exploration touched off, as one commentator describes it, not the discovery of a new world but "a sudden and harsh encounter between two old worlds that transformed both and integrated them into a single New World."[38] For many years now, and certainly since the 1972 publication of Alfred Crosby's classic *The Columbian Exchange*, we have gotten used to thinking of the Atlantic as the setting for a two-way (at least) process with global consequences. With the Europeans came cattle, horses, sheep, and other livestock, but also deadly smallpox; they sailed back to their home countries with a comparable array of blessings and curses: potatoes, beans, maize, manioc, cacao, but also syphilis.[39] Tallying the costs and benefits of this exchange is nearly impossible: how does one measure the lethal effects of smallpox on millions of Amerindians against the benefits of diversified livestock and crops on all continents? Undeniably, though, both America and Europe emerged from the interpenetration of each other's ecologies utterly transformed. The "Columbian exchange" is a classic illustration of the point that the panoramic, transnational purview of "oceanic" histories allows us to uncover crucial stories about the human past that would otherwise go untold.

That is not to say that all oceanic history has to be told on a grand scale: in many cases, historians have used the wider framework of intercontinental mobility to illuminate a specific locale. Two books published in 2004 offer complementary examples of this approach on either side of the Atlantic. April Hatfield's *Atlantic Virginia* describes the ways in which seventeenth-century Virginians learned their trade routes from the Powhatan Indians while adapting their models for slaveholding from Caribbean societies, especially Barbados; different parts of the state were connected, via groups of immigrants, to various French, Spanish, and British Caribbean colonies. Across the ocean, as Juan Javier Pescador shows in *The New World inside a Basque Village*, migrants returning from Latin America with new wealth undermined the social structure and cultural traditions of the small Basque town of Donostia, as some inhabitants came to rely more on imperial connections than local ones.[40] Thanks to environmental historians of North

---

38. D. W. Meinig in 1986, as quoted in Bailyn, *Atlantic History*, 55.

39. Alfred Crosby, *The Columbian Exchange: The Biological and Cultural Consequences of 1492* (Westport, CT: Greenwood Publishing, 1972).

40. April Lee Hatfield, *Atlantic Virginia: Intercolonial Relations in the Seventeenth*

America, we have come to understand the ways in which far-flung migration and commerce reshaped specific local landscapes such as the Connecticut River valley, as French Protestant refugees showed British colonists how to exploit trees for turpentine, or the desire of Europeans for luxurious pelts resulted in the disappearance of beaver dams.[41]

Atlantic history can even take the form of individual biography. One of the downsides of recent trends toward transnational and global history is that privileging the larger scale can make it difficult to focus on small groups and individual destinies. Historians have of late been finding ways of combining geographic sweep with the story of ordinary people, for instance, by tracking individuals who moved across borders and even oceans.[42] A recent book by James H. Sweet, for instance, tells the story of Domingos Álvares, an enslaved African transported to Brazil who worked on a sugar plantation in the north, was sold to another master in Rio de Janeiro, and eventually was manumitted only to be arrested by the Inquisition. The Catholic authorities shipped him to Portugal where he was tortured and nearly executed, before disappearing into the Iberian countryside. What made Álvares unusual among the millions who shared experiences like his—besides his three-continent odyssey—was his skill as a healer/priest, probably learned from his African parents: his status as a "fetisher" gave him some purchase on the worlds into which he was thrust, as his masters both feared and relied upon him. Only because of his success as a freelance healer in Rio did Álvares come to the attention of the religious authorities, only because

Century (Philadelphia: University of Pennsylvania Press, 2004); Juan Javier Pescador, *The New World inside a Basque Village: The Oiartzun Valley and Its Atlantic Emigrants, 1550–1800* (Reno: University of Nevada Press, 2004).

41. William Cronon, *Changes in the Land: Indians, Colonists, and the Ecology of New England,* 2nd ed. (1983; New York: Hill and Wang, 2003); Strother E. Roberts, "The Commodities of the Country: An Environmental History of the Colonial Connecticut Valley," PhD diss., Northwestern University, 2011.

42. For instance, Natalie Davis, *Trickster Travels: A Sixteenth-Century Muslim between Worlds* (New York: Hill and Wang, 2007); Linda Colley, *The Ordeal of Elizabeth Marsh: A Woman in World History* (New York: Pantheon, 2007); Rebecca Scott and Jean Hébrard, *Freedom Papers: An Atlantic Odyssey in the Age of Emancipation* (Cambridge, MA: Harvard University Press, 2012). A searching discussion of the issue is Amy Stanley, "Maidservants' Tales: Narrating Domestic and Global History in Eurasia, 1600–1900" *American Historical Review* 121 (April 2016): 437–60.

he had been freed was he vulnerable to arrest, and only because of the Inquisition's six-hundred-page dossier do we know his life story. The accidentally documented saga of Domingos Álvares affords us a close-up look at the transmission and transformation of cultures (Álvares converted to Catholicism without giving up his African beliefs) and at the way in which practices such as healing protected and perpetuated, in other contexts, the cultures from which millions had been ripped away.[43]

Central aspects of Álvares's story also remind us that Atlantic currents ferried cultures and ideas as well as persons and goods. The classic, and most familiar, version of this theme has the wind of freedom gusting back and forth across the water in the later eighteenth century, in what a venerable study called the "Age of the Democratic Revolution" (note the singular—this was *one* revolution): the French Enlightenment stirred leaders in the Thirteen Colonies, whose self-emancipation inspired the French in 1789; the French Revolution in turn moved Haitian slaves and free blacks to ask why they were not included in the Declaration of the Rights of Man, and their successful insurrection after 1791 fueled both revolutionary hopes (for blacks) and repressive paranoia (among whites) throughout the Americas for many decades.[44] The story of the eighteenth-century Atlantic revolutions is still often presented as the opening act of humanity's progress toward the modern world: in this vision, the intellectual and political dynamic between late eighteenth-century France and America provided the template for democratic revolution the world over, a precondition for the

43. James H. Sweet, *Domingos Álvares, African Healing, and the Intellectual History of the Atlantic World* (Chapel Hill: University of North Carolina Press, 2011).

44. The classic study of the "Atlantic revolutions," focusing only on Europe and North America, is R. R. Palmer, *The Age of the Democratic Revolution: A Political History of Europe and America*, 2 vols. (Princeton, NJ: Princeton University Press, 1959–1965). For more specific studies, see Bernard Bailyn, *The Ideological Origins of the American Revolution* (Cambridge, MA: Harvard University Press, 1967); Durand Echeverria, *Mirage in the West: A History of the French Image of American Society to 1815* (New York: Octagon Books, 1966); Laurent Dubois, *A Colony of Citizens: Revolution and Slave Emancipation in the French Caribbean, 1787–1804* (Chapel Hill: University of North Carolina Press, 2004); David Geggus, ed., *The Impact of the Haitian Revolution in the Atlantic World* (Columbia: University of South Carolina Press, 2001).

advent of that nebulous entity known as "modernity."[45] Historians now routinely include the Caribbean and Latin American revolutions of this period under the umbrella term "Atlantic revolutions," but the narrative arc often remains the classic tale of contagious freedom, with progressive or revolutionary European ideas spreading to other parts of the world.

It was this narrative that a sociologist named Paul Gilroy challenged in his celebrated 1993 book *The Black Atlantic*, a history of the intellectual and cultural legacy of Atlantic slavery. In the classic narratives, Atlantic history focuses mainly, if not entirely, on what was done to Africans and their descendants. Gilroy's study is instead about what the descendants of slaves did—what they wrote and created, and how it has for many decades provided an alternative to the triumphalist story of the European Atlantic. Gilroy posits that blacks in the modern West, whether in Europe or America, have created cultural and intellectual traditions that escape and challenge national frameworks: black culture, whether the writings of intellectuals like W. E. B. Du Bois or Richard Wright, or the music of funk or rap singers, is rooted in the transnational experience of slavery. African-Americans and European blacks inhabit, he argues, what Du Bois called a "double consciousness," a condition of alienation from the places in which they live that makes ultimate identification with any national entity impossible. What Gilroy calls the "Black Atlantic" is the cultural space occupied by the descendants of black slaves, whose ancestors' "modernity" was made up of whips, shackles, and slave ships. In contrast to traditional narratives of "Atlantic modernity," which have emancipatory ideas careening back and forth between the old and new worlds, Gilroy's *Black Atlantic* posits a "counterculture of modernity," a nationless space of resistance, and presents a striking example of how to write intellectual and cultural history outside of, and indeed *against*, national frameworks.[46]

Ocean-centered history—Atlantic, Pacific, Indian—has shown that challenging traditional geographies can radically change our understanding of

45. Palmer, *Age of the Democratic Revolution*; Jacques Godechot, *France and the Atlantic Revolution of the Eighteenth Century, 1770–1799*, trans. Herbert Rowen (New York: Free Press, 1965). On the concept of modernity in history, see "AHR Roundtable: Historians and the Question of 'Modernity,'" *American Historical Review* 116 (June 2011): 631–751.

46. Paul Gilroy, *The Black Atlantic: Modernity and Double Consciousness* (Cambridge, MA: Harvard University Press, 1993).

the past, just as extending our attention to previously overlooked people has. If you carve out space differently or redirect your gaze from the obvious places you are likely to come up with different actors and different stories. Traditional nation-based histories work from the center outward as accounts of how ruling elites "built the nation," sometimes with the help of uprisings by "the people." Standard historical narratives usually privilege capital cities or other urban centers, and while their tone is not always triumphalist they typically take for granted an endpoint at which everyone eventually becomes "British," "Polish," or "Australian." A typical example might be Eugen Weber's *Peasants into Frenchmen* (1976), a vivid account of how illiterate, dialect-speaking, witchcraft-believing peasants came, between 1870 and 1914, to consider themselves members of the French nation thanks to railways, free and compulsory primary schooling, and universal conscription.[47]

But what if we take the opposite view—that identities are constructed not at the center but on the periphery, that only in the remote regions where one people encounters another does it become important to define who you are and why? Such is the assumption behind the large and growing field known as "borderlands" history. In contrast to Weber's national history, Peter Sahlins's *Boundaries: The Making of France and Spain in the Pyrenees* (1989) focuses on a tiny, remote area: the Cerdanya, a high valley in the Pyrenees mountains bisected by the frontier between France and Spain. The area saw warfare in the seventeenth century and was divided between the two countries in 1660, though the border was not precisely defined until 1868. The inhabitants of the tiny villages of Cerdanya shared the same culture and the same language—Catalan—but fell under different national jurisdictions. Over the decades, they came increasingly to assert claims—to use pastures, to dam a river, diverting its flow to serve their needs—by appealing to the authorities of their respective nations. A 1740 petition by the inhabitants of the village of La Tor de Carol to the French authorities over a disputed tract of land contains many references to "the haughty and insulting manners of the Spaniards," described as "foreign neighbors" despite being fellow Catalans from a nearby village with whom the petitioners were heavily intermarried.[48] Because of disputes over land,

47. Eugen Weber, *Peasants into Frenchmen: The Modernization of Rural France, 1870–1914* (Stanford, CA: Stanford University Press, 1976).

48. Peter Sahlins, *Boundaries: The Making of France and Spain in the Pyrenees*

boundary areas are the first places to experience the modern definition of the nation as a territory rather than a jurisdiction. Thus, some inhabitants of the Cerdanya probably began to identify themselves as "French," not just "subjects of the King of France," earlier than most of their compatriots. The idea of "France" as an expanse of territory with fixed boundaries, Sahlins suggests, first took shape at the margins, in places like the Pyrenees.

Interest in borderlands is even more pronounced in United States history than in that of most other places since the emergence of what we now call "America" was a complex and lengthy process of conflict and negotiation among many populations. One of the earliest statements of the view that the center of a nation is defined by its margins is the "frontier thesis" articulated at the end of the nineteenth century by the historian Frederick Jackson Turner. In "The Significance of the Frontier in American History," a paper he delivered to the American Historical Association in 1893, Turner proposed that the central features of American politics and culture emerged from the process of westward expansion. The experience of those who, over several generations, pushed ever further west gave America its worst and best features. Violence, individualism, and hostility to high culture, but also energy, courage, and a democratic aversion to inherited privilege: these traits, honed at the edges of the nation, came to define its cultural core. Turner's thesis represented in his time a novel and provocative statement of American exceptionalism: "America" was in no sense an extension of Europe, as the refined urbanites of its Atlantic seaboard liked to imagine, but a unique society defined by a restless push into unknown wilderness: "The American frontier is sharply distinguished from the European frontier, a fortified boundary line running through dense populations," Turner wrote. "The most significant thing about the American frontier is that it lies at the hither edge of free land."[49]

Turner's vision of early Americans marching into "free land" is today discredited by our awareness that in most cases the lands European pioneers trekked into and grabbed already had owners, namely indigenous peoples,

---

(Berkeley: University of California Press, 1989), 162–63.

49. Frederick J. Turner, "The Significance of the Frontier in American History" (1894), https://www.historians.org/about-aha-and-membership/aha-history-and -archives/archives/the-significance-of-the-frontier-in-american-history (accessed January 22, 2016).

and were not theirs to claim by right or destiny.[50] Where Turner granted historical agency only to white pioneers, subsequent historians have told more complex stories of encounter and negotiation. The areas we now think of as "America" and "Canada" were for a very long time the edges of empires, places where French, British, and Spanish traders, warriors, and missionaries encountered each other and indigenous populations. These contact zones between different populations are known as "borderlands," a term that designates not so much a type of place as an approach to national history. To quote an influential article on the subject, "If frontiers were the places where we once told our master American narratives, then borderlands are the places where those narratives come unraveled. . . . If frontiers are spaces of narrative closure, then borderlands are places where stories take unpredictable turns and rarely end as expected."[51] Only when nations establish firm legal boundaries do these internal frontiers and border zones lose their strategic and cultural importance: when borderlands become "bordered" lands, everyone within those borders acquires an identity, either as a citizen or as an alien.[52]

"Borderlands" history sometimes concerns history that happens at those officially designated borders of modern nations that we call frontiers, where rigid boundaries are undermined by migrants, by smugglers, or just by shared language and custom. And sometimes it charts the messier interactions in places where great powers meet, at the edges of empires. Richard White's classic work *The Middle Ground* (1991) tells the story of political and cultural encounters between the French, Native Americans, and English in the western Great Lakes region of North America, the areas bordering lakes Michigan and Superior, in the seventeenth and eighteenth centuries. There, French and English administrators, soldiers, and traders encountered a multiethnic constellation of Native American communities, mostly settled in

50. For an influential critique of Turner by an eminent historian of the American West, see Patricia Nelson Limerick, *The Legacy of Conquest: The Unbroken Past of the American West* (New York: W. W. Norton, 1987).

51. Pekka Hämäläinen and Samuel Truett, "On Borderlands," *Journal of American History* 98 (September 2011): 338.

52. Jeremy Adelman and Stephen Aron, "From Borderlands to Borders: Empires, Nation-States, and the Peoples in Between in North American History," *American Historical Review* 104 (June 1999): 814–41.

villages. As White points out, his is a story set within a world system of imperial ambition—the French and British early-modern expansion—but it takes place at the edges, where empire is at its weakest and minor players without much military clout are forced to improvise.[53] The French and British, competing with each other far from their home bases, had to rely on the indigenous population, while the latter relied on Europeans: no single group could get its way through force. The result was a remarkable process of interpenetration and mediation, as Europeans and indigenous people tried to understand and navigate each others' cultures. In 1682, for instance, two sons of an Ojibwe leader and another warrior murdered two French traders and stole their goods. The local Algonquian tribes intervened to keep the peace by offering to smoke the calumet with the French and to give them slaves to "cover" their dead. This was not to the liking of the French leader, Daniel Dulhut, who tried to impose some form of French law on the proceedings while still including the Indians by inviting his native allies—Ottawa, Chippewa, and Huron-Petun headmen—to participate in a trial and asking them to carry out the execution of the guilty parties. The Algonquians, in turn, were upset and confused by the refusal of their offer of slaves—in their culture, a means to resolve a murder between allies—and the prospect of an execution, which to them would have amounted to a declaration of war. In the end, the French tried to mollify the Native Americans by executing only two of the three murderers, taking a life for a life. Even so, the Indians were shocked by what they viewed as another murder, and the French subsequently made a series of ritual gestures to placate them.[54] This incident shows the tensions between two cultural approaches (one centered on individual guilt, the other organized around the principle of alliance) but also the efforts by both sides to navigate a foreign system of meaning by drawing analogies between different ideas of justice. White's title, *The Middle Ground*, refers not just to a geographical location, the middle of a continent where cultures came into contact with each other, but to a metaphorical place, constituted by the strategies that actors adopted, the shared culture they created, "finding the middle ground" in a historical situation where powers were balanced

53. Richard White, *The Middle Ground: Indians, Empires and Republics in the Great Lakes Region, 1650–1815* (Cambridge: Cambridge University Press, 1991), xi.
54. Ibid., 77–82.

and cooperation was vital. (Once power was consolidated in the hands of a single entity, the American Republic, the government had the resources to wage war against the Indians and this political-cultural middle ground disappeared.)

The words historians use to describe experiences of contact in areas remote from centers of power matter a great deal, and White carried out something of a conceptual revolution by labeling the area he wrote about a "middle ground" rather than a "frontier," since the latter implies, as in Turner's thesis, the one-sided activity of explorers or pioneers pushing up against an empty wilderness. Histories can change dramatically not just when you look to the margins, but also when you tell the story from both sides.

Like White's *Middle Ground*, Timothy Snyder's *Bloodlands: Europe between Stalin and Hitler* (2010), a history of mass murder in Eastern and Central Europe in the 1930s and 1940s, is notable for telling a familiar, atrocious story in a new way.[55] The histories of the mid-twentieth century's mass atrocities are usually told separately: on the one hand, the Soviet Union's labor camps, organized famines, and political exterminations; on the other, the massacre of Jews and other non-Aryans by Hitler's Reich. When we think of Stalin's crimes, the Siberian Gulag comes to mind, while the Holocaust conjures up visions of Auschwitz and other death camps. But as Snyder points out, a vast majority of European noncombatants killed in the 1930s and 1940s perished in fields, forests, villages, and cities rather than death camps, starved to death or summarily shot, not methodically transported and gassed. Most remarkably, the bulk of both Stalin's and Hitler's civilian victims, fourteen million of them, lived and died in an area of Europe sandwiched between Germany and Russia that Snyder calls the "bloodlands": the region from the Baltic in the north to the Black Sea in the south that includes Estonia, Latvia, Lithuania, Poland, Belarus, Ukraine, and Russia's western borderlands. "Stalin's crimes are often associated with Russia," Snyder writes, "and Hitler's with Germany. But the deadliest part of the Soviet Union was its non-Russian periphery, and Nazis generally killed beyond Germany."[56] Fixing our gaze on this region as a whole, without regard to national frontiers—which in any case shifted a great deal throughout the

55. Timothy Snyder, *Bloodlands: Europe between Hitler and Stalin* (New York: Basic Books, 2010).
56. Ibid., xi.

period—allows us to approach the unfathomable yet all too familiar atrocities of this period in a new way.

Over three million people, mostly Ukrainians, died in the 1933 famine that resulted from forced collectivization and food requisitions linked to Stalin's Five-Year Plan for the Soviet economy. When the Germans invaded the Soviet Union in 1941, they too caused a horrific famine, which killed over four million Russians, Belarussians, and Ukrainians, both civilians and prisoners of war; this is in addition to the 5.4 million Jews—as well as Roma, gays, and others—murdered in this part of Europe in the Nazis' pursuit of racial "purification." The methods behind these horrific episodes seem to differ across the Communist-Nazi divide, as do the rationales. Yet hundreds of thousands of other civilians, in Poland and Belarus especially, perished at the hands of both sides in acts of repression and reprisal, most notably among the Polish elites, whom both the Germans and the Russians wanted to eliminate. Why were the same populations so often victims of both Stalin and Hitler? Why did so many die, and why in this particular area?

There is a long tradition, especially prominent during the Cold War, of equating Hitler and Stalin by parking both of their regimes under the umbrella term "totalitarianism." Snyder's approach, however, is based not on symmetrical blame ("Communists were just as bad as Nazis") but on an analysis of the similar geopolitical needs and ambitions of two political monsters with utopian visions for their peoples. Both dictators eyed the same regions—including the vulnerable but geopolitically important buffer state of Poland and the giant "bread basket" of Ukraine. Stalin had given up for a time on expanding the Soviet revolution worldwide, but his dedication to the success of "socialism in one state" required consolidating crucial areas on its periphery; Hitler nourished imperial ambitions—in part due to his obsession with overmatching Britain—and had long dreamed of expanding eastward to lands where he would colonize the locals and relocate the Reich's undesirables.[57] Both mobilized their compatriots by identifying and eliminating scapegoat populations: Stalin justified his mass murder of Poles with conspiracy theories; Hitler held the Jews responsible for most of Europe's problems. Once the two dictators went to war with each other, the casualties increased as noncombatants were accused of sabotage and resistance or simply dispatched for utilitarian reasons.

57. Ibid., 156–58.

Hitler and Stalin, in short, did not carry out their worst political massacres in the geographical heart of their empires but on their margins. Snyder's transnational and geographic focus enables us to see something even more staggering than we had imagined—fourteen million victims in a relatively small area of Europe—and to grasp the interlocking stories that resulted in this protracted atrocity. *Bloodlands* is an example of a book that recasts familiar accounts by adopting a transnational approach based not on the centers of regimes but on their margins.

As we saw in the previous chapter, the kinds of questions historians ask and the stories they tell are radically recast when the spotlight is trained on new groups of people. Reconfiguring historical space has much the same effect: when we look from the margins in, or at the messy boundaries where populations meet and nations clash, or when we put water rather than land at the core of an analysis, we can track histories that remain hidden in a more traditional framework centered on nations and capital cities. Sometimes, finding new stories in new geographies involves, as we have seen, framing a small area in a new way: historians have bought to light the ways in which pressures from distant parts of the world have converged on communities in the Pyrenees, the Basque country, coastal Virginia, the Great Plains. Other narratives, in contrast, require a vast scale, the perspective not of an anthropologist but of an astronaut.

THE RISE OF GLOBAL HISTORY

This large-scale history, whose popularity has increased steadily in recent years, is what is called "global" or "world" history (the terms have slightly different meanings but in practice are used interchangeably).[58] If the tropes of national history are familiar—the story of the origins and development of a nation as made manifest in its leaders or its people, usually told in positive terms and implicitly contrasted to the fate of less admirable others—

---

58. "World history" is the more neutral and capacious term, meaning history on the broadest, in some cases planetary, scale. "Global history" is usually understood to have a more specific meaning: it is related to the term "globalization," which Lynn Hunt defines as "the process by which the world becomes more interconnected and more interdependent." Hunt, *Writing History in the Global Era* (New York: W. W. Norton 2014), 52. In sum, "world" emphasizes scale, while "global" stresses interdependence. See also Pamela Kyle Crossley, *What Is Global History?* (Cambridge: Polity Press, 2008).

"world" history is considerably harder to imagine: what kind of approach, what sort of analysis, could make sense of the experience of the entire planet? Just as no national history can be even remotely comprehensive, world history is a matter of choosing what to highlight and why. A pragmatic definition might be that world or global history usually concerns phenomena that transcend national boundaries and unite different parts of the planet. Some of these, and among the earliest studied, are economic and more generally material in nature: as in the instance of the Atlantic trade, commerce builds connections between distant regions. So too do financial institutions like multinational banks and businesses, or means of long-range communication such as printing or the internet. Also transcending national and even continental boundaries are biological or ecological events such as the spread of disease: the so-called Black Death, an eruption of bubonic plague that killed as many as two hundred million people in an area stretching from Asia to Western Europe in the fourteenth century, was clearly a "world historical" event, as is the current warming of the planet. Culture has also bridged distant parts of the world, as is most clearly the case with influential religions: Islam, Christianity, Judaism, and Buddhism, to name the biggest, have connected communities worldwide and need to be understood in their global scope as well as their local instantiations.[59] All of these phenomena have in common what is called "deterritorialization": the focus of world history is usually not on specific places but on the dynamic intangibles that connect far-flung populations, such as trade, credit, disease, or faith, even as those intangibles have very concrete and sometimes devastating effects.[60] The curiosity that historians and students nowadays harbor for these past instances of worldwide "connectivity" clearly mirrors the daily experience of global interconnection among wealthier, literate populations. World history is perhaps today's most "usable past."

Many older forms of world history have existed for a long time, including mythologies and religious accounts such as the book of Genesis, all of which propose theories of the origins, development, and nature of human life on the planet. Decades ago, back when most history concerned the ruling classes, transnational research frequently fell into the category of "international" or "diplomatic" history, which chronicled transactions be-

---

59. Jerry H. Bentley, "The New World History," in Kramer and Maza, *Companion to Western Historical Thought*, 393–416.

60. Hunt, *Writing History*, 54–55.

tween the political elites of the world's nations.[61] But just as the emergence of social history was driven by a critical awareness of social inequalities, so the central analytical concerns of world history have revolved around disparities in wealth and power between areas of the world, a concern that has generated influential theories known as "world systems."

Approaches that emphasize the socioeconomic development and relation between states on a planetary scale are all in one way or another indebted to the writings of Karl Marx. Marx, who published the first volume of *Das Kapital* in 1867 and died in 1883, identified what he saw as a uniform pattern in the development of societies based on a dynamic rooted in the material world of resources, wealth, and social power. In a range of publications, often written in collaboration with Friedrich Engels, Marx described the transition of societies from tribal to slavery-based to feudal, capitalist, and in the near future, socialist. The forces that, in his theory, provoke transitions are complex, but they include contradictions within the economy (as when increases in production paradoxically lower the value of goods, touching off a search for new sources of profit), or within the social order, when a group (the bourgeoisie or working class) becomes aware that it is producing wealth but being denied the profits generated by its industry and the power that should devolve from them. Marx's theories offer a comprehensive interpretation of worldwide conditions based not on subjective judgments about the attributes of races or nations but on a putatively objective measure, stages of socioeconomic development. In his own time, Marx believed, Europe had advanced furthest in the direction of industrialization and capitalism, North America lagged at an earlier stage, and Asian societies had not yet effected the transition away from feudalism. Some areas of the world, such as the southern United States, combined elements of different stages, while deviations from the pattern in areas like Africa had led to stasis.[62]

Although the idea that all areas of the world go through similar stages of socioeconomic development is no longer widely accepted, Marxism remains highly influential with world historians, not only for its analytical categories (few would question the world-historical significance of something

61. David Washbrook, "Problems in Global History," in Maxine Berg, ed., *Writing the History of the Global: Challenges for the Twenty-First Century* (Oxford: Oxford University Press, 2013), 21.

62. Crossley, *What Is Global History?*, 54–65.

called "capitalism"), but because it allowed later scholars to conceptualize relations between states in ways that are analogous to those between social groups. If Marx is the granddaddy of modern world history, its father might be the historical sociologist Immanuel Wallerstein, who forty years ago began to articulate what remains the best-known historical version of the approach known as "world systems." In 1974 Wallerstein, an Africanist by training, published the first book of his multivolume magnum opus, *The Modern World System.* In his account, our planet started to become a world system in the early modern period, between about 1450 and 1650, when Europe experienced a protracted economic crisis linked to bad weather (a "mini ice age") and collapsing profits. The major states in Western Europe—England, France, Spain, the Netherlands—responded by centralizing power in the form known as "absolute monarchy." The great voyages of discovery, from the fifteenth century forward, were financed by these powerful states and the joint-stock companies they patronized, and whatever the avowed purpose of early modern exploration (finding a route to China, locating Eden, converting the heathen), it resulted in the appropriation of both natural and human resources—raw materials and slaves—which buoyed Europe out of its economic slump. From then on a pattern of exploitation and dependency was established between regions that Wallerstein calls the "core" and those he designates as "periphery." Domination and dependency did not result in a simple binary, since some less unified and industrialized areas of Europe, the German and Slavic states in the east, functioned as "semi-peripheries," providing markets as well as raw materials. Wallerstein's hierarchy of world regions—core, semi-periphery, and periphery—mirrors the relation between bourgeoisie, petty bourgeoisie, and proletariat in Marxian thought. The core-periphery distinction is not, in Wallerstein's view, a fixed state of affairs, since some areas rise into the core (North America) while others decline into semi-periphery (Spain): following Marx, Wallerstein posits that recurring crises within capitalism generate searches for both new markets and new resources in expanding peripheries, periodically destabilizing existing patterns. Wallerstein's work has been predictably debated, criticized, and repudiated by many, but it remains a landmark attempt to make sense of interdependent patterns of worldwide development within a single framework.[63]

63. Ibid., 89–95; Hunt, *Writing History,* 56–57.

Following other pioneering world historians, Wallerstein framed the question that has come to dominate historical accounts on this scale: why and how did Europe—and later America—come, in the last five centuries, to dominate the world materially, militarily, and culturally? The major debates shaping the field of world history in recent decades revolve around, first, the possible answers to this question and, second, whether it should be posed in this way in the first place. A vocal minority of historians continues to insist that Euro-Americans emerged on top because of the positive attributes of Western culture: ingenuity, individualism, industriousness, the stabilizing effects of increasingly enlightened legal and political institutions. Recent evocatively titled books on the subject include *The Wealth and Poverty of Nations: Why Some Are So Rich and Some Are So Poor* (1998) by the prominent economic historian David S. Landes and *Civilization: The West and the Rest* (2011) by the Harvard historian Niall Ferguson.[64] More frequently, though, the starting point for this debate is to note that in the period Europeans call the Late Middle Ages, Asian and Middle Eastern societies were every bit as powerful and sophisticated as their European counterparts. The agenda thus consists in identifying the reasons for what economic historians refer to as the "European miracle" or the "great divergence": how and why did Europe, and later the United States, become the world's dominant powers for most of the nineteenth and twentieth centuries?

The most notable recent contribution to this debate, Kenneth Pomeranz's *The Great Divergence: Europe, China, and the Making of the Modern World Economy* (2000), is also one of the most cited works in the burgeoning field of world history. Classic narratives of the "European miracle" trace the roots of the continent's dominance at least two or three centuries into the past (the Reformation, the Scientific Revolution, the Enlightenment, with some accounts stretching back to the Middle Ages) and stress Europe's deep-rooted institutional, cultural, or geographic exceptionalism. In contrast, Pomeranz, a historian of China, argues that only after 1750 did the West pull ahead of Asia, and that the causes of this later divergence were accidental. Pomeranz describes the world economy before 1800 as a polycentric system with several cores—densely populated and

---

64. David S. Landes, *The Wealth And Poverty of Nations: Why Some Are So Poor and Some Are So Rich* (New York: W. W. Norton, 1998); Niall Ferguson, *Civilization: The West and the Rest* (London: Allen Lane, 2011).

industrialized regions—rather than one dominant center. Comparisons deeming pre–nineteenth century "Europe" more advanced than contemporary "Asia" have been skewed, Pomeranz suggests, by issues of scale: Asia comes across as doing worse, on average, because any one of its larger countries (India for instance) could easily contain Western Europe. A more appropriate comparison would be between units of roughly equal size, population, and wealth: thus the prosperous Yangtze Delta region of China, which around 1750 had thirty-one to thirty-seven million inhabitants, many living in the large cities of Shanghai, Nanjing, and Hangzhou, provides a more apt equivalent to Britain than does China as a whole. "Unless state policy is at the center of the story being told," he writes, "the nation is not a unit that travels very well."[65] Once units of comparison are more closely matched, he concludes, the world before 1800 shows less a European advantage over Asia than a pattern of highly industrialized and populated cores at either end of the Eurasian landmass.

If that is the case, he asks, what accounts for Europe's spectacular nineteenth-century surge in wealth and world power? By the end of the early modern period, the core regions of Europe and Asia were facing similar crises of overpopulation and ecological depletion, with growing numbers of people crowded onto exhausted lands subjected to extensive deforestation.[66] At this juncture, two contingent historical developments allowed the western edge of Europe, and Britain most especially, to pull ahead. One of these was a piece of geological good luck, the proximity of coal to England's industrial core; China had huge coal deposits in its northern and northwestern provinces, but these regions were geographically remote from prosperous and populated areas like the Yangtze Delta.[67] As a result, England could more readily make the transition from timber to coal, which boosted iron production and powered the industrial processes of a new economy. Coal crucially offset deforestation, but could not on its own remedy England's (and more generally Western Europe's) increasing imbalance between population and resources. The main reason Britain and Europe were able to escape this "Malthusian trap" sooner and more decisively than

65. Kenneth Pomeranz, *The Great Divergence: Europe, China, and the Making of a Modern World Economy* (Princeton, NJ: Princeton University Press, 2000), 7, 12.
66. Ibid., chapter 5.
67. Ibid., 57 ff.

comparable regions elsewhere in the world was access to colonial labor and products. Europe avoided an ecological dead end because its colonial periphery (the Americas and the Caribbean) kept it supplied with food and textiles at very low cost, absorbed its surplus population, and provided markets for its manufactured products. Europe even drew wealth from its Asian competitors by selling large quantities of American silver on the Chinese market. For both of these reasons, coal and colonies, Western Europe enjoyed "breathing space" to develop technological means of bringing population and productivity into balance, which in turn allowed it to outstrip its Asian competitors.

The Great Divergence is emblematic in several respects of world history as practiced today. While the argument does not encompass all parts of the world—the author acknowledges that some regions, such as Africa, while mentioned, are not central to the book's analysis—its scale is planetary. But Pomeranz's book is also representative of a field many of whose practitioners are looking to displace Europe—and "the West" more generally—from its position as model and leader for "the rest." In earlier generations even scholars critical of Western hegemony such as Immanuel Wallerstein reasoned from a Eurocentric stance: whether celebratory or censorious, the agenda was to explain how Europe and North America "got there" (capitalism, industrialization, imperialism) sooner than anyone else. To be sure, Pomeranz is also explaining a period of European dominance, but coming at the question from a Chinese perspective makes for a very different story, in which East and West were commensurate for centuries and Europe's advantages came about accidentally and quite late. World history as practiced by scholars like Pomeranz offers another instance of a geographic reframing of the past leading to conceptual breakthroughs.

DISPLACING EURO-AMERICA

By pulling the camera back and embracing a planetary scale, the practice of world history offers a perspective from which to question narratives in which Euro-American dominance is both central and somehow preordained. Eurocentric tendencies are deeply embedded in historical writing, in the West and beyond, because professional historical scholarship—departments, journals, professional associations—took shape in the later nineteenth century in Europe and America when those regions did indeed dominate most of the world's peoples, and that moment's supremacy was read back into humanity's past. In the West well into the twentieth century, academic fields were divided up such that historians dealt only with Europe while orientalists studied the "sophisticated but traditional" cultures of Asia and anthropologists the "primitive and unchanging" societies of Africa and Oceania.[68] The process of correcting for the assumption that Europe and America had "history" while other world areas were exotic "lands out of time" has been lengthy: as late as 1959, out of 1,735 history graduate students in the United States, only *one* specialized in Africa.[69]

Since professional historical scholarship came of age in the heyday of European imperialism, that continent's history from the start served as a yardstick and model not only for Euro-American historians but their counterparts in Africa, Asia, and Latin America. As Dipesh Chakrabarty puts it in his influential *Provincializing Europe* (2000), "'Europe' remains the sovereign, theoretical subject of all histories, including the ones we call 'Indian,' 'Chinese,' 'Kenyan,' and so on. There is a peculiar way in which all these other histories tend to become variations on a master narrative that could be called 'the history of Europe.'" "Third world" academics, he points out, have always been required to know European history and the theories of historical change that go with it, whereas Western academics are mostly ignorant of histories other than their own (he calls this "asymmetrical ignorance").[70] And interpretive models developed in the West often make little sense when taken out of context. The African historian Steven Feierman points to a classic definition of societies with mature "civilizations" as opposed to more primitive "cultures": civilizations are dynamic, and their characteristics include political and economic hierarchy, writing, the plow, and significant population densities, especially in towns. The problem, Feierman points out, is that in many areas of Africa some of these features have long existed for a very long time while others are absent: the Igbo-speaking areas of southeastern Nigeria for centuries had dense population

68. Jerry H. Bentley, "Globalizing History and Historicizing Globalization," *Globalizations* 1 (September 2004): 70–71.

69. Steven Feierman, "African Histories and the Dissolution of World History," in Robert H. Bates, V. Y. Mudimbe, and Jean O'Barr, eds., *Africa and the Disciplines: The Contributions of Research in Africa to the Social Sciences and Humanities* (Chicago: University of Chicago Press, 1993), 168.

70. Dipesh Chakrabarty, *Provincializing Europe: Postcolonial Thought and Historical Difference* (Princeton, NJ: Princeton University Press, 2000), 27–28.

and markets, including long-distance trade, as well as sophisticated agriculture, in the absence of both political hierarchy and writing. European categories of development cannot make sense of whether Igbo society was a "culture" or a "civilization."[71]

More broadly stated, the "West versus the rest" problem in historical interpretation is an issue that conflates space and time within the concept of modernity. "Modern" has been a shifting temporal category (at any given point in time it stretches one or two centuries into the past from where the observer stands) but also a normative one that includes certain features presumed to be positive, such as the nation-state, urbanization, participatory politics, industrialization, education, and human rights.[72] The concept of modernity has become controversial since it once was used, along with "civilization," as a justification for Western colonialism, and later, in what is known as modernization theory, as a category by which to judge how far a society had progressed along a developmental path modeled on that of Europe. A uniform view of time held that the present was Western, and that it behooved other societies to scramble as fast as possible out of their pastness and catch up. To quote Chakrabarty again, "Historicism . . . came to non-European peoples in the nineteenth century as somebody's way of saying 'not yet' to somebody else."[73] Scholars belonging to the movement known as "postcolonialism"—many of them South Asian intellectuals—argue that, because this Western narrative was embraced by native elites and imposed upon "subalterns" in places like India, even after the end of empire postcolonial subjects remain alienated from their authentic, autonomous selves.[74]

Historians of Asia, Africa, Latin America, and Oceania have for several decades rebelled against the assumption whereby the societies they study are viewed as "backward." As one Africanist describes it, African history "came into being partly by challenging racist, teleological, and condescending

71. Feierman, "African Histories," 176–77. The definition of "civilization" was articulated in 1987 by the French world historian Fernand Braudel.

72. Carol Gluck, "The End of Elsewhere: Writing Modernity Now," *American Historical Review* 116 (June 2011): 676–77.

73. Richard Wolin, "'Modernity': The Peregrinations of a Contested Historiographical Concept," *American Historical Review* 116 (June 2011): 743; Chakrabarty, *Provincializing Europe*, 8.

74. For an overview of this influential school, see Prasenjit Duara, "Postcolonial History," in Kramer and Maza, *Companion to Western Historical Thought*, 417–31.

presumptions embedded in such conceptions of the modern."[75] The dilemma these historians face, however, is that most of them embrace as positive ideals such features of modernity as democracy and human rights, and readily acknowledge that the inhabitants of the areas they study rightfully aspired, and still do, to many aspects of the modern, including forms of material comfort and security. The way out of this contradiction has been, for many, to shift modernity into the plural and describe their agenda as the study of "modernities": societies have aspired to, and attained, increasing freedom, education, and prosperity in an infinite variety of incommensurate ways, and the task of the historian is to describe the multitude of ways societies have become modern on their own terms.[76]

It has been common, for instance, to think of changes in African societies in the eighteenth and nineteenth centuries as driven by worldwide European-led phenomena such as the Atlantic slave trade and the rise of capitalist trading networks. But if these developments are all we see, we fail to apprehend or fully understand other historical dynamics of much greater relevance to the actual inhabitants of particular regions. Feierman offers as an example the story of Narwimba, a woman who lived in the area between what are now Tanzania and Zambia in East Africa in the late nineteenth century. Narwimba's life was one of peril because the early death of her husband and her lack of resources rendered her vulnerable: she was once taken captive and almost sold as a slave but escaped, and she unsuccessfully begged a relative of her husband's to marry her as protection from bondage. As a result of Narwimba's marginal status, her daughter was forced to enter a low-status union with a man who paid no bridewealth, an arrangement that in turn placed her daughter (Narwimba's granddaughter) in jeopardy as a vulnerable member of the chief's household. The young girl was eventually given away in payment for a debt. What is the broader context for this story? The conventional answer would involve the pressures exerted on Narwimba's society (specifically her Ngonde people) by global commerce and the slave trade, since that area of Africa had recently opened up to the Indian Ocean and slave trading. But the Ngonde themselves would have explained the changes their society experienced in those years as the results of dynastic marriage patterns that shifted trade patterns eastward, and Nar-

---

75. Lynn M. Thomas, "Modernity's Failings, Political Claims, and Intermediate Concepts," *American Historical Review* 116 (June 2011): 727.

76. Ibid., 731.

wimba's vulnerability as the result of her family's dispossession following a raid by Ngoni warriors from southern Africa. The distinction here is not between a "broader" and a "local" context, but between European- and African-centered readings of the same set of events.[77]

While African historians are showing that the long and complex history of that continent need not and should not revolve around its encounter with European trade and colonialism, postcolonial historians of Asia insist that the traditional/modern binary cannot make sense of cultural patterns in places like India. To categorize the culture of twentieth-century Indian peasants as "archaic" or "prepolitical," writes Chakrabarty, is to adhere to "the idea of a single, homogeneous and secular idea of human time." Instead, we should strive to understand the ways in which experiences of modernity were braided with other forms of subjectivity. To study modernity in this context is not a problem of *transition* from one phase of history to the next, but of *translation*: "European thought is at once both indispensable and inadequate in helping us to think through the experiences of political modernity in non-Western nations, and provincializing Europe becomes the task of exploring how this thought . . . may be renewed from and for the margins."[78] Just as Benedict Anderson arrived at his transformative insights about the construction of nationhood after many years of studying Indonesian history, Chakrabarty and his colleagues in postcolonial studies suggest not only that Western historicism cannot be simply mapped onto other contexts, but that shifts in the geographical center of gravity of research and analysis pose productive challenges to the central categories of Western historical thought.

Thinking about the "where" of history raises complex and controversial questions about the very nature of historical inquiry as practiced today. Nearly all historians still operate within the parameters of a national field, commonly organized around one or more defining big events or concepts: the Chinese Revolution, the Italian Renaissance, the Third Reich, the British Industrial Revolution, Indian Independence. Brilliant books on each of those topics cannot be ignored, and historians' training and imagination remain more often than not framed in national terms, but we have long since lost our innocence about what nations are and how they came

77. Feierman, "African Histories," 193–99.
78. Chakrabarty, *Provincializing Europe*, 16.

about. Both developments within Euro-American fields and critiques by scholars outside of those traditions have made it increasingly difficult to posit the nation-state as the natural and inevitable unit of history. World historians and postcolonial scholars have called for "provincializing Europe," by which they mean not just marginalizing Europe as a place, but also questioning the imposition on the past of Euro-American categories, most notably the division of societies into "backward" and "modern." In its most radical form, this line of inquiry questions the very possibility of writing a history that is not Eurocentric, since most writing that we recognize as such today is framed by ways of thinking about time, space, and human progress first articulated when the West held sway over all others both materially and culturally: how is it possible, these critics ask, to write of historical change in a way that escapes the categories of European culture?[79]

In sum, the "where" questions about history are destabilizing the discipline nowadays as radically as the "who" questions did a generation ago, if not more so. Not all challenges to conventional geographies pack the same controversial punch. Much "oceanic," "transnational," or "borderlands" history is multinational rather than antinational; these genres tell new stories, sometimes brilliantly, by focusing on the times before or the spaces between nations. Global and postcolonial history, on the other hand, constitute more radical critiques, the first by pulling back and inviting us to take an intellectual perspective that decenters the West, the second by zooming in to take in local, unexpected instantiations of what it means to be "modern." There is a significant price to pay, however, for thinking outside of "the nation" and "modernity": it entails letting go of familiar stories (the "rise," "development," or "triumph" of . . .), and possibly of any all-encompassing stories about the past whatsoever. How, historians are currently wondering, can we continue to write our particular histories if they are no longer framed by a grand narrative, national or worldwide, that gives them meaning?

79. Nicholas Dirks, "History as a Sign of the Modern," *Public Culture* 2, no. 2 (1990): 25–32; Arif Dirlik, "Is There History after Eurocentrism?," *Cultural Critique* 42 (Spring 1999): 1–34.

THE HISTORY OF WHAT? 3

FROM IDEAS TO THINGS

The "what" of history may seem more self-evident than the "who" and the "where": history is about human beings. A classic statement to this effect was penned in 1944 by the historian Marc Bloch in his widely read introduction to the craft of history: "The good historian is like the giant of the fairy tale. He knows that wherever he catches the scent of human flesh, there his quarry lies."[1] The simile is striking and might have seemed less obvious when Bloch wrote it. He was arguing for "history from below" before such approaches became standard in the discipline. Just as ogres (and ogresses) don't care about your status or occupation if they want to make a meal out of you, so should historians be indiscriminately and equally interested in people of all kinds.

History is, indeed, about people. As later chapters will explain in more detail, the study of the past revolves around questions about human identity (how are we similar to, and how did we become different from, people in past generations?) and the creation of meaning (how did our predecessors make sense of the world?). Women and men engage with the world in countless ways, from collecting refuse to devising mathematical theorems to having sex. Their activities are affected by material conditions—the opportunities and obstacles presented by such things as the natural environment, weather, animal life, and their own bodies. So while history always ultimately concerns human beings, historians have long sorted out their "what" inquiries into a long list of ways in which people in the past have interacted with the world around them.

Traditionally the "what" of history has mapped closely onto the "who." A century or more ago, when the default actors of history were male elites, chronicles of the past centered on the ways men established dominance over other men and over the world: military and political achievements primarily,

1. Marc Bloch, *The Historian's Craft*, trans. Peter Putnam (New York: Vintage, 1953), 26.

but also institutional and intellectual prowess, as recorded, for instance, in histories of the church or of great artists, thinkers, and scientists. It would be possible to describe the "what" of history in this chapter as evolving along with the "who," with the focus on women, for instance, opening up the history of the family, interest in workers leading to something called labor history, or the discovery of the gay and lesbian past creating "the history of sexuality." The who-to-what equation has much going for it but also presents some problems, beginning with the fact that some "whats" have no corresponding "whos": environmental history is not linked to a specific group of actors, economic history can in some cases involve no visible people at all, intellectual and cultural history can take very abstract forms.

The story in this chapter is more complicated, and also more interesting, than a straightforward account of new objects appearing along with new actors. Historians have long recognized that their craft concerns a wide range of human activities, often conventionally ordered along a hierarchy from spiritual to material, with the history of religion and ideas at the top and topics like farming and mining at the bottom. This hierarchy was enshrined in the academic world starting in the nineteenth century, with the history of the "higher" endeavors getting their very own departments: the histories of art, religion, literature, and philosophy have long been central to a traditional liberal arts curriculum, but not the histories of farming or fishing. In the last half century, however, books about food, clothing, objects, consumer culture, bodily habits and practices, the natural environment, and many other conventionally "mundane" matters have become part of the historical canon, deemed just as important to the discipline as studies of political life or religious conflict.[2]

The two previous chapters in this book have described challenges to established hierarchies: a traditional focus on social and political elites displaced by an explosion of interest in the poor and obscure, and the nation as default setting—with its Eurocentric connotations—starting to give way to other geographic configurations. The "what" story does not unfold in the same way. In the 1960s and 1970s many historians insisted, on ideolog-

---

2. A major marker of this reorientation occurred in the 1980s, when a team of the most prestigious historians in France, headed by Philippe Ariès and Georges Duby, published a five-volume history of everyday life (*Histoire de la vie privée*, 1985), which was soon translated into many languages.

ical grounds, that studies of peasants, workers, slaves, and women should be more important to democratic and progressive societies than the history of a small white male elite, and in the late twentieth and early twenty-first centuries another generation questioned the historical primacy of the nation-state, also on political grounds. But where realms of human experience are concerned, it would be utterly foolish to mount an ideological assault on "ideas," "religion," or "science," claiming that food, furniture, or forests are more politically urgent concerns for historians. While the occasional crank from either end of the ideological spectrum can be heard to suggest that the history of childbirth is trivial or that intellectual history should be abandoned as elitist, the vast majority of historians believe that all areas of experience, all forms of action and creation, are important to understanding humanity's past and can be studied in illuminating ways.

Renewal has come to these areas of historical inquiry not through a challenge to higher "whats" on behalf of lower ones, but through methodological innovations that have brought the range of human experiences closer together. This chapter describes the transformation of some subfields of history and the appearance of new ones by arguing that historians have in recent decades made the conventionally "higher" realms more material and the allegedly "lower" ones more cultural, while at the same time challenging the idea that humans have an unlimited capacity to mold the world as they please. The classic concept of "humanism" as first defined during the Italian Renaissance held that "man" occupied an exceptional place in creation: on a chain of being that stretched from God and the angels on high to inanimate matter at the bottom, he stood poised at the juncture between the world of spirit and that of matter, uniquely able to move closer to the deity or succumb to baser animal instincts (women, closer to the material realm, enjoyed no comparable freedom). The burden of choice made for man's greatness, his ability to bend the world to his will.[3] Historical scholarship of the last few decades has chipped away at this classically humanistic perspective by reshuffling the high-to-low classification and casting significant doubts on the ability of humans to act upon the world around them

---

3. Arthur Lovejoy, *The Great Chain of Being: A Study of the History of an Idea* (Cambridge: Cambridge University Press, 1936); E. M. W. Tillyard, *The Elizabethan World Picture* (London: Chatto & Windus, 1943); Paul Oskar Kristeller, *Renaissance Thought: The Classic, Scholastic, and Humanistic Strains* (New York: Harper & Bros., 1961).

without limits or adverse consequences. This chapter traces the emergence of new objects of historical study, such as environmental history, but it also describes some of the ways in which traditional areas of inquiry have been renewed by new approaches.

THE CHANGING HISTORY OF IDEAS

The most abstract and elusive object of historians' attention is also one of the most traditional: the history of ideas. While the expression is familiar, its meaning presents something of a challenge: what does it mean to write the history of an idea, or of a set of ideas? One type of commonsense answer treats ideas like biological phenomena: they are passed down from one thinker to the next like a genetic inheritance, or they spread like a disease, and the historian's task is to follow the transmission and mutations of ideas from one thinker to the next down the generations. Arthur Lovejoy, who founded the field in the United States in the early twentieth century, also launched the *Journal of the History of Ideas* in whose very first issue (1940) he called for articles exploring "the influence of classical on modern thought, and of European traditions and writings on American literature, arts, philosophy, and social movements."[4]

Methodologically, traditional approaches to the history of thought sometimes proceed by reifying ideas—approaching them as objects. Lovejoy himself was famous for inventing the term "unit ideas": in his view there existed a finite set of basic philosophical ideas, which thinkers over the centuries combined into different arrangements. In his best-known book, *The Great Chain of Being: A Study in the History of an Idea* (note the singular), he explained the long-lived Western idea of creation as a hierarchical "chain of being" as a series of reshufflings of three unit-ideas: "plenitude," first formulated by Plato, and "continuity" and "gradation," which we owe to Aristotle.[5] Ideas, in this sort of approach, are like a set of building blocks with which thinkers play and from which the occasional genius constructs

4. Arthur Lovejoy, "Reflections on the History of Ideas," *Journal of the History of Ideas* 1 (1940): 7.

5. Lovejoy, *Great Chain of Being*, 3–5. For a good discussion of Lovejoy's approach, see William F. Bynum, "The Great Chain of Being after Forty Years: An Appraisal," *History of Science* 13 (1975): 1–28. See also Darrin McMahon, "The Return of the History of Ideas?" in McMahon and Samuel Moyn, eds., *Rethinking Modern Intellectual History* (Oxford: Oxford University Press, 2014), 15–16.

something dazzling—as in fact did Lovejoy and others working in the same vein.

The "history of ideas" tradition has produced, and continues to yield, fascinating scholarship, from Frank and Fritzie Manuel's survey of utopias in the Western world (1979) to recent histories of the concepts of "happiness," "genius," and "common sense."[6] In its most simplified form, still common in textbooks and survey courses, the history of ideas consists of a series of biographies of great thinkers, each one of whom makes an important contribution to the cumulative progress of human understanding: Machiavelli disconnected politics from religion, which allowed Hobbes to come up with the premise of contractual government, which Locke adapted for democracy and Rousseau for more radical and egalitarian purposes, later influencing Marx, and so on. Even in its most linear and teleological form, the history of ideas has always included some attention to context: you need to know something about sixteenth-century Italian city-states to understand Machiavelli's writings, and Hobbes's harsh views of human motivation and of the origins of government are surely related to his generation's experience of violent civil wars in England. In more conventional approaches, however, "context" merely serves as background for the emergence of ideas whose greatness lies precisely in the fact that they "transcend their time."

For decades after it was created as a field, the history of ideas was understood as a genealogy of great canonical thinkers conversing with, building upon, and sometimes repudiating each other's ideas across the centuries. In the 1960s younger scholars, most notably the Oxford historian Quentin Skinner, began to undermine the traditional approach by pointing out that it took notice only of thinkers later enshrined as intellectual giants, ignoring now obscure figures who were important in their own time: in short, intellectual history as practiced was ahistorical and elitist. In "Meaning and Understanding in the History of Ideas" (1969), Skinner skewered both "internalist" methods, which posit the autonomy of ideas, and traditional appeals to "context" as equally inadequate ways of approaching

---

6. Frank Manuel and Fritzie Manuel, *Utopian Thought in the Western World* (Cambridge, MA: Harvard University Press, 1979); Darrin M. McMahon, *Happiness: A History* (New York: Atlantic Monthly Press, 2006); McMahon, *Divine Fury: A History of Genius* (New York: Basic Books, 2013); Sophia Rosenfeld, *Common Sense: A Political History* (Cambridge, MA: Harvard University Press, 2011).

ideas in the past. It is silly, he wrote, to assume that some ideas—say, "progress" or "equality"—were born at a specific time and then struggled to
come into their own, sometimes "dropping out of sight," and just as ridiculous to argue that thinker X provided the script for development Y centuries later ("Rousseau is responsible for totalitarianism") or to fault thinkers for "failing to see" certain implications of their writings. Nor should
intellectual historians be in the business either of imposing coherence on
the writings of an author or of trying to pin down the "essential meaning"
of a body of work.[7] Scathingly dismissive of essentialist approaches to the
study of ideas, Skinner was kinder to standard contextual interpretations,
though not uncritical: "historical" approaches, he pointed out, have frequently resulted in crudely reductionist interpretations, as when Hobbes is
read as the first great "bourgeois" thinker or Locke as a theorist of nascent
capitalism.[8]

Skinner himself advocates a contextualist approach rooted in a deep
knowledge of the intellectual landscape of a writer's time. He offers this
example: when Machiavelli writes that "a prince must learn how not to be
virtuous," we can interpret this prescription in various ways—as a com-
monplace that echoes many other writings, as a radical statement, or as a
joke. Only a solid grasp of a wide range of contemporary writings will allow
us to determine which it is, since "the understanding of texts . . . presupposes the grasp both of what they were intended to mean, and how this
meaning was intended to be taken."[9] In our own world, for instance, the
proper answer to the question "Do you have the time?" is not "Yes" (as in
the old joke about the miserly New Englander) but "Yes, 2:45." Someone
from another culture, or possibly another planet, might assume that the
logical response to this query is simply "Yes," but our grasp of the relevant
context clues us in that the question actually means "Do you have the time,
and could you please share that information with me?" This kind of implicit knowledge, Skinner argued, is what intellectual historians must set
out to understand: every text is an utterance proffered in a specific context, drawing on a set of contemporary understandings and aimed at an
audience equipped with its own cultural expectations. While a philosopher

7. Quentin Skinner, "Meaning and Understanding in the History of Ideas,"
History and Theory 8 (1969): 4–35.
8. Ibid., 39–41.
9. Ibid., 48.

might be interested in the "timeless" meanings of Plato's or Hobbes's writings, an intellectual historian must find out how every text participates in a conversation with other texts in its own time. Methodologically, Skinner's approach implies the need to read every canonical text alongside a wide range of other, less famous writings that it was building upon and responding to—a form of contextual analysis that could be understood as "democratizing" the history of ideas, since for purposes of interpretation it knocks famous works off their solitary perch.[10]

As a result of challenges from people like Skinner, the phrase "history of ideas" has mostly fallen out of favor. Nowadays, scholars are more likely to describe themselves as "intellectual historians" even though, as in other subfields, no agreement exists as to what exactly constitutes "intellectual history." Peter Gordon has defined the field concisely as "the study of intellectuals, ideas, and intellectual patterns over time," while another scholar describes it as including the biographies of thinkers, the history of books and reading, and that of institutions such as universities and more informal learned societies, as well as patterns and currents of thought.[11] The only consensus seems to be that most of today's practitioners are adamant that they are *not* engaged in a "history of ideas" in the style of Arthur Lovejoy. Many styles of intellectual history continue to flourish, with some works so abstract and cerebral that they resemble philosophy. Since the 1960s, however, following the advent of modern social history, the field overall has moved in the direction of more concrete approaches grounded in specific social realities.

One of the symptoms of this trend is the emergence of something called the "social history of ideas," one of whose pioneers and best-known practitioners is the historian of eighteenth-century France Robert Darnton. In

10. Some of Skinner's best-known colleagues are the historian of political thought J. G. A. Pocock and the scholar of eighteenth-century French intellectual history Keith Michael Baker. Recently, at least one prominent younger intellectual historian has pointed to some downsides of the Cambridge school's insistence on strict contextualism: Peter E. Gordon, "Contextualism and Criticism in the History of Ideas," in McMahon and Moyn, *Rethinking Modern European Intellectual History*, 32–55.

11. Peter E. Gordon, "What Is Intellectual History?," http://projects.iq.harvard.edu/harvardcolloquium/pages/what-intellectual-history (accessed February 1, 2016; cited with permission); Daniel Wickberg, "Intellectual History vs. the Social History of Intellectuals," *Rethinking History* 5 (2001): 383.

one of his earliest articles, published in 1971, Darnton took on a classic question in the history of ideas: what was the link between the Enlightenment and the French Revolution? The answer to that question had always seemed obvious, including to most scholars in the field: the radical thinkers of the French Enlightenment known as the *philosophes* undermined the status quo of old regime France by writing and (illegally) publishing works scathingly critical of the church, the monarchy, and the aristocracy. Darnton proceeded to poke many large holes in this tidy scenario: none of the major *philosophes* ever questioned the legitimacy of the monarchy, most were either nobles themselves or closely connected to the aristocracy, and in any case none of them lived to see the outbreak of the Revolution. "The Enlightenment," as conventionally defined, challenged intellectual orthodoxies but not the political or social order, and the most radical literature circulating on the eve of the French Revolution was not penned by the likes of Voltaire and Rousseau. Delving into police archives and booksellers' records, Darnton discovered that the best-sellers of the 1780s included many works of gossipy pornography with titles like *The Nun in a Nightgown* or *The Pastimes of Antoinette* (a reference to the queen). To understand where these works came from, he dug into the sociology of the eighteenth-century literary world and discovered that the authors of these so-called *libelles* were hacks, marginalized writers unable to succeed in the rarefied world of intellectual salons and aristocratic patronage who supported themselves and vented their bitterness through a corpus of steamy, scandal-mongering pamphlets. These, rather than the classic works of the "High Enlightenment," he argued, provided the ammunition for the French Revolution's outbreak and radicalization.[12]

Darnton has deepened and expanded his "Grub Street" thesis since the 1970s, and it has also come in for its share of criticism and revision.[13] Regardless of how much of the original the argument still stands, Darnton's work provided an early and influential example of how our understanding of the relation between ideas and events can be transformed when scholars leave the library and go rooting around in the archives. The field of intel-

12. Robert Darnton, "The High Enlightenment and the Low-Life of Literature in Pre-Revolutionary France," *Past & Present* 51 (May 1971): 81–115.

13. For instance, Haydn Mason, ed., *The Darnton Debate: Books and Revolution in the Eighteenth Century* (Oxford: Voltaire Foundation, 1998).

lectual history, broadly construed, now involves teams of scholars tracking the production and dissemination of books and pamphlets, and the histories of publishing houses, authors, publishers, best-sellers, popular literature, romance novels, and much else. It extends even to such fascinating specialties as the history of reading practices: At what points in history did people, and which sorts of people, read? Did they do so alone or in groups, aloud or silently, revisiting the same book over and over or engaging a wide range of material, with what forms and degrees of emotion and concentration?

Trends toward diversity have been brought to bear on the field of intellectual history as on others. Since the 1970s feminist scholars have brought to light the contributions of women to the life of the mind in the past: early feminist thinkers like Mary Wollstonecraft, celebrated female intellectuals of early modern Italy like Laura Bassi, the *salonnières* of eighteenth-century France and nineteenth-century Germany—highly educated hostess-mediators who played crucial roles in the intellectual life of their time—have all claimed their place in our histories of thought.[14] In sum, the history of ideas has been transformed by the multiplication of texts and voices and the anchoring of intellectual life in the concrete worlds of intellectual networks, in the business of producing and consuming books and other material, in the social worlds of writers, in the sensory and emotional worlds of readers. Intellectual history is no longer only, as one scholar has put it, "history from the neck up."[15]

THOMAS KUHN'S SCIENTIFIC REVOLUTION

Along with "ideas," another great intangible object of history is "science," although differences between the two spring readily to mind. Science has usually been the most "social" of intellectual endeavors, involving groups

14. Deborah Hertz, *Jewish High Society in Old Regime Berlin* (New Haven, CT: Yale University Press, 1988); Dena Goodman, *The Republic of Letters: A Cultural History of the French Enlightenment* (Ithaca, NY: Cornell University Press, 1994); Paula Findlen et al., eds., *Italy's Eighteenth Century: Gender and Culture in the Age of the Grand Tour* (Stanford, CA: Stanford University Press, 2009).

15. David Armitage, "The International Turn in Intellectual History," in McMahon and Moyn, *Rethinking Modern European Intellectual History* 233.

of people and institutions, and while its results may be abstract, the mechanics of much scientific life—experiments, laboratories, practical applications—stand in sharp contrast to the more solitary and cerebral activity of philosophers or political theorists.[16] Furthermore, "science" is often used as a synonym for "knowledge," while "ideas" shade toward "opinions": we readily assume that multiple theories about the best form of government or the nature of the good life can and should be in play at one time, whereas even when its answers are provisional and evolving, science strains toward the one correct understanding of gravity or the ultimate explanation of genetics. Even more than the canonical history of Western ideas, the history of science traditionally consisted in the epic tale of a succession of geniuses standing on each others' shoulders, each improving on his predecessors' achievements. From the later nineteenth century through the Cold War, historians of science, many of them eager to pit the story of their field against supposed religious obscurantism, described the march of scientific progress as "an accumulation of empirical findings subsumed into ever-broader covering laws."[17]

In many ways, the history of science has evolved since the mid-twentieth century in the same way as other fields in history, away from unitary, top-down approaches (to wit, great upper-class male geniuses) toward much more eclectic views of who "did science" in the past and how. The field is particular, however, in that it changed course more abruptly than others in response to the extraordinary impact of a single book. In 1962 a Harvard physicist named Thomas Kuhn published *The Structure of Scientific Revolutions*, an essay on the sociology of science that went on to become the most cited book in the arts and humanities of the later twentieth cen-

---

16. This contrast between more abstract "ideas" and more concrete "science" can and should be qualified in many ways. The entire field of mathematics can be said to fall in between ideas and science, and its practitioners, such as the seventeenth-century thinker René Descartes, include major scientists whose work is entirely abstract. Similarly, the philosophy of science—the process of exploring the foundations of scientific inquiry—as elaborated in a tradition stretching from Aristotle to Karl Popper, Thomas Kuhn, and Ian Hacking, bridges the areas of intellectual history and the history of science.

17. Ken Alder, "The History of Science, or, an Oxymoronic Theory of Relativistic Objectivity," in Lloyd Kramer and Sarah Maza, eds., *A Companion to Western Historical Thought* (London: Blackwell, 2002), 303–9, quote p. 306.

tury.[18] The book was itself revolutionary, its effect analogous to the process it describes: Kuhn advanced the argument that changes in scientific understanding do not occur incrementally, as conventional wisdom held, but by means of the conceptual leaps known as scientific revolutions. One of the book's most celebrated propositions is that scientists operate within "paradigms," which Kuhn defines as "universally recognized scientific achievements that for a time provide model problems and solutions to a community of practitioners."[19] Most of the time, in periods of what Kuhn labels "normal science," the reigning paradigm goes unchallenged and indeed sometimes unnoticed. Eventually, though, the accumulation of empirical work reveals anomalies and produces results that are impossible to square with the existing paradigm. The resulting crisis can be resolved only through the creation of a radically new paradigm "incommensurable" with the older one. The most famously dramatic example of such an upheaval occurred in the mid-sixteenth century when the Polish astronomer Nicolaus Copernicus suggested that discrepancies in contemporary calculations of planetary motion could be resolved by assuming that the earth revolved around the sun rather than vice versa. The shift from a geocentric to a heliocentric view of the cosmos (radically incommensurable paradigms) is a textbook example of a scientific revolution. Controversially, Kuhn's argument implied that science does not yield perennial truth, only provisional solutions expressed within the context of transient, historically determined paradigms.

A landmark work in the sociology of knowledge, *The Structure of Scientific Revolutions* proved particularly important in redirecting the field of the history of science. Kuhn did have interesting observations to make

18. Thomas Kuhn, *The Structure of Scientific Revolutions*, 2nd ed. (Chicago: University of Chicago Press, 1970). Edward Garfield, "A Different Sort of Great Books List: The 50 Twentieth-Century Works Most Cited in the *Arts & Humanities Citation Index*, 1976–1983," *Current Comments* 10, no. 16 (April 20, 1987): 3–7. Since the book's publication, its key terms ("normal science," "paradigm," "incommensurability") and Kuhn himself have been the objects of a substantial academic literature. See most recently, for instance, Vasso Kindi and Theodore Arabatzis, eds., *Kuhn's "The Structure of Scientific Revolutions" Revisited* (New York: Routledge, 2012).

19. Kuhn, *Structure*, viii. The concept of "paradigm" touched off an avalanche of scholarly discussion, starting with Kuhn himself, who in his book's second edition (1970) devoted most of a postscript to clarifying its meaning; ibid., 174–98.

about the individuals who touched off scientific revolutions: they were typically young and/or newcomers or outsiders to the field they changed (as was, interestingly, Kuhn himself, a scientist with no formal training in the social sciences).[20] The more important thrust of the book, however, was toward understanding scientific life and change as a matter of communities rather than individuals: how and why do scientists in a specific place and time embrace a paradigm as plausible and productive, and how and why does that same paradigm become dysfunctional? Around the same time that the historical discipline was turning to the "new social history" (E. P. Thompson's masterpiece was published the year after *Structure*), Kuhn's book conveyed in lucid and persuasive form the message that professional structures and dynamics mattered more than individual genius for understanding scientific change.

A second, even more controversial message was contained in Kuhn's notion of "incommensurability." Years later, Kuhn traced the roots of this concept to an epiphany he experienced while preparing his first course on the history of science. Poring over Aristotle's writings on mechanics, he marveled that such a brilliant thinker, admired through the centuries for his skills at logic and observations in biology, had gotten so many things wrong when it came to physics. Staring out of his Harvard office window, he suddenly intuited the answer: any given item in Aristotle's theories of motion might seem ridiculous from a post-Newtonian perspective, but looked at together they added up to a perfectly cogent system, "an integral whole . . . that had to be broken and reformed on the road to Newtonian mechanics."[21] *The Structure of Scientific Revolutions* provided a compelling theoretical framework for an evolution that was already, as he noted, under way in the field. Historians of science were turning away from cumulative histories: "Rather than seeking the permanent contributions of an older science to our present vantage," he wrote, "they attempt to display the historical integrity of that science in its own time."[22] The implication of Kuhn's emphasis on ruptures and discontinuities was that the history of science was one not of linear "progress" but of successive worldviews, each

20. Ibid., 89–90.

21. Thomas Kuhn, "What Are Scientific Revolutions?," in James Conant and John Haugeland, eds. *The Road since Structure* (Chicago: University of Chicago Press, 2000), 13–20, quote p. 20.

22. Kuhn, *Structure*, 3.

of which had its own coherence—until it didn't. (Historians who write in this tradition prefer to talk of scientific "change" rather than "progress," although Kuhn firmly described himself as a believer in scientific progress.[23]) Kuhn's approach initiated a tradition sometimes called "constructivism," which one scholar defines as "the belief that scientific knowledge is a human creation, made with available material and cultural resources, rather than simply the revelation of a natural order that is pre-given and independent of human action."[24]

Constructivism encountered resistance, especially in its early years, with Kuhn and like-minded scholars accused of undermining the authority of science by questioning the boundary between better or worse practices and the validity and usefulness of scientific results—in short, by adopting a stance of irresponsible relativism.[25] But constructivists are quick to respond that they do not seek to weigh in on questions of truth or validity (and equally quick to specify that they would rather have major surgery now than in the seventeenth century). Their project is to explain how knowledge is produced and validated in specific historical contexts while bracketing the issue of scientific "truth" by adopting a neutral stance known as the "symmetry postulate"—the premise that their function as historians or sociologists is to describe, not to adjudicate between, different scientific views.[26]

The ultimate effect of what one might call the Kuhnian revolution on the practice of the history of science was the eclipse of macro narratives that charted the "march of science" over the centuries in favor of "snapshot" studies of particular institutions, sets of people, and (most typically) moments of crisis that pitted competing paradigms against one another.[27] Once the field became, for constructivists, a matter of understanding scientific ideas in context, without worrying about who was right or wrong,

23. Ibid, 205–6.

24. Jan Golinski, *Making Natural Knowledge: Constructivism and the History of Science* (Cambridge: Cambridge University Press, 2012), 6.

25. Kindi and Arabatzis, "Introduction," in *Kuhn's "Structure,"* 1–12. A sustained (and intemperate) attack on constructivism is Paul Gross and Norman Leavitt, *Higher Superstition: The Academic Left and Its Quarrels with Science* (Baltimore: Johns Hopkins University Press, 1994).

26. Golinski, *Making Natural Knowledge*, 7–9.

27. Ibid., 26–27.

scholars began to produce deeply researched social and cultural studies of specific episodes of scientific controversy.

SCIENCE IN HISTORICAL CONTEXT

One of the earliest contextual studies of this sort has endured as a classic: Steven Shapin and Simon Shaffer's *Leviathan and the Air-Pump* (1985) examines the clash between Robert Boyle and Thomas Hobbes in the early 1660s over the question of whether a vacuum could exist and how that fact could be plausibly demonstrated. A prominent scientist barely into his thirties, Boyle was a founding member of England's newly created Royal Society for the Advancement of Science, a body committed to the collective, experimental pursuit of modern science along the lines advocated in the previous century by Sir Francis Bacon. The seventy-two-year-old Thomas Hobbes, author of *Leviathan*, an infamous defense of absolute rule, was dogged by suspicions of atheism and had been excluded from the Royal Society on account of his rigid opinions and overbearing demeanor.[28] In 1658–1659 Boyle had commissioned a staggeringly expensive new machine ("the cyclotron of its age," as one scholar has put it), a device comprising a thirty-quart glass globe fitted with an elaborate wood and brass pumping mechanism, for the purpose of conducting experiments to confirm the existence of a vacuum. In 1660 he published *New Experiments Physico-Mechanical*, a narrative of forty-three trials made with the contraption, touting his success. The following year Hobbes fired off his own pamphlet, *Dialogus Physicus* (*A Physical Dialogue*), taking issue not only with Boyle's results but with the entire principle of experimentation as the basis for arriving at scientific truth.

Looking back from our own time there seems no contest between Boyle's enthusiasm for experimental testing and Hobbes's insistence that experiments were not the path to scientific certainly: Boyle won, Hobbes lost, and no more need be said. But Shapin and Schaffer make the case that such moments of scientific controversy allow us to question our assumptions because they took place at a time before many aspects of scientific practice we now take for granted had congealed into self-evidence; Hobbes could mount an attack on scientific experimentation precisely because the

28. Steven Shapin and Simon Schaffer, *Leviathan and the Air-Pump: Hobbes, Boyle and the Experimental Life* (Princeton, NJ: Princeton University Press, 1985). The reasons for Hobbes's exclusion from the society are discussed on pp. 129–39.

latter was still in its infancy. Because of its distance from us in time, the seventeenth-century context allows us better to grasp that matters of fact are not established by "holding a mirror to reality." In Boyle's case, the validity of experimental activity and the resulting "facts" he described depended both on a new machine, which like the contemporary microscope and telescope "disciplined" the senses, and on the public performance of experiments in the Royal Society's assembly room before carefully selected witnesses. Boyle further disseminated these results before a virtual public of readers through narratives crafted in a particular style (civil, modest, unadorned) aimed at like-minded practitioners. "The objectivity of the experimental matter of fact," the authors conclude, "was an artifact of certain forms of discourse and certain modes of social solidarity."[29]

Hobbes stringently disagreed with Boyle on grounds that could be called both methodological and philosophical. Hostile to the very idea of a vacuum or "incorporeal substance," he feared that such a notion would play into the hands of the priesthood, a group he deeply distrusted. He also viewed the sorts of experiments carried out by Boyle as at best irrelevant to determining the ultimate truths of natural philosophy. For Hobbes, the only reliable science was mathematical deduction, known at the time as "geometry," whose logical truths could be made clear to anyone with the power to reason; where scientific experiments yielded variable results, the truth of mathematical demonstration was irrefutable.[30] As might be expected in a country that had just emerged from two decades of civil war and dictatorship, the argument about science veered constantly into a struggle over political principles: Boyle and his followers thought of their experimental community as an embodiment of freedom responsibly exercised, while for Hobbes only unitary principles, in science as in the polity, could guarantee peace and stability in the commonwealth. Shapin and Schaffer provocatively conclude that "solutions to the problem of knowledge are solutions to the problem of social order."[31] In sum, they do not frame the story of the air-pump debate as that of a retrograde crank defeated by a young champion of experimental science, but as a struggle to frame "truth" within competing worldviews.

29. Ibid., chapter 2, quote pp. 77–78.
30. Ibid., chapters 3 and 4.
31. Ibid., 332.

In contrast to an older tradition in which scientific insights sprang from the disembodied minds of brilliant thinkers, recent generations of historians of science have located the production of truth in science within the dynamics of particular societies and institutions. "Truth," they argue, is a concept inseparable from "trust," since we all process information on the basis of our confidence in those who provide it. (The book you are reading includes footnotes, a convention designed to convince you to trust its author as someone who relies on the writings of equally trustworthy people with academic credentials.[32]) How, in past societies, were reputations for trust established? Steven Shapin provides an example in his follow-up to the air-pump study, a monograph entitled *A Social History of Truth: Civility and Science in Seventeenth-Century England*.[33] Experimental science flourished in seventeenth-century England, Shapin argues, because it was conducted by a group of elite practitioners—"gentlemen," members of the landed upper class—who both trusted one another and had moral authority in the society at large. Belonging to the gentlemanly class conferred credibility because its members were assumed to be both materially independent and virtuous adherents to the Christian values of modesty and integrity. A gentleman was beholden to nobody, and his word was his bond—accusing a gentleman of untruth was so serious an affront to his being that the only conceivable response was a duel. The Royal Society was an environment propitious to the pursuit of "truth," Shapin argues, because its members, all gentlemen, could trust one another and because their scientific discoveries were vouchsafed by their social status.

Two centuries later, trustworthiness was established via expertise backed by numbers rather than genteel status, as the historian of science Theodore Porter has shown in a series of remarkable studies: comparing nineteenth-century Britain, France, and the United States, he demonstrates that the larger, younger, and more democratic the society, the more its administrative elites are likely to resort to statistics as "technologies of trust" to convince or even manipulate the citizenry; the resort to numbers to justify policies, he argues, emerges from sociopolitical vulnerability rather than

32. The story of how this convention came about is told by another trustworthy scholar, Anthony Grafton, in *The Footnote: A Curious History* (Cambridge, MA: Harvard University Press, 1999).

33. Steven Shapin, *A Social History of Truth: Civility and Science in Seventeenth-Century England* (Chicago: University of Chicago Press, 1994).

strength.[34] In sum, constructivists have moved the history of science away from the realm of pure ideas and into the messy realities of social and political life, an approach summed up by the tongue-in-cheek title of Shapin's latest collection of essays, *Never Pure: Historical Studies of Science as if It Was Produced by People with Bodies, Situated in Time, Space, Culture, and Society, and Struggling for Credibility and Authority.*[35]

Other, related ways in which the history of science has been brought "down to earth" are through the opening up of our definitions of what science is and our knowledge of who practiced it. Traditional accounts of the birth of "modern" science have scientific truth rising from the ashes of such discredited beliefs as "magic" or "superstition." In the later twentieth century, however, much creative work was devoted to breaking down barriers between "good" and "bad" science to show that these latter-day categories were hardly water-tight three or four centuries ago. The divide that hardened, starting in the eighteenth century, between "occult" pursuits such as alchemy and legitimate science was before then far more porous: scholars like Richard Westfall and B. J. T. Dobbs have shown that the intellectual breakthroughs leading to Isaac Newton's formulation of the law of universal gravitation—usually considered the pinnacle of the Scientific Revolution—were rooted in the great scientist's avid and extensive research into the "dark arts" of alchemy.[36]

Even more rigid than the conventional division between "science" and "magic" has been the association between "science" and "modernity" and the corollary belief that what we call science could not flourish in "traditional" societies. While Western scholars have long acknowledged the existence of Asian and the Middle Eastern scientific traditions operating within parameters of thought similar to their own, the expression "African science"

34. Theodore Porter, *The Rise of Statistical Thinking, 1820–1900* (Princeton, NJ: Princeton University Press, 1986); Porter, *Trust in Numbers: The Pursuit of Objectivity in Science and Public Life* (Princeton, NJ: Princeton University Press, 1995).

35. Baltimore: Johns Hopkins University Press, 2010.

36. Richard Westfall, *Force in Newton's Physics: The Science of Dynamics in the Seventeenth Century* (London: Macdonald and Co., 1971); Betty Jo Teeter Dobbs, *The Foundations of Newton's Alchemy or "The Hunting of the Greene Lyon"* (Cambridge: Cambridge University Press, 1975); Dobbs, *The Janus Faces of Genius: The Role of Alchemy in Newton's Thought* (Cambridge: Cambridge University Press, 1991).

was long viewed as an oxymoron: it seemed impossible to compare such practices as healing and divination to the abstract thinking held to govern properly scientific thought. Around the same time that Kuhn was describing scientific change as a succession of incommensurable paradigms, however, the Africanist Robin Horton produced a series of now-classic articles proposing that what he called "traditional African thought" shared many theoretical properties with European science. African cosmologies, for instance, have the same unifying and simplifying function as the natural or inanimate items to which Western science resorts as metaphors: "Like atoms, molecules, and waves . . . the gods serve to introduce unity into diversity, simplicity into complexity, order into disorder, regularity into anomaly."[37] In traditional societies, he argued, the world of people, highly structured and predictable, is a plausible ground on which to build theory; in complex societies, by contrast, the social world offers no such reassurance and thinkers look to inanimate and natural objects to get to the theoretical essence of things.[38] The particulars of Horton's theses have long been debated, but in demolishing the notion that "theory" only happens in certain kinds of society his work laid the foundation for a rich vein of studies of African scientific practices such as healing.[39]

All in all, challenges to conventional definitions of science have shattered the common view of its practitioners as educated, specialized men operating in some old-time version of a laboratory. In some times and places such men did exist, congregate, collaborate, and correspond, but the world of science was a lot more capacious and diverse, historians argue, than we once believed. In early modern Europe, science took place in royal and aristocratic courts where virtuosi "performed" their discoveries for the benefit of their patrons. Galileo, for instance, read his works aloud at mealtimes to his protector, the Grand Duke Cosimo II de' Medici, and presented him with his newly discovered moons of Jupiter as a gift, naming

37. Robin Horton, "African Traditional Thought and Western Science, Part I: From Tradition to Science," *Africa: Journal of the International African Institute* 37, no. 1 (January 1967): 52.

38. Ibid., 64–66.

39. Steven Feierman, *Peasant Intellectuals: Anthropology and History in Tanzania* (Madison: University of Wisconsin Press, 1990); David Schoenbrun, "Conjuring the Modern: Durability and Rupture in Histories of Public Health between the Great Lakes of East Africa," *American Historical Review* 111 (2006): 1403–39.

them the "Medicean Stars"—the famous astronomer's status, career, and livelihood depended on the production of science for his patron, and what he chose to study was informed by that fact.[40] "Science" also happened in the workshops of artisans and artists who scrutinized the natural world in order to reproduce it in startlingly realistic paintings, drawings, and sculptures, and in the "cabinets of curiosity" and private museums of rulers and wealthy men who amassed vast collections of natural and man-made wonders.[41] Science, in short, was not just produced by savants in learned societies but practiced by all sorts of people with very concrete needs and agendas—performing at court, impressing wealthy friends, firing an intricate piece of pottery, or, in the case of wives and family members, providing unacknowledged assistance of every sort.[42] It engaged bodies as well as minds, rested on practices as well as theories. And of course science has always centrally involved objects, from the simplest vials to the *machina Boyleana* to miles-long particle colliders.

THE NEW HISTORY OF THINGS

Half a century ago, "things" rarely featured in the work of academic historians. Furniture, clothing, table- and kitchenware, and food were the domain of archaeologists, antiquarian specialists, and lay enthusiasts adept at pinpointing the date of a piece of pottery, identifying the style of an armchair, or trying out a medieval recipe on long-suffering friends. Except for archaeology, which formed its own discipline and generated sources for textually poor fields of history, the study of material culture was largely ignored by historians, dismissed as the province of museum curators and set designers for costume dramas. The stuff of the past was deemed interesting at best, but trivial, fodder mostly for the sort of old-style social history long on details about post-horses and chamber pots. The "new social historians" of

40. Mario Biagioli, *Galileo, Courtier: The Practice of Science in the Culture of Absolutism* (Chicago: University of Chicago Press, 1993).

41. Pamela Smith, *The Body of the Artisan: Art and Experience in the Scientific Revolution* (Chicago: University of Chicago Press, 2004); Paula Findlen, *Possessing Nature: Museums, Collecting and Scientific Culture in Early Modern Italy* (Berkeley: University of California Press, 1994); Helmar Schramm, *Collection, Laboratory, Theater: Scenes of Knowledge in the Seventeenth Century* (Berlin: Walter de Gruyter, 2005).

42. On the work of women and other "invisible technicians," see Shapin, *Social History*, chapter 8.

the 1960s and 1970s were not concerned with such matters either: writing the story of (male) artisans, peasants, and slaves, they focused their attention on producers rather than consumers, all the more so given the era's deep suspicion of consumer culture: the new left historians of the 1960s operated within a worldview in which producing signaled authenticity, and shopping—the pastime of the rich and of misguided women—meant alienation.

How did historians come to pay attention to things in their own right rather than as negligible elements of local color? The story could be told in a Kuhnian vein: the rise of social and economic history generated research in which, in some contexts, the importance of changes in material culture were simply impossible to ignore and required a new explanatory paradigm. Scholars working on highly commercialized societies like seventeenth-century Holland and eighteenth-century England were confronted with what Simon Schama termed an "embarrassment of riches," an unprecedented riot of consumer goods, and began to advance the thesis of an eighteenth-century "consumer revolution" on a par with the political and industrial revolutions of the age.[43] Women's and gender history no doubt played a big role as well, with feminist scholars insisting that private spaces were as socially and politically relevant as the public world. Cultural historians influenced by literary theory introduced such terms as "performance" and "self-fashioning" into their colleagues' vocabularies, and with them the suggestion that the props and costumes people adopted in past societies were as vital to their identities as income and occupation.[44] Finally, the study of objects and material culture became prominent in the 1980s and 1990s when historians were starting to lose faith in huge abstractions like "class" as the key to explaining social relations. Starting with tangible things, whether consumer goods like coffee or cloth, dishes and wallpaper,

43. Simon Schama, *The Embarrassment of Riches: An Interpretation of Dutch Culture in the Golden Age* (New York: Knopf, 1987); Neil McKendrick, John Brewer, and J. H. Plumb, *The Birth of a Consumer Society: The Commercialization of Eighteenth-Century England* (London: Europa, 1982); John Brewer and Roy Porter, eds., *Consumption and the World of Goods* (London: Routledge, 1993).

44. Important influences from outside the field of history include Stephen Greenblatt, *Renaissance Self-Fashioning: From More to Shakespeare* (Chicago: University of Chicago Press, 1980), and Judith Butler, *Gender Trouble: Feminism and the Subversion of Identity* (New York: Routledge, 1990).

or homemade items like quilts or clothing, offered a promising way of exploring a wide range of social relations without forcing the subject matter into preconceived explanatory patterns. It was, in short, a new way of doing social history.

What stories do objects tell? Historians of Europe agree that the eighteenth century was a watershed: you need only compare etchings or paintings of upper-class seventeenth-century interiors, sparsely furnished with a few heavy items of furniture and the odd tapestry, to similar homes a century later, with their upholstered armchairs, colorful wallpaper, and an abundance of knickknacks, to realize that something big had happened to people's material environments, at least for those not living in poverty. Proposed reasons for this change have been endlessly debated and analyzed, ranging from the manufacturing and marketing genius of people like the china manufacturer Josiah Wedgwood, to the impact of ever-accelerating colonial trade, which swamped the old continent with new "luxuries," to the idea of an early "industrious revolution" that had people working harder to purchase consumer goods rather than using homemade products.[45] Cause and effect are notoriously difficult to disentangle where consumption is concerned, but the eighteenth-century consumer revolution was certainly linked by contemporaries to the erosion of traditional status hierarchies. Research into probate records in eighteenth-century France, for instance, shows that by the end of the century women from the middle and upper working classes owned many more clothes than their predecessors had a few decades earlier; their wardrobes now included one-piece dresses instead of just skirts, petticoats, and waistcoats, bringing their style closer to that of women in the social elites, and they had access to such goods as silk stockings, unimaginable in previous generations. The meaning of fashion in France and elsewhere shifted gradually from an emphasis on clothes as a sign of rank, with aristocratic men just as decked out as women in lace

45. McKendrick, Brewer, and Plumb, *Birth of a Consumer Society*; Arjun Appadurai, ed., *The Social Life of Things: Commodities in Cultural Perspective* (Cambridge: Cambridge University Press, 1986); Sidney W. Mintz, *Sweetness and Power: The Place of Sugar in Modern History* (London: Penguin, 1986); Nicholas Thomas, *Entangled Objects: Exchange, Material Culture, and Colonialism in the Pacific* (Cambridge, MA: Harvard University Press, 1991); Jan de Vries, *The Industrious Revolution: Consumer Behavior and the Household Economy, 1650 to the Present* (Cambridge: Cambridge University Press, 2008).

and ribbons, to an expression of individual (and for the French, national) style, associated with women rather than men.[46]

Historians have shown that consumer goods, cultures, and behaviors can have political as well as social dimensions. Colin Jones, for instance, has suggested that the social origins of the French Revolution can be found in a "great chain of buying," the networks of consumers of the century's new commodities who participated in the egalitarian dynamics of the marketplace. Similarly, Timothy Breen has traced the origins of the American Revolution to the mobilizing power of the 1765 boycott of British goods, which had previously been so central to the colonists' lives.[47] In a different context, Lizabeth Cohen argues that the consumer boom of the decades after World War II in the United States, celebrated by politicians and business leaders as the quintessential expression of American egalitarianism, was a sham covering up a highly segmented marketplace in which white men reaped disproportionate rewards from the GI Bill and new tax laws.[48] Not only have the political origins and consequences of consumption varied widely over time and place, but so has the meaning of acquiring and "consuming" goods: historians distinguish between older patterns of acquisition and use that reinforce hierarchies—getting and employing things to maintain status or to participate in a gift economy—and newer consumer cultures in which goods are imagined as identity-changing (this car will make me sexy!) and the anarchic potential of consumer desire is ceaselessly manipulated by advertising mavens.[49]

46. Jennifer M. Jones, *Sexing la Mode: Gender, Fashion, and Commercial Culture in Old Regime France* (Oxford: Berg, 2004).

47. Colin Jones, "The Great Chain of Buying: Medical Advertisement, the Bourgeois Public Sphere, and the Origins of the French Revolution," *American Historical Review* 101 (February 1996): 13–40; T. H. Breen, *The Marketplace of Revolution: How Consumer Politics Shaped American Independence* (Oxford: Oxford University Press, 2004).

48. Lizabeth Cohen, *A Consumer's Republic: The Politics of Mass Consumption in Postwar America* (New York: Knopf, 2003).

49. Colin Campbell, *The Romantic Ethic and the Spirit of Modern Consumerism* (Oxford: Basil Blackwell, 1987); Roland Marchand, *Advertising the American Dream: Making Way for Modernity, 1920–1940* (Berkeley: University of California Press, 1986); T. J. Jackson Lears, *Fables of Abundance: A Cultural History of Advertising in America* (New York: Basic Books, 1995).

The historical studies mentioned so far approach goods as an aggregate: even as they provide vivid details about clothing, furniture, and people's daily habits they seek to understand what difference wanting, owning, and even boycotting certain goods made to the social and political dynamics of a given society. But what if instead of starting with the cumulative impact of goods one were to begin with a specific object and try to reconstruct the social world that produced it? This approach, akin to that of museum curators, has been adopted by some historians, perhaps most famously Laurel Thatcher Ulrich in her 2001 *The Age of Homespun: Objects and Stories in the Creation of an American Myth*. Ulrich organizes her book around a dozen specific objects ranging in time from 1676 (an Indian basket) to 1837 (an unfinished stocking), working from the sparse information accompanying museum displays to increasingly broader contexts. The Indian basket, for instance, was presented to the Rhode Island Historical Society in 1842 along with a note explaining that it was given in the late 1600s to the wife of a garrison officer, Dinah Fenner, by a grateful Algonquian woman, "a native of the forest," as thanks for the gift of a drink of milk. Ulrich's painstaking reconstruction of the donor's family history exposes telling incongruities in the basket's official provenance tale (why would a member of a lactose-intolerant population come begging for milk?) and relates the object, whose materials included bark, wool, and cornhusk, to the convergence of British and Algonquian weaving practices and the larger history of Dinah's family's role in the violent settlement of Rhode Island and the atrocities of King Philip's War. The basket, in short, literally weaves together Native American and British colonial histories and has come down to us accompanied by a narrative of female peacemaking that obscures a story of male violence.[50] Along with the other objects in Ulrich's book, it makes up a gallery of handmade objects with complicated histories which, starting in the 1850s, were pressed into the myth of "the age of home-spun," the idealization of colonial American handicraft by women proposed as a soothing counterpoint to the emergence of factories and the work of women outside the home. "The mythology of homespun persists," Ulrich concludes, "because it allows us to forget that greed and war were so much part of the American past. . . . [P]eople make history not only

50. Laurel Thatcher Ulrich, *The Age of Homespun: Objects and Stories in the Creation of an American Myth* (New York: Knopf, 2001), chapter 1.

in the work they do and the choices they make, but in the things they choose to remember."[51]

All of the thing-centered histories mentioned so far approach objects as, well, objects. Humans fabricate goods and then use, sell, trade, display, covet, or tell stories about their inert creations. But is it really the case, historians have recently been asking, that the relation between people and things works only one way? The current proliferation of increasingly smart devices in our daily lives constantly invites us to ponder the line between human and nonhuman, and to wonder whether and in what ways things can affect, even shape, their makers. One area of fruitful inquiry along these lines is the history of food, a very particular category of "object" partaking equally of nature and culture. Food stands apart in the history of material culture, a ubiquitous and indispensable commodity laden with cultural significance, both necessity and luxury, by nature ephemeral since it disappears when used, consumed in the most intimate fashion.[52] As we are reminded by antacid commercials showing diners being attacked by their pizza or spaghetti ("Are your favorite foods fighting you?"), food is a commodity that can act at least semi-independently on our bodies, making us fat or sick, shaping our tastes and cravings.

In her landmark essay "Tasting Empire," Marcy Norton historicizes the somatic effects of foodstuffs on human culture. How, Norton asks, did Europeans come to accept and eventually crave chocolate from Central America, a food whose taste, at first repellent to most of them, was without parallel in their countries of origin?[53] The conventional answer is that Spaniards, in America and in their home country, "corrected" the unfamiliar foodstuff by eliminating native spices and adding sugar. Only once chocolate had been made acceptable to European taste buds did Spaniards and others become enamored of its addictively stimulating properties. This

---

51. Ibid., 414.

52. Brewer and Porter, "Introduction," in *Consumption and the World of Goods,* 5–6. See, for instance, Sidney Mintz, *Tasting Food, Tasting Freedom: Excursions into Eating, Power, and the Past* (New York: Beacon Press, 1997); Rachel Laudan, *Cuisine and Empire: Cooking in World History* (Berkeley: University of California Press, 2013).

53. Marcy Norton, "Tasting Empire: Chocolate and the European Internalization of Mesoamerican Aesthetics," *American Historical Review* 111 (June 2006): 660–91.

version of chocolate's transmission was first articulated by eighteenth-century Spanish chroniclers, but according to Norton it does not stand up to scrutiny. Spaniards in the New World encountered chocolate in an overwhelmingly Indian environment and were introduced to the material culture of cacao consumption by servants, especially women. In their homes and in public spaces, they learned to partake of the drink in the native fashion—hot, cold, at room temperature, sometimes mixed with maize, seasoned with honey and chili peppers, on occasion topped with foam produced by pouring the mixture of cacao paste and water from one container to another from a certain height. They imbibed the beverage from special vessels, lacquered gourds made for the purpose, in settings such as the houses of religious orders where Indians and Europeans encountered one another.

Traveling back to the mother country, Spanish soldiers, sailors, and priests brought chocolate, which they prepared and consumed in the Mesoamerican fashion: "In the first years of chocolate's diffusion in Europe," Norton writes, "there was little difference between the types of chocolate consumed by creoles, Indians, and Iberians. . . . European chocolate was not just similar to American chocolate, it *was* American chocolate."[54] Even as Spaniards adopted the beverage, some among them worried that that its association with American idolatry would tempt their compatriots into heresy, seducing them into the cultural degeneracy attributed to New World creoles. In sum, while the conventional view presumes that Europeans controlled and dominated chocolate, domesticating it to their taste, Norton argues that her story reveals the fragility of colonialism in the face of native cultures, with chocolate "Indianizing" its consumers. The transmission of taste, in this instance, flowed in the reverse of the expected direction, "from the colonized to the colonizer, from the 'barbarian' to the 'civilized.' "[55]

The complicated history of chocolate involves not just the encounter between two worlds but the way in which, via foodstuffs, culture can travel through bodily experience quasi-independently of human volition, in this case upsetting established hierarchies. Norton's analysis of taste as an autonomous force is a particular instance of the more general point that objects can be active agents in history. Ritual objects, such as the crown placed on a monarch's head or the rings exchanged in a marriage ceremony, transform a person's status. After the invention of moveable type, books and

54. Ibid., 681–82.
55. Ibid, 670.

newspapers did more than convey entertainment and information; they also, as Benedict Anderson noted, created a lateral sense of kinship with other readers that had previously been unimaginable. Glass-paned windows, some historians argue, sharpened people's sense of the division between public and private worlds.[56] Humans are constantly devising objects that affect how men and women perceive the world around them. Starting in the fifteenth and sixteenth centuries, for instance, Europeans created increasingly accurate and beautiful clocks, objects that became central to the lives of the elites; clocks, in turn, made people, philosophers and scientists in particular, think differently about nature, to the extent that human and animal bodies, and the cosmos itself, were commonly described as working like clocks. Studying clocks and ideas in relation to each other partakes, as Jessica Riskin writes, of an approach that connects intellectual history to material culture: some physical objects "are inseparable from ideas because people incessantly used them as models and examples to think with and, reciprocally, designed and built the machines on the basis of (implicit or explicit) philosophical principles."[57]

Whether we start from the more conventional premise that things are the products of human creativity and as such completely in our power, or venture into less familiar notions that objects can affect their makers in unexpected ways, the assumption has always been that humans and their material creations belong together in the realm of "culture." That is not the case, in contrast, for the natural environment, including the animal world, which obviously can exist and flourish in the absence of human beings, evolving, if left undisturbed, within a temporal realm incommensurate with the time of hominids.

NATURE AND OTHER NONHUMAN ACTORS

The very term "history" includes an implicit qualifier: historians employed in academia actually work in departments of "human history," a discipline that has from its beginning stood in implicit contrast to "natural history," the study of natural organisms in their environments. For centuries the

56. Leora Auslander, "Beyond Words," *American Historical Review* 110 (October 2005): 1017–18. On Benedict Anderson, see chapter 2.

57. Jessica Riskin, "The Restless Clock," in Paula Findlen, ed., *Early Modern Things: Objects and Their Histories, 1500–1800* (London: Routledge, 2013), 84–101, quote pp. 97–98.

supremacy of humans over the natural world was taken for granted; in Western culture it followed from God's decree in the book of Genesis that man should "have dominion over the fish of the sea, and over the fowl of the air, and over the cattle, and over all the earth, and over every creeping thing that creepeth upon the earth."[58] The biblical view of nature as a lesser realm and the legitimate object of human domination was gradually displaced starting in the eighteenth century by a romantic tradition, articulated by writers from Jean-Jacques Rousseau to Henry David Thoreau, that enshrined the natural world as the virtuous alternative to human decadence. Until the middle of the nineteenth century, as Andrew Isenberg notes, most scholars drew a sharp distinction between "harmonious, self-regulating" nature and the purposeful, dynamic human world. This idealization of a passive, unchanging nature, and its elevation into victimhood, lay behind the earliest writings on environmental history in the late nineteenth and early twentieth century. Long the barely noticed backdrop to human activity, the natural world initially entered history as the vulnerable object of human hubris and greed.[59]

The field that came to be known as "environmental history" first took shape in the United States, a place whose myths of origin revolve around the conquest of nature. In nineteenth-century America, triumphalist histories, in the mode of Frederick Jackson Turner, of a nation born of the arduous, intrepid settlement of the wilderness competed with increasingly influential declensionist chronicles of man's destructive impact on nature, which converged with the efforts of early conservationists like John Muir and Aldo Leopold.[60] Even more than other areas of historical writing, this field has, since taking shape in its modern form starting in the 1970s, been closely connected with a specific political project, that of environmental conservation. While it is probably the case that most practitioners of environmental history support the aims of environmentalists, as the field has matured into more complexity it has lost, according to leading commentators, some of its political edge and jettisoned its more romantic

58. Genesis 1:26, King James Version.

59. Keith Thomas, *Man and the Natural World: A History of the Modern Sensibility* (New York: Pantheon, 1983); Andrew Isenberg, "Historicizing Natural Environments: The Deep Roots of Environmental History," in Kramer and Maza, *Companion to Western Historical Thought*, pp. 372–75, quote p. 374.

60. Ibid., 374–80.

illusions.[61] The theory, for instance, eagerly espoused in the early days of the field, that only Westerners and capitalism were ever responsible for the careless depletion of natural resources, has not withstood careful scrutiny. While high population density and industrialization have no doubt done more harm to nature than has anything else, studies show that Native Americans, for instance, felt no compunction about overfishing and over-hunting when they got a chance to do so; Indian beliefs in animal reincarnation may in fact have encouraged the heedless mass killing of animals such as bison.[62] While not minimizing the worldwide depredation that has resulted over time from specific aspects of Euro-American culture, environmental historians are currently backing away from the view that Judeo-Christian norms were intrinsically more villainous with respect to the environment than those of other cultures.[63]

While retaining most of its political edge, the field of environmental history has become in recent years more analytically complex by, as Paul Sutter has put it, "the troubling of nature as a category of analysis." Where earlier work posited a stark division between "nature" and "culture," current scholarship mostly rejects the myth of a pure, unsullied nature in favor of the view that "all environments are hybrid." For instance, writes Sutter, where the first generation of environmental historians would have described the building of a river dam in the western United States as an act of destructive domination, "the second generation has been more likely to characterize such an intervention as creating a 'second nature,' of the river . . . an 'organic machine.'" Viewing the relationship between humans and nature as "hybrid" or mutually interactive has allowed historians of the environment to "replace a fortified border between nature and culture with an in-

61. J. R. McNeill, "Observations on the Nature and Culture of Environmental History," *History and Theory* 42 (December 2003): 34; J. Donald Hughes, *What Is Environmental History?* (New York: Polity, 2006), 94–97.

62. Isenberg, "Historicizing Natural Environments," 383–84. For a classic, still popular account of the effects of capitalism on the environment, see Donald Worster, *Dust Bowl: The Southern Plains in the 1930s* (New York: Oxford University Press, 1979). Anti-"romantic" arguments about Native Americans and the environment can be found in Arthur McEvoy, *The Fisherman's Problem: Ecology and Law in the California Fisheries, 1850–1980* (Cambridge: Cambridge University Press, 1986), and Shepard Krech III, *The Ecological Indian: Myth and History* (New York: W. W. Norton, 1999).

63. McNeill, "Observations," 7.

creasingly expansive borderland."[64] The assumption, for instance, that "the environment" means "nature" has been seriously challenged by a growing subfield of urban environmental history, devoted to showing the ways in which natural environments shape cities and vice versa, or to demonstrating the socially unequal impact of urban physical environments on people of different classes.[65]

Environmental history has rescued the natural world from its onetime status as mere backdrop to human activity while raising intriguing questions about power and agency in the human/nature relationship. Unlike the other "whats" discussed in this chapter, nature is not the result of human activity, and our natural environment is at once vulnerable and dangerously powerful (earthquakes, stampedes, microbes). As a result, most definitions of environmental history stress the dynamic and reciprocal relationship between humankind and nature. In the words of J. R. McNeill, "Environmental history pleads for recognition that nature not only exists, but changes. Moreover it changes both of its own accord and on account of human actions, and in doing so changes the context in which human history unfolds."[66]

Modern classics in environmental history vary a good deal in the degree of agency they ascribe to humans and nature respectively. Earlier works in the field, inspired by ecological activism, most often highlighted the deleterious effects of human activity. This was true even of the most sophisticated scholarship, such as William Cronon's celebrated *Changes in the Land* (1983), an account of the environmental effects of the transition in the seventeenth and eighteenth centuries from Native American to European dominance of the New England landscape.

Europeans drastically altered the New England ecology, in particular by means of extensive deforestation. Even so, Cronon does not frame the story as one of villains and victims but as an analysis of the shift from one set of cultural practices to another and its impact on the local environment. Native Americans adapted to the changing seasons by moving seasonally

---

64. Paul S. Sutter, "The World with Us: The State of American Environmental History," *Journal of American History* 100 (June 2013): 96.

65. Ibid., 113–15. See, for instance, Andrew Hurley, *Environmental Inequalities: Class, Race, and Industrial Pollution in Gary, Indiana, 1940–1980* (Chapel Hill: University of North Carolina Press, 1995).

66. McNeill, "Observations," 42.

to wherever the greatest food supplies were available: clustering around a waterfall when the fish were spawning, spreading out over a larger area in the hunting months, in some cases staying put to raise crops. Less concerned than their European counterparts with storing food, Indians prided themselves on their ability to go without sustenance for days at a time, a capacity to survive at starvation level that paradoxically ensured a relative abundance by limiting the human population. When the Europeans arrived, they remade the land according to their own sedentary traditions and understanding of property rights, their moral and economic imperative of land "improvement," and their approach to natural goods as commodities rather than resources.[67] The arrival of humans from a different culture did not just result in the introduction of discrete plant and animal species; it involved a whole series of linked cultural and ecological changes: "The pig was not merely a pig," Cronon writes, "but a creature bound among other things to the fence, the dandelion, and a very special definition of property."[68] While telling a story triggered by human agency—the arrival of Europeans in the place they came to call New England—Cronon is careful to stress throughout the dynamic, reciprocal relationship between humans and nature. Deforestation, for instance, affected seasonal air and soil temperatures, changed the composition of tree and animal species, caused floods and droughts, and created swamps. All of these, and more, deeply conditioned human lives.[69]

Cronon's early classic, like many other studies in environmental history, begins with human events, a story of cultural encounter. At the other end of the spectrum are works in which the physical environment utterly determines the fate of those who dwell in it. Jared Diamond's *Guns, Germs, and Steel*, for instance, enjoyed huge popular success after its 1997 publication because of its clear and engaging style and provocative thesis. A work of serious, if controversial, scholarship, Diamond's best-seller proposed an answer to the question of why Eurasian societies came to dominate the rest of the world in modern times. Why, he asks, "weren't Native Americans, Africans, and Aboriginal Australians the ones who decimated, subjugated,

67. William Cronon, *Changes in the Land: Indians, Colonists, and the Ecology of New England*, 2nd ed. (1983; New York: Hill and Wang, 2003), especially chapters 2 and 3.

68. Ibid., 14.

69. Ibid., chapter 6.

or exterminated Europeans and Asians?"[70] In a deliberate rebuttal to theories of cultural or genetic superiority, Diamond argues that Europeans and Asians were geographically and environmentally lucky. The planet's largest east-west landmass, located mostly in a temperate zone, Eurasia enjoyed an unusual abundance of plant and animal species, which multiplied as humans increasingly circulated across its landmass. Thanks to the planet's most effective nutrition (grasses with large, storable seeds spread from the Mediterranean across the continent) people and animals proliferated in close quarters, with humans as a result acquiring or developing resistance to viruses such as smallpox, measles, and influenza, which would prove deadly when exported to other continents. Increasing population density over time allowed Eurasian societies to develop specialized sectors such as standing armies—the guns and steel in the title—which gave them a further edge. In short, you don't need Christianity, capitalism, or the Chinese work ethic, let alone the putative superiority of Caucasian or Asian genes, to account for the Eurasian advantage. While many have disputed Diamond's stark environmental determinism, arguments like his have the merit of drawing our attention to the power of physical environments in history and, in the process, helping to wean us from anthropocentric arrogance.

Somewhere between approaches that highlight the effects of human activity upon nature (which then reacts in ways hard to predict and control) and studies like Diamond's in which geography and biology play the central roles, are historical accounts that combine human and natural agency, even as they highlight the latter in sometimes surprising ways. Alfred Crosby's 1986 *Ecological Imperialism* has become such a classic that its arguments are widely known. Unlike Diamond, Crosby starts with the European desire to conquer other worlds but seeks to explain why it was successful against apparent odds: "European emigrants and their descendants are everywhere," he writes, "which requires explanation."[71] Europeans tried and failed to settle in many places—the Vikings trained their sights on Greenland, crusaders made a grab for the Holy Land, imperialist zealots sought to settle Africa and the Caribbean—but they were only successful on a massive scale in the places Crosby calls "neo-Europes": areas

70. Jared Diamond, *Guns, Germs and Steel: The Fates of Human Societies* (New York: W. W. Norton, 1997), 15.

71. Alfred Crosby, *Ecological Imperialism: The Biological Expansion of Europe, 900–1900*, 2nd ed. (1986; Cambridge: Cambridge University Press, 2004), 2.

with climates similar to those of the Old World and low density populations, such as North America and the south of South America, Australia and New Zealand. And while the first small bands of European explorers and conquerors were vastly outnumbered by native warriors, they came with invisible and ultimately irresistible biological allies: weeds, proliferating livestock such as rabbits and pigs, and above all pathogens. Arriving in North America, southeast Australia, Brazil, and Argentina, Europeans and their "portmanteau biota" cleared all before them. Native flora were no match for the speedy march of aggressive European grasses, fragile South American guanacos yielded the pampas to cattle and horses, and heretofore isolated populations succumbed to European typhus and smallpox. In a matter of a few centuries, as Crosby puts it, the sun never set on the empire of the dandelion.[72] The story of conquest and settlement by the Old World of the New is, in short, unintelligible if we do not take into account the role of Europeans' nonhuman allies.

One of the best illustrations of nonhuman agency in history can be found in J. R. McNeill's *Mosquito Empires*, which tracks the role of those tiny and often deadly creatures in the geopolitics of the late eighteenth-century Caribbean. Although the author warns that his book is "not quite an essay in mosquito determinism," it is humbling for a human reader to discover just how significant a role *Aedes aegypti* played in the power struggles of this time and place.[73] The female of the species is the carrier of disease, most especially of the deadly yellow fever (known variously at the time as "yellow jack" or "black vomit"). The Atlantic trade, and the ports and sugar cane plantations of the early modern Caribbean, proved uncommonly hospitable to *A. aegypti*: pots of stagnant water were plentiful on board ships; clay vessels draining sugar offered ideal room and board; and massed and immobilized populations of soldiers, indentured servants, and slaves provided the insects with a smorgasbord of "blood meals." The constant presence of these tiny carriers of death was therefore closely connected to the human endeavors of travel, war, and plantation agriculture, but their ravages affected groups of people differently.

72. Ibid., 7.

73. J. R. McNeill, *Mosquito Empires: Ecology and War in the Greater Caribbean, 1620–1914* (Cambridge: Cambridge University Press, 2010), 6.

The geopolitical effects of mosquito activity stemmed from what McNeill calls "differential immunity": populations exposed earlier to yellow fever built up resistance and a resulting advantage over vulnerable latecomers, especially if they could manipulate the circumstances of an encounter. The Spaniards, for instance, were in a weak position overall by the eighteenth century, their Caribbean possessions threatened by wealthier ambitious rivals like Britain and France. They had, however, built up not only a degree of immunity to the disease but redoubtable stone fortresses at strategic points along sea routes, at Havana, San Juan, Cartagena, and elsewhere. Experience had taught the Spaniards that if an attacking European army could be held at bay and stationary thanks to fortifications for a month or more, disease would do their fighting for them. And so it went: in the early 1740s, 74 percent of the British soldiers sent to the Caribbean perished, but only 6 percent died in combat; among troops from North America, the overall toll was 65 percent, but only 3 percent in action. More British troops succumbed to the "yellow jack" in the 1762 siege of Havana than died in all of North America during the Seven Years' War.[74] Thanks to their insect allies and despite the weakness of their home country, the Spanish held on to their empire. Mosquitoes inflected the course not just of wars but of revolutions as the insurgent armies of leaders like Toussaint Louverture and Simon Bolívar made tactical use of their enemies' vulnerability to yellow fever. In McNeill's story, nature—not just mosquitoes but the weather, crops, and human bodies that allowed them to flourish—had the power to shape international relations.

McNeill's inquiry into the historical role of mosquitoes returns us to the ways in which all of the currents in scholarship described in this chapter have destabilized, indeed fatally undermined, the conventional tenets of "humanism" as once represented in the idea of a chain of being with man as mediator between the realms of spirit and matter, standing atop a hierarchy of creatures. The history of animals, a growing field, tracks the multiple and shifting status of animals in human societies: hunters and prey, bred, slaughtered, feared, domesticated, protected, worshipped.[75] (In many

74. Ibid., chapter 5.

75. For instance, Harriet Ritvo, *The Animal Estate: The English and Other Creatures in the Victorian Age* (Cambridge, MA: Harvard University Press, 1987); Ritvo, "Animal Planet," *Environmental History* 9 (April 2004), 204–20; Erica

instances in the past, "higher" animals—the falcons, dogs, and steeds of hunters and warriors, for instance—enjoyed higher status than "servile" men.[76]) Historians of animals have shown that what it means to be "human" in the past and present is revealed not only by the triumphs and sins of our species but also by the labile, emotionally charged dividing line between ourselves and other creatures. All in all, we seem to be on our way to fulfilling William Cronon's hope that "someday no historian will write as if people and their societies can be understood purely on their own terms, with no reference to natural systems and no acknowledgment of the other creatures with whom we share this planet."[77]

Enemies of the traditional canon in the humanities used to ridicule the old-fashioned curriculum by saying that that it consisted only of "dead white men" or "pale males." Historians' subjects remain, in their vast majority, dead—exceptions do exist—but a crowd of other characters has, in the past decades, joined the white men. The "who" of history has extended to every conceivable group of actors in past societies, an expansion that has productively challenged historians to ask different questions and hunt down different sources. White men have been further sidelined by the reframing of historians' "where" from landmasses to oceans, from nation-states to borderlands, from the single location to transnational and global expanses, all of which have entailed challenges to Eurocentrism. Finally, "men" no longer hog the limelight, not only because women have demanded their historiographic due, but also, as this chapter has shown, because of a productive scrambling of the old spirit-to-matter hierarchy: great ideas and inventions have been dragged into the real world of things, bodies, social status, and ambition, and we now recognize that humans everywhere have shaped and been shaped by objects, food, animals, and their natural environment. A similar upheaval has completely reshaped one of the most tra-

Fudge, "A Left-Handed Blow: Writing the History of Animals," in Nigel Rothfels, ed., *Representing Animals* (Bloomington: Indiana University Press, 2002), 3–18; Susan Pearson, *The Rights of the Defenseless: Protecting Animals and Children in Gilded Age America* (Chicago: University of Chicago Press, 2011).

76. See another illuminating essay by Marcy Norton, "Going to the Birds: Animals as Things and Beings in Early Modernity," in Findlen, *Early Modern Things*, 53–83.

77. Cronon, *Changes in the Land*, 173.

ditional topics within the discipline, the history of religion. Once centered on institutions, spiritual leaders, and theological disputes, the history of religion shifted its purview to the lives of the faithful, merging long ago with various strands of social and cultural history; at the same time, since most faiths embrace bodily experiences—fasting, celibacy, pain, but also sounds, sights, and smells—as a portal to religious experience, historians of religion have long been on the vanguard of inquiries into the physical context of immaterial experience in past societies.[78]

That said, a lot of historical writing, possibly most of it, still centers on traditional topics, often approached in old-fashioned ways: both inside and outside of the academy, political, military, diplomatic, and intellectual history still flourish, even if all of those subfields have been productively shaken up by post-1960s developments in the discipline. As a group, historians are by nature respectful of the past, which includes past scholarship in their fields and discipline, disinclined to throw out the baby of solid research with the bathwater of superannuated questions and approaches. More than practitioners of some other disciplines, historians tend to resist the tyranny of the extreme scholarly fad. The practice of history accommodates, as noted in the introduction to this volume, a near infinity of subjects and styles, yet it is also the case that historical inquiry tends to cluster at various times around certain themes, questions, and controversies. It is to the nature and dynamics of historical practice, to the questions and stakes behind the writing, that we turn in the second part of this book.

78. Miri Rubin, "Religion," in Ulinka Rublack, ed., *A Concise Companion to History* (Oxford: Oxford University Press, 2011), 317–30. Two masterpieces of historical writing on the link between social, bodily, and religious experience are Caroline Walker Bynum, *Holy Feast and Holy Fast: The Significance of Food to Medieval Women* (Berkeley: University of California Press, 1987), and Peter Brown, *The Body and Society: Men, Women and Sexual Renunciation in Early Christianity* (New York: Columbia University Press, 1988).

HOW IS HISTORY PRODUCED? 4

FROM CHRONICLERS TO ACADEMICS

Anyone can write history. Or rather, anyone equipped with some basic pre-requisites—literacy, time, and access to books and archives—can produce a nonfictional account of some aspect of the past. In this respect, history stands out among academic disciplines: it requires no equipment, labora-tories, or elaborate research protocols, nor does it usually involve the mas-tery of highly specialized concepts or technical terms. Here is how Adam Hochschild, a widely admired popular historian, described his method a few years ago: "If there is a special new technique of writing history, I cer-tainly have not discovered it. All the lessons I try to follow are very ancient ones. Read widely; 'Read,' G. M. Young, the historian of Victorian England, once said, 'until you can hear people talking.' Try like hell to be accurate. Remember how much you don't know. Write in a way that will make your reader keep on reading."[1] Producing history is no simple matter, of course, even when difficult languages and illegible documents are not an issue. Lo-cating and examining sources, of which there are typically either too few or too many, involves a particular blend of imagination, ingenuity, and mul-ish persistence, nor does the alchemy that turns stacks of disparate notes into graceful prose come easily to even the most experienced practitioners. The unspecialized nature of historical research and writing, however, ex-plains why of all the subjects taught in the academy, history has the largest popular following. History as a practice is unusual in the extent to which it flourishes simultaneously inside and outside of academia, not only in its scholarly and popular guises, but also in the form of "public history," of-fered up in museum exhibits, monuments, historical sites, and the like.

Although they connect in multiple ways, however, popular and profes-sional history tug the writing of the past in different directions, which, to oversimplify, one might describe as the production of new information,

---

1. Adam Hochschild, "Statement about Writing," http://www.liquisearch.com /adam_hochschild/statement_about_writing (accessed January 27, 2016).

on the one hand, and the dissemination of history to a broad public, on the other. This chapter focuses on the production of history by what are known as popular, public, and academic historians. It surveys some of the similarities and differences between various ways of representing the past in contemporary culture, showing that all such presentations involve choices and points of view, though this may be more evident in some cases than in others. The chapter explains why historians choose the topics they do, and why history in the academy is always framed, if only implicitly, by a debate between practitioners. Finally, it describes the building blocks of historical writing—sources—and explores the ways in which onetime unproblematic notions such as "archives" and "documents" have become controversial. This chapter seeks, in short, to explain what goes on behind the scenes of history "products," from best-selling biographies to documentaries to academic monographs. If the production of history in all of these formats sometimes touches off heated debates, it is because many people care viscerally about the past, and for excellent reasons: controversy and disagreement are what keeps the discipline vital and relevant to the contemporary world.

Today the word "historian" brings to mind a history professor, but that association is comparatively recent, going back less than two centuries. Well into the nineteenth century, history was mostly written by all-purpose "men of letters" (men nearly always): wealthy and leisured gentlemen, civil servants, politicians, and often persons who combined several of these identities.[2] Two writers now considered the foremost historians of the European Age of Enlightenment, for instance, the Frenchman Voltaire and the Englishman Edward Gibbon, were both comfortably off and successful writers independent of any institution, although both also had tenuous political careers, Gibbon as a low-profile member of Parliament, and Voltaire, briefly and unhappily, as historiographer royal at the court of Louis XV.

Before the nineteenth century, historians were frequently associated in one way or another with the world of politics. Over the centuries, their ranks have included notable individuals who wrote historical works during or after careers in public life, often as a means of understanding and sharing with others what they had learned. The first-century Roman historian

---

2. For an account of how women were marginalized by the professionalization of historical studies in Europe, see Bonnie Smith, *The Gender of History: Men, Women and Historical Practice* (Cambridge, MA: Harvard University Press, 1998).

Tacitus produced his accounts of recent regimes, *The Histories* and *The Annals*, between stints as a senator and as governor of an Asian province of Rome. Niccolò Machiavelli, an official of the Florentine Republic, was imprisoned and tortured after the Medici family regained control of the city in 1512 and wrote his celebrated works of history and political science in the wake of his very personal experience of regime change. The tradition of politician-historians endured into the twentieth century, with Winston Churchill writing a multivolume *History of the English-Speaking Peoples* (started in 1937, published 1956–1958) while he was steering Britain through World War II and the difficult postwar years.

Historians in past societies were often officially attached to governing bodies. Government-sponsored history writing in China, for instance, began in the second century BC under the Han Dynasty and flourished especially under the Tang Dynasty (seventh to ninth centuries AD): the Tang emperors established a "historiographical office" at court, which oversaw the production of court diaries, administrative records, and daily calendars that later fed into an official "national history" of the dynasty. In early modern India, likewise, Mughal emperors employed scores of literary bureaucrats, some of whom produced chronicles of the reign while others recorded the past for different purposes as they drew up documents establishing property rights.[3] The post of "historiographer royal," meanwhile, was a coveted position in many premodern European courts, typically occupied by less dyspeptically critical characters than Voltaire. The association of history with the exercise of power came naturally in premodern societies where no distinction existed between the state and society, history consisted in chronicling the lives of the great, and national or popular histories had yet to emerge.

While many people imagine the first chroniclers of the past etching their words on tablets or parchments, history has not always taken written forms. In ancient Ireland, Yugoslavia, Polynesia, and Benin the past was preserved and transmitted orally, by performers who specialized in the recounting of epic narratives or dynastic chronicles. In Peru oral chroniclers used sets of colored and knotted ropes of different lengths, known as *quipu*, as mne-

3. Denis Twitchett, *The Writing of Official History under the T'Ang* (New York: Cambridge University Press, 1992); Rosalind O'Hanlon, "'Premodern' Pasts: South Asia," in Prasenjit Duara, Viren Murthy, and Andrew Sartori, eds., *A Companion to Global Historical Thought* (London: Wiley Blackwell, 2014), 107–21.

monic devices to help recall both quantitative and qualitative information—not just the years of a monarch's rule, for instance, but also whether he was deemed just or brave. In Polynesia and West Africa, historians belonged to professional lineages of singers who transmitted their knowledge from father to son, each serving as a sort of walking reference library. In these societies "griots" recited history—dynastic successions, for instance—on specific occasions such as a coronation or a meeting of chiefs. As a saying of the West African Akan people put it, "Ancient things remain in the ear."[4] The social identities and practices of historians have been far more varied than is conveyed by the usual image of them as scholarly hermits.

For Western societies, the nineteenth century proved a watershed in both the organization and nature of the historical enterprise. Not only did the American and French Revolutions crystallize the idea of the "national" history of a "people," but the institutional upheavals that followed the Napoleonic wars resulted in significant change in the organization of knowledge. One consequence of the "age of revolutions" was the rapid expansion of state bureaucracies and with it the need for institutions to train civil servants, a task that included fostering enlightened loyalty to the nation through a knowledge of its past. The result was the creation or expansion of modern national universities, the prototype of which was the University of Berlin, founded in 1810.

Older universities had long existed in other European nations (Oxford, Cambridge, the Sorbonne, as well as several Italian and Spanish institutions all have medieval origins), but what distinguished nineteenth-century German academia was its early dedication to two powerful new ideals, scientific inquiry and nationalism. German historians of the early nineteenth century, most notably Leopold Von Ranke (who famously declared that the historian should describe the past "as it actually occurred"—*wie es eigentlich gewesen*), saw their mission not just as one of teaching, as in older universities, but of producing new information through original research.[5] Where historians of prior generations, the Voltaires and Gibbons, had been celebrated above all for their synthetic and literary skills, their

4. Jan Vansina, *Oral Tradition as History* (Madison: University of Wisconsin Press, 1985), 27–44.

5. Georg G. Iggers, *Historiography in the Twentieth Century: From Scientific Objectivity to the Postmodern Age* (Hanover, NH: Wesleyan University Press, 1997), chapter 1.

nineteenth-century counterparts, eager to align their discipline with the natural sciences, then at the peak of their prestige, enshrined "research" as the historian's central task. Starting in the mid-nineteenth century, an intense new focus on sources as the all-important building blocks for an unimpeachably "scientific" history led to the publication of massive collections of documents as the backbone for the study of national histories: the *Monumenta Germaniae Historica, Collection des documents inédits sur l'histoire de France,* and *Chronicles and Memorials of Great Britain and Ireland* were all launched before the 1860s. With these volumes, historians announced to the world that their efforts did not belong in the speculative or decorative realm of belles-lettres; their work, like that of scientists, would produce solid, incontrovertible, verifiable "research."[6]

No longer a pastime for well-heeled amateurs, university-based history evolved into a career akin to law or medicine, with all the expected markers of academic professionalism: the Germans were once again at the forefront, with the first major journal, *Historische Zeitschrift* (1859), and other countries followed suit, launching the flagship publications that exist to this day (*Revue historique, English Historical Review, American Historical Review*) from the 1870s to the 1890s. Following the German lead again, universities broke with the tradition of the uncredentialed gentleman-scholar by conferring doctoral degrees in history. Harvard awarded its first research-based PhD to a historian in 1873, and the Johns Hopkins University, founded in 1876 in deliberate imitation of German models, came close to cornering the market on such degrees until the end of the century (Oxford and Cambridge did not award history doctorates until 1917 and 1920, respectively). Not only are history PhDs a recent invention, their numbers were for a long time minuscule. In the 1870s there were only a dozen or so academic historians in the United States, and only after 1900 did more than twenty students a year earn PhDs. In his autobiography Henry Adams describes being hired as an assistant professor of medieval history at Harvard in 1870 mostly on the strength of personal connections, even though he had no doctorate and by his own account knew no history: "Down to the moment he took his chair and looked his scholars in the face, he had given, as far as he could remember, an hour, more or less, to the Middle

6. Ibid.; Georg G. Iggers, "The Professionalization of Historical Studies," in Lloyd Kramer and Sarah Maza, eds., *A Companion to Western Historical Thought* (London: Blackwell, 2002), 226–29.

Ages."[7] The decades before 1900 did, however, lay the bases for what we know now as professional history, with its journals, credentials, and professional associations such as Britain's Royal Historical Society (1868) and the American Historical Association (1885).[8]

Newly "professional" and "scientific," history became, over the course of the nineteenth century, mostly university-based and, in the process, ever more closely bound to secular and democratic states with nationalist ideals. In nations like France and Germany, the study of history was increasingly confined to the universities, themselves directly funded by the state and devoted to the training of teachers and other civil servants: German historians in the early twentieth century, for instance, coordinated closely with the government to provide accounts of the causes of and responsibility for the outbreak of World War I.[9] Formal links between the state and academic institutions were less pronounced in Britain and the United States, but in both the professoriate belonged to a small, homogeneous elite with close ties to governing circles.[10] In late nineteenth-century America, for instance, wealthy donors directly influenced hiring decisions and curricular orthodoxy, while leaders of the historical profession eagerly adopted "Anglo-Saxonism," the post-Reconstruction faith in the superiority of the Aryan races over not only blacks but Catholics and people of Celtic, Latin, and Semitic descent. In all of these national contexts, professionalism—the belief in an autonomous historical profession devoted to the pursuit of "objective" truth—coexisted paradoxically with the expectation that academic historians would promote consensual and patriotic narratives of the past that mirrored the views of a small intellectual and political elite.[11]

Not until the largest share of history writing came under the purview of professionally organized scholars did the distinction between "academic"

7. Henry Adams, *The Education of Henry Adams* (Boston: Houghton Mifflin, 1974), 300. I thank Daniel Immerwahr for drawing my attention to this passage.

8. Iggers, "Professionalization," 230–31; Robert Townsend, *History's Babel: Scholarship, Professionalization, and the Historical Enterprise in the United States, 1880–1940* (Chicago: University of Chicago Press, 2013), chapters 1, 2, 4; Peter Novick, *That Noble Dream: The "Objectivity Question" and the American Historical Profession* (Cambridge: Cambridge University Press, 1988), chapter 1.

9. Iggers, "Professionalization," 234–35.

10. Peter Mandler, *History and National Life* (London: Profile Books, 2002), chapter 2.

11. Novick, *That Noble Dream*, chapter 3.

and "popular" (or "lay") historians become operative, and for some decades the line remained blurry: in the first few decades of its existence, only half of the members of the American Historical Association worked as teachers, and only around a quarter at the college or university level, as compared to well over three-quarters belonging to the professoriate today.[12] With the rapid expansion, in the twentieth century, of both higher education and a large reading public, writings about the past increasingly fell into distinct categories of "academic" and "popular."[13]

POPULAR AND PUBLIC HISTORY

What distinguishes academic from so-called popular history? Not, as it happens, the identities of "popular" historians, many of whom occupy distinguished positions within the academy. In addition to successful non-academic historians such as Barbara Tuchman, David McCullough, or Doris Kearns Goodwin, the ranks of best-selling historical writers have included a stream of professors, many of them from leading institutions, such as Simon Schama, Joseph Ellis, Jill Lepore, David Hackett Fisher, James McPherson, and Richard Evans.[14] Among the features of a successful popular history, one is paramount: vivid, elegant prose and a subject framed in a way that makes it accessible to nonspecialists by assuming no prior knowledge of the field and its debates. Other ingredients of popular history are frequently but not inevitably present. One of these is narrative form. Nearly all popular histories include stories, and most are written *as*

12. Townsend, *History's Babel*, 31–35. In 2014 the American Historical Association counted 13,693 members, of whom 16.2 percent reported their area of employment as "Four-Year College" and 57.3 percent as "University." The 21.7 percent who did not answer the question probably also included many in these categories, so it is reasonable to assume that professors make up 80 percent or more of the current AHA membership. 2014 Membership report provided by Liz Townsend, AHA coordinator, via email, January 28, 2014.

13. Ian Tyrrell describes the complicated relation between academic and popular history in the United States before the 1960s in *Historians in Public: The Practice of American History, 1890–1970* (Chicago: University of Chicago Press, 2005), chapters 3 and 12. Unfortunately, there seems to exist no comparable synthesis for the more recent era.

14. For a discussion of "celebrity historians" in Britain, including notably Simon Schama, see Jerome de Groot, *Consuming History: Historians and Heritage in Contemporary Popular Culture* (London: Routledge, 2009), 17–22.

stories, including the very large categories of military history—most frequently the accounts of campaigns and battles—and historical biography. The latter, if well done, pulls readers in on several levels: biography typically concerns an exceptional individual—famous or infamous—includes intimate details and an evolving psychological portrait, features a cast of usually well-known secondary characters, and above all occurs in storied form with predictable triumphs and reversals. The massive, enduring popularity of historical biography—the number of books about Abraham Lincoln, most in biographical form, is currently estimated at around sixteen thousand—comes from the fact that readers can easily connect with the story of another person's life and learn valuable historical information along the way.[15]

The subject matter of popular history books tends to be more traditional than that of academic history. This should come as no surprise. Scholars are explicitly in the business of pushing the boundaries of knowledge, of finding new subjects or new approaches to old ones. Mass-market authors, in contrast, need to connect with readers on the basis of the already known, hence the endless stream of volumes on Henry VIII and his wives, the American Founding Fathers individually or collectively, Napoleon Bonaparte, the Third Reich, and the two world wars. Biographies of statesmen and military history loom large in the corpus of historical best-sellers, even as the bulk of academic historians have long since turned away from great leaders and feats of arms. Gordon Wood, a distinguished academic historian, noted a decade ago, reviewing yet another biography of George Washington, that his fellow scholars' enthusiasm for the study of racial, class, and gender tensions, especially among the masses of ordinary people, did not align with the tastes of a broader public. "Based on sales figures alone" he wrote, "it seems clear that most Americans want to read about the dead white males who created the nation—that is, the very subjects most academics do not want to write about."[16]

15. Stefanie Cohen, "Fourscore and 16000 Books," *Wall Street Journal*, October 12, 2012. Ford's Theatre Museum in Washington, DC, features a thirty-four-foot tower of books about Lincoln.

16. Gordon Wood, "The Man Who Would Not Be King," *New Republic Online*, December 16, 2004, https://newrepublic.com/article/ . . . /george-washington -founders-gilbert-st (accessed January 27, 2016).

While Wood's conclusion about the conservative tastes of nonspecialist history readers may prove generally true, there have been many exceptions. Books by Dava Sobel about little-known figures in the history of science (*Longitude* in 1995, *Galileo's Daughter* in 2000) occupied prime spots on the best-seller lists for many months, and works such as Erik Larson's intertwined story of the nineteenth-century Chicago architect Daniel Burnham and the serial murderer H. H. Holmes (*Devil in the White City*, 2003) and Laura Hillenbrand's biography of the Olympic runner and World War II survivor Louis Zamperini (*Unbroken*, 2010) have achieved even more massive success. Popular acclaim for a history book does not always require a famous event or protagonist. Solid research and superior style are essential, but even more crucial is narrative form: in most cases nonspecialist readers expect, and respond best to, a well-crafted, suspenseful story.

Therein resides the essential difference between popular and academic history. The motivation for both writing and reading "lay" history is most often basic curiosity: typically, both writer and reader are spurred by a straightforward desire to know about the subject. That said, anyone proposing to write, for instance, yet another biography of Queen Victoria must have either a new angle or some radically new information in order to sell the project to a publisher. Indeed, examples can be readily found of popular histories shaped around a distinctive approach or argument. Doris Kearns Goodwin's *Team of Rivals* recounted the political history of Abraham Lincoln's 1860 presidency through the prism of Lincoln's determination to cooperate with his erstwhile competitors for the position. Simon Schama's *Citizens: A Chronicle of the French Revolution*, a best-seller after its 1989 publication, took a sharply critical view of that event, arguing that the blood-soaked excesses of the 1793 Reign of Terror took shape during the revolution's allegedly moderate early years. Jared Diamond's *Guns, Germs, and Steel*, discussed in chapter 3, is unusual among best-selling histories in that it does not follow a consistent narrative form, is not confined to a single national history, and advances a strong thesis about geographical determinism. Popular histories do sometimes take a strong position, but the debates in which they engage are usually more straightforward (Napoleon Bonaparte: revolutionary hero or tyrannical dictator?) than the more complex issues that fuel arguments among scholarly historians. Typically, though, a work of non-academic history is judged and succeeds to the extent that it offers readers sound information and superior writing.

So-called popular history produced outside academia includes many important and influential books. Most academic historians can only dream of their work having the impact of *King Leopold's Ghost* by journalist and non-fiction writer Adam Hochschild.[17] First published in 1998, Hochschild's book is a horrific account of how King Leopold II of Belgium acquired and from 1885 to 1908 ran the Congo Free State, a chunk of Central Africa that, as the monarch's personal property, escaped his government's control. After obtaining the vast territory with international support thanks to a publicity campaign for which he enlisted the help of the famous explorer Henry Morton Stanley, Leopold and his agents engaged in over two decades of savage exploitation of its people for the sole purpose of filling the king's personal coffers with profits from the ivory and rubber trades. Inhabitants of the Congo were dragooned into what amounted to slave labor, working under the control of officers and overseers who starved, whipped, and mutilated them. Belgian soldiers presented their commanders—some of them sociopaths who decorated their gardens with skulls—with baskets of severed hands as proof of having carried out orders to wipe out entire villages, and limbs were amputated from the living wives and children of men who resisted work. Over the course of this period, by Hochschild's estimate, half of the area's population, around ten million people, died from the effects of forced labor, starvation and associated diseases, or outright murder.[18]

Much of the information in Hochschild's book, as the author acknowledges, had been uncovered by other scholars but published only in lengthy volumes from obscure presses (some of the most important work was previously available only in Flemish). Hochschild added his own research to his expertly written narrative, much of which centers on vivid portrayals of King Leopold, his associates, and the growing phalanx of human-rights crusaders who uncovered the Belgian atrocities and successfully campaigned against them, forcing the king to give up his territory: the African-American historian and activist George Washington Williams, the Anglo-Irish politician Sir Roger Casement, the writers Arthur Conan Doyle and Joseph Conrad, and British journalist Edmund Morel, who worked as a clerk for a Liverpool shipping firm and first observed that ships bound for the Belgian

17. Adam Hochschild, *King Leopold's Ghost: A Story of Greed, Terror, and Heroism in Central Africa* (New York: Houghton Mifflin, 1999).

18. Ibid., chapters 8–11, 15.

territory left with only men and weapons but returned laden with riches. *King Leopold's Ghost* sold hundreds of thousands of copies, and its 1999 translation had a huge impact in Belgium, shocking many people who still thought of their nation's colonial past as relatively benign. The nation's main colonial museum immediately planned an exhibition to explore the memory of colonialism in Belgian public life, and there followed an explosion of historical research and documentary filmmaking on the subject that continues to this day.[19] Hochschild's book does not revolve around the complex set of arguments engaged by most academic histories: its impact comes from superior style wedded to a morally urgent tale that has obvious ramifications in the present day.

Not all history produced and consumed outside of academia takes the form of books. Laying aside the huge category of historically inspired movies (and more recently, video games), which may be based on historical fact but supplement it with, for instance, invented dialogue, the popular form that lays the greatest claim to "truth" is the historical documentary, with its seductive shuffling of images, documents, and landscapes set to "authentic" or melodramatic soundtracks—pipes, fiddles, soaring strings. Arguably the most influential American historian of the last quarter century has been Ken Burns, the mop-topped, boyishly enthusiastic filmmaker whose documentaries on such topics as the Civil War, jazz, baseball, and Prohibition have drawn viewers in the tens of millions.[20] Documentaries about the past produce a strong illusion of truthfulness in several ways. Their authors' presence is usually hidden, since most historical documentarians do not make their directorial activity or agenda visible Michael Moore–style, preferring a godlike voice-over narration by a third party. Viewers experience a documentary's visuals—images, documents, physical

19. Alan Riding, "Belgium Confronts Its Heart of Darkness: Unsavory Colonial Behavior in the Congo Will Be Tackled by a New Study," *New York Times*, September 21, 2002; Debora L. Silverman, "Diasporas of Art: History, The Royal Tervuren Museum, and the Politics of Memory in Belgium, 1885–2014," *Journal of Modern History* 87 (September 2015): 16–18.

20. "Ken Burns is the most famous historian in the country," wrote David Harlan, noting that over twenty-three million people saw the first two episodes of Burns's Civil War documentary and fourteen million watched all nine. Harlan, "Ken Burns and the Coming Crisis of Academic History," *Rethinking History* 7, no. 2 (2003): 169.

artifacts—as unmediated contact with primary sources, and such films are typically punctuated by sober commentary from credentialed "talking heads" delivering brief chunks of seemingly dispassionate expertise.[21]

The "reality effect" of documentaries, as well as their immense popularity, have drawn the ire of some academic historians. British "telly dons" like Simon Schama regularly come in for their share of criticism from (possibly jealous) fellow academics, and in the United States Ken Burns's wide range and spectacular success have made him a favorite target. Leading scholars of the Civil War era have been sharply critical of Burns's film on that subject, complaining that it downplays the war's origins in slavery and the racial iniquities and violence of its outcome during the subsequent Reconstruction era. According to some prominent historians of nineteenth-century America, like Eric Foner and Leon Litwack, Burns reduces the war to a melodrama of white-on-white fratricide and subsequent redemption that mostly writes African-Americans out of the story.[22] Burns, a lifelong liberal, fully acknowledges the nation's past conflicts and atrocities, from the extermination of Native Americans by Civil War heroes Custer and Sherman (in his film *The West*), to Thomas Jefferson's ownership and callous treatment of slaves, to the longtime exclusion of black athletes and exploitation of working-class players (in *Baseball*). But even as he portrays prejudice and oppression in the past, Burns's ultimate message is one of patriotic optimism: the strength of American history and culture, he maintains, is its ability to wrest greatness—jazz, baseball, democracy itself—from diversity, a greater unity from tragedy. His documentaries pursue what he himself has called an "emotional consensus" around a common core of American culture.[23]

21. De Groot, *Consuming History*, 149–60; Marnie Hughes-Warrington, *History Goes to the Movies: Studying History on Film* (London: Routledge, 2007), chapter 6.

22. Eric Foner, *Who Owns History?* (New York: Hill and Wang, 2002), chapter 9; Robert Brent Toplin, ed., *Ken Burns's The Civil War: Historians Respond* (Oxford: Oxford University Press, 1996), chapters 6 and 7 (and see in the same volume critiques by historians of women and of the military, chapters 4 and 8).

23. Even a commentator more sympathetic to Burns, David Harlan, notes that the filmmaker's overall approach is more sanguine and less critical than that of most academic historians. Harlan, "Ken Burns," 171–80.

Such idealism rarely aligns with the perspective of the academic world, where scholars devoted to critical inquiry rarely promote "emotional consensus" about the national past, still less optimism about the near future. Some academic historians dismiss enterprises like Burns's as part of a mind-numbing "heritage" enterprise in which history becomes nostalgia-infused, sepia-toned entertainment. In a much noticed 2001 essay, "America Made Easy," Princeton historian Sean Wilentz excoriated contemporary popular history as "a passive nostalgic spectacle." Exhibits A and B in Wilentz's diatribe were David McCullough's admiring biographies of Theodore Roosevelt, Harry Truman, and John Adams ("yet another genre of spectatorial appreciation") and Ken Burns's *Civil War*, "brilliant in its detail, evocative in its storytelling, but crushingly sentimental and vacuous in its historical judgment of the war's origins and meaning."[24]

In a similar vein, the form of lay access to history known as "heritage"—the preservation of national sites and recreation of settings and events—has come in for criticism from some scholars. David Lowenthal, the most prominent and vocal academic foe of the "heritage industry," has repeatedly pointed out how much invention goes into revered national sites: the tourist-friendly lump of stone known as Plymouth Rock was not identified as such until the nineteenth century, and considerable doubts have long surrounded the history of Masada, the much-visited symbol of Israeli nationalism, a set of ruins on a barren plateau where in the first century AD some 960 Jewish defenders allegedly killed themselves rather than surrender to Roman besiegers.[25] The point for Lowenthal, however, is less that some sites traffic in fakery or distortion than the function served by heritage as a solipsistic and exclusive use of the past: "History is for all, heritage for us alone."[26] Carefully tended sites, from castles to battlefields, encourage com-

24. Sean Wilentz, "America Made Easy," *New Republic*, July 2, 2001, 35–40.

25. For a short and especially pugnacious statement of Lowenthal's position, see his "Fabricating Heritage," *History and Memory* 10 (Spring 1998): 5–24. See also Lowenthal, *The Past Is a Foreign Country* (Cambridge: Cambridge University Press, 1985), chapter 6; Lowenthal, *The Heritage Crusade and the Spoils of History* (Cambridge: Cambridge University Press, 1998). On Masada, see Yael Zerubavel, "The Death of Memory and the Memory of Death: Masada and the Holocaust as Historical Metaphors," *Representations* 45 (1994): 72–100; Zuleika Rodgers, ed., *Making History: Josephus and Historical Method* (Leiden: Brill, 2007).

26. Lowenthal, "Fabricating Heritage,"8.

munion and veneration, he argues, rather than insight and debate; the more you try to preserve the past "just as it was" the more you foreclose discussion. For Lowenthal, "heritage" is history's opposite.

If many heritage sites invite reverence and nostalgia by presenting one-sided or sanitized versions of the past, that is far from inevitable. A case in point is the increasingly conspicuous and frequently contentious introduction of the realities of African-American slavery into some of America's most hallowed historical sites, from Civil War battlefields to public spaces in Richmond, Virginia, to Thomas Jefferson's Monticello. The presence of slaves at Monticello (no longer concealed under the sanitized term "servants") has in recent years been openly acknowledged and addressed, as have Jefferson's relationship and children with his slave Sally Hemings, and while this evolution has met resistance in some quarters, most visitors are appreciative of this more honest portrayal of social realities on the estate.[27]

Most controversial have been the reenactments of slavery at the living-history museum Colonial Williamsburg in Virginia. Since 1979, African-Americans have portrayed members of the original town's large slave population, to the discomfort of some visitors, but the sharpest controversy erupted in 1994 over the decision to reenact a slave auction. Opinions diverged widely both between and within different constituencies. Some liberal groups, like the NAACP, protested the event as racist, while equally progressive parties, including academic specialists and some African-Americans, defended the reenactment on the grounds that it effectively conveyed a horrific reality at the heart of the slave experience. The defenders, however, were well aware of the serious issues raised by a slave-auction reenactment: Is it right to stage something so deeply upsetting to many actors and spectators? And how does one draw a firm line between historical integrity and entertainment or exploitation?[28] Clearly, heritage sites can provoke and nourish debates, both about the authenticity of their contents and the ways in which these are presented to the public.

27. James Oliver Horton and Lois E. Horton, eds., *Slavery and Public History: The Tough Stuff of American Memory* (Chapel Hill: University of North Carolina Press, 2006); on Monticello, see chapter 7.

28. James Oliver Horton, "Slavery in American History: An Uncomfortable Debate," in ibid., 49–53.

The same is true of historical museums, another major site for the practice of what is known as public history.[29] Today's public museums descend from both private collections—such as Renaissance cabinets of wonders amassed by gentlemen scientists—and research institutions. The United States Smithsonian Institution, for instance, was established thanks to the bequest of a nineteenth-century British scientist as a repository for the findings of geologists, archaeologists, and ethnographers. Only in the early twentieth century, when leading academics became increasingly critical of the Smithsonian's "oversimplifying" impulse in its treatment of collections, did it shift its focus to one of public education rather than scholarship.[30] At the same time that the Smithsonian moved away from its initial scholarly vocation, other institutions came into existence thanks to private initiatives. For much of the late nineteenth and twentieth centuries, many American history museums and heritage sites owed their existence to local enthusiasts, amateurs, and philanthropists like John D. Rockefeller, who established Colonial Williamsburg. Because such initiatives typically focused on the domestic and the everyday—presidential homes, displays of clothing, crafts—and because they blurred the line between education and entertainment, professional organizations like the American Historical Association long kept a distance from what they deemed overly emotional and "feminine" displays aimed at middlebrow audiences.[31]

The general public seems to respond better to museums than to any other form of historical presentation. When Roy Rosenzweig and David Thelen conducted a survey among a representative sample of 808 Americans in the early 1990s, they found that "visiting a history museum or heritage site" received the second highest score when rated on "how connected to the past do you feel on a scale of 1–10?"—only "gathering with

29. "Public history" is usually taken to designate the work done by historians in institutions that make the past available to the public, such as heritage sites, museums, national parks, and archives, but practitioners disagree about whether "public" means publicly funded, open to the public, devoted to public service and a progressive agenda, or some combination of these, and about what the field's relationship should be with academia. See Denise D. Meringolo, *Museums, Monuments and National Parks: Toward a New Genealogy of Public History* (Amherst: University of Massachusetts Press, 2012), xiii–xxv. For an account of the field's origins in the United States, see Tyrrell, *Historians in Public*, chapter 9.

30. Meringolo, *Museums*, chapter 3.

31. Ibid., 160–63.

your family" elicited higher scores. Museums came in first in response to a question about trustworthiness in portraying the past: 80 percent of respondents gave them the highest marks in that respect, well ahead of college history professors (54.3 percent) and high school teachers (35.5 percent), but also decisively edging out grandma and grandpa (69 percent).[32] The comments elicited from interview respondents confirmed that, much more than books, documentaries, or classes, museums offer the sort of unmediated access to the stuff of the past that convinces visitors what they are seeing is untainted by bias. Direct contact with artifacts allows you to "come to some conclusions on your own instead of listening to someone else's conclusions," offered one interviewee; another agreed that a museum "isn't trying to present you with any points of view. . . . You need to draw your own conclusions." "When you sit and look at an object," observed a middle-aged woman respondent, "your own senses come into play."[33]

Close exposure to physical artifacts from the past certainly elicits powerful emotional responses. Even seasoned researchers can feel their pulse quicken when handling an original document, whether a handwritten letter from a world leader or a marriage contract bearing the scrawled names of ordinary people whose lives are otherwise lost to us. For visitors to museums, exposure to this aura of pastness can mask the reality that every museum exhibit results from a series of highly conscious choices about selection and presentation. In one particularly severe verdict, Ludmilla Jordanova writes that museums "work in insidious ways," presenting carefully chosen objects that have been "cleaned, mended, 'restored' and packaged," and papering over gaps and silences. Museum displays, she argues, often revolve around simple, melodramatic story lines in which, for instance, life in the past is portrayed either as dirty and dangerous or as idyllically simple and safe. Paradoxically, the very concreteness and visibility of museum displays serves to conceal carefully calculated strategies of selection and presentation that remain invisible to patrons.[34]

32. Roy Rosenzweig and David Thelen, *The Presence of the Past: Popular Uses of History in American Life* (New York: Columbia University Press, 1998).

33. Ibid., 106–7. In the years since Rosenzweig and Thelen's survey, attendance at historical museums has suffered a steady decline. See Cary Carson, "The End of History Museums: What's Plan B?," *Public Historian* 30 (Fall 2008): 9–27.

34. Ludmilla Jordanova, *History in Practice*, 2nd ed. (London: Bloomsbury Academic 2006), 126–31.

There are times, however, when the choices that go into museum exhibits become utterly clear because of the controversies they ignite. In the United States, no instance of this has been more wrenching in recent times than the fight, in 1993–1995, over the Smithsonian National Air and Space Museum's plans for an exhibit about the decision to drop atomic bombs on Japan as World War II was drawing to a close.[35] The event, planned to coincide with the 1995 half-century commemoration of the war's end, was to center around the *Enola Gay*, the B-29 aircraft used to drop the "Little Boy" bomb on Hiroshima at the cost of some seventy to eighty thousand Japanese lives and as many thousands grievously wounded. Since the 1980s, veterans had been urging the museum to display the *Enola Gay*, which was housed at the museum's Paul E. Garber preservation facility; planning for such an exhibit began in earnest in 1990, but tensions among various constituencies were in evidence from the earliest days. On the one hand, the museum's director since 1987, Martin Harwit, a distinguished astrophysicist and a member of the postwar generation, saw this and other exhibits as a way of moving the National Air and Space Museum away from simply serving as a showcase for aircraft and toward more historically framed exhibits. On the other hand, once news got out that the museum was planning to frame the display of the *Enola Gay* with the controversial decision to drop the bomb, veterans' groups began to object strenuously, pointing to the museum's original mission statement: "The valor and sacrificial service of the men and women of the Armed Forces shall be portrayed . . . as an inspiration to the present and future generations of America."[36]

A three-hundred-page script for the exhibit, produced by museum curators with the help of academic historians, was completed in January 1994. The show was first to set the scene by chronicling the end of the European war and the expansion of conflict in the Pacific Theater, including accounts of Japanese aggression and atrocities. The second and most controversial section was to focus on the decision to use the atomic bomb, incorporating the sorts of questions and arguments raised in academic debates:

35. The following account draws upon Edward Linenthal, "Anatomy of a Controversy" in Linenthal and Tom Englehardt, eds., *History Wars: The* Enola Gay *and Other Battles for the American Past* (New York: Henry Holt, 1996): 9–62.
36. Ibid., 20.

Would a bomb of this sort have been dropped on the Germans? Did the United States ignore Japanese peace initiatives? To what extent did nuclear devastation serve, beyond ending the war, as an opening act of "atomic diplomacy" aimed at the Soviets? The script also addressed the debates surrounding estimates of the number of Americans (ranging from fifty thousand to half a million) who might have perished in an invasion of Japan had the bombs not been dropped. Finally, the exhibit was to include relics from Hiroshima, poignant reminders of lost Japanese lives: a wristwatch marking the exact time of the explosion, infant garments, a schoolgirl's lunchbox.

As the exhibit plans were made public, the Air Force Association, the American Legion, and members of various veterans' organizations reacted with anger to what they perceived as a devaluation not only of their wartime activities but of their very survival, believing as they did that the bomb had saved their lives and those of their comrades. In their view, the script put Japanese suffering ahead of the sacrifices of American soldiers and airmen. As museum staff scrambled to revise the script to placate critics, the controversy spilled into the popular press, which tilted heavily toward the veterans over the museum curators and their academic advisers, while members of Congress called for Harwit's resignation. On January 30, 1995, Smithsonian Secretary Michael Heyman canceled the planned exhibit, and Harwit resigned from his directorship on May 2. The aircraft's fuselage alone went on display from 1995 to 1998.

Triggered by the prospect of a single exhibit, the *Enola Gay* affair brought into the open the divisive potential of both permanent collections and special exhibits in history (and other) museums: the choice of items on display and the presentation and commentary that goes with them are just as much a form of argument as the contents of books and articles. The particular slant of a presentation is often visible only to specialists, though in the case of the *Enola Gay*, controversy over the exhibit's plans erupted as the result of broad ideological and generational tensions: at the time veterans of World War II were still numerous and active, while members of the postwar baby boom generation, many of them skeptical of patriotic militarism, were coming into their own as academics and museum staffers.

Beyond the single-exhibit controversy, the very existence and purpose of some historical museums can trigger soul-searching or debate. Well into the twentieth century, for instance, nobody objected to museums in Western nations exhibiting the "primitive" customs and arts of countries deemed "backward," usually places colonized by Europeans, who proudly displayed imperial loot as legitimate by-products of their "civilizing mission." But in the face of rising awareness of the depredations of colonialism, how should European nations exhibit, if at all, the treasures they acquired in the heyday of empire? France's brand-new museums of "first"—that is, "native"—art (*arts premiers*), in Paris, and of European and Mediterranean civilizations, in Marseille, opened in 2006 and 2013, respectively, and have come under fire for downplaying or ignoring their collections' links to the nation's colonial past: sometimes the very *absence* of historical commentary amounts to an interpretive choice.[37]

Even more problematically, Belgium is still home to the lavish museum built by Leopold II on his Tervuren estate as a showcase for the natural resources and native arts and crafts that advertised the Congo Free State to the world. The Royal Congo Museum opened in 1905, showcasing colonial products, African objects, stuffed beasts, huge maps, and massive allegorical statues of Belgium bringing "security" and "well-being" to the Congo. Throughout the twentieth century no mention was made of the millions of Congolese killed or maimed by their Belgian overlords: "It was as if," writes Adam Hochschild, "there were a huge museum of Jewish art and culture in Berlin that made no mention of the Holocaust."[38] Things began to change with the appointment in 2001 of a new director, and the museum's 2005 centennial was marked by an exhibit titled *The Memory of the Congo: The Colonial Era*. One historian has described the display as "an exercise in tepid and reluctant revisionism": under the headings "Transactions" and "Encounters," the exhibit portrayed Belgian occupation as mostly beneficial to both parties, while misrepresenting routine atrocities as occasional abuses and underplaying the catastrophic toll of colonialism on

37. For synthetic treatments of the debates that have surrounded the historical approaches—or lack thereof—of Paris's Musée du Quai Branly and Marseille's Musée des civilisations de l'Europe et de la Méditerrannée, see Caroline Ford, "Museums after Empire in Metropolitan and Overseas France," *Journal of Modern History* 82 (September 2010): 625–61, and Daniel J. Sherman, *French Primitivism and the Ends of Empire, 1945–1975* (Chicago: University of Chicago Press, 2011), 191–211.

38. Adam Hochschild, "In the Heart of Darkness," *New York Review of Books* 52, no. 15 (October 6, 2005).

the population.[39] The Tervuren Museum's half-hearted display of postcolonial remorse demonstrates how hard it can be to expunge entrenched biases from museums marked by the imprint of their own historical beginnings.

Some forms of popular history, then, lend themselves to controversy more than others. The latest best-selling biography of Thomas Jefferson or documentary about World War II might offer interpretations just as debatable as the National Air and Space Museum's projected *Enola Gay* exhibit, but acquiring the book or turning on the History Channel are private decisions involving no public establishments or finances. Museums, on the other hand, are public institutions in many senses—publicly funded, physically conspicuous, representing the nation's past to itself and to the world—and also monopolies of knowledge, since there can be only one National Museum of Whatever: citizens, and the politicians who represent them, have an obvious stake in the narrative displayed in "their" building, bankrolled by their taxes. Ironically, the most resonant debates tend to erupt around the *least* accessible form of popular history, which for most people requires an expensive and time-consuming trip to a distant city. The combination of taxpayer money, politics, and visibility, however, makes "public" history a prime arena for controversy about how the past is represented.

ORTHODOXY AND REVISIONISM: HOW DEBATE SHAPES HISTORY

Museum directors rarely court or welcome controversies that can cost them their jobs. For academic historians, on the other hand, debate, however civil, and disagreement, however small, are the motors that propel inquiry—and in the process build careers. In the heyday of positivistic ideals, the nineteenth and early twentieth centuries, leading historians in Europe and the United States believed that their field should consist in an exhaustive gathering of all the available evidence, ideally culminating in a definitive, unassailable account of some aspect of the past: with all knowable facts assembled and "objectively" presented, what need would there be for debate?[40] As we will see in chapter 6, the notion of a completely and objectively knowable past lost currency decades ago, giving way to the general view nowadays

39. Silverman, "Diasporas of Art," 16.
40. Novick, *That Noble Dream*, Chapter 1.

that historical knowledge progresses via a combination of new questions, new information, and new interpretive moves. Disagreement with what has been written before, ranging from friendly debate to career-rattling slugfest, powers most historical research and writing.

Academic disputes about history usually remain unknown outside of universities, since in most cases you need training in the field just to understand the terms and stakes of the debate. Around 1990, for instance, leading early modern British historians were at each other's throats over the role of Viscount Saye and Sele in the 1647 English Parliament: to what extent did he and his network of clients control the House of Commons? The question is of vital importance to specialists in that field—the larger issue is the role of the nobility in the English Revolution of the 1640s—but the articles in which leading scholars pounded away at one another are nearly impenetrable to those outside the field.[41] When academic controversy does spill over into the public arena, it is because it touches on areas about which people care a great deal and is framed in terms that most people can understand.

The history of Nazi Germany may be the prime instance of a field of study that makes regular incursions into public life: the Third Reich and the Holocaust matter viscerally, not only to two obvious constituencies, Jews and Germans, but also to the massive numbers of people horrified at the idea of a quintessentially "modern" and "civilized" European nation carrying out the methodical genocide of millions. Salient scholarship in this field often revolves around basic moral and psychological issues readily accessible to a general public that often approaches this area of history with strong feelings and opinions.

A dramatic example of the passions that surround clashing interpretations in this field came about in the 1990s with the publication of two high-profile books, Christopher Browning's *Ordinary Men: Reserve Police Battalion 101 and the Final Solution in Poland* (1992) and Daniel Jonah Goldhagen's *Hitler's Willing Executioners: Ordinary Germans and the Holocaust* (1996), the latter written in large part as a response to Browning. Both scholars grappled with the issue captured by the philosopher Hannah

41. J. S. A. Adamson, "The English Nobility and the Projected Settlement of 1647," *Historical Journal* 30 (1987): 567–602, and Mark Kishlansky, "Saye What," *Historical Journal* 33 (1990): 917–37, were the opening salvos in a protracted kerfuffle.

Arendt's memorable phrase "the banality of evil": what made "people like us," law-abiding citizens, pious churchgoers, and devoted family members, condone or actively cooperate in the mass murder of people who had done them no harm?

Browning's study is based upon a set of remarkable records, the judicial interrogations, in the 1960s, of 125 members of Reserve Police Battalion 101, a company of German reservists who over the course of 1942–1943 carried out orders to shoot and kill some thirty-eight thousand Polish Jews in a dozen different locations. Browning's protagonists were indeed "ordinary": middle-aged men of modest standing from the German city of Hamburg, most of whom held blue-collar jobs in civilian life. Only a quarter of them belonged to the Nazi party.[42] At the time of their first operation, on July 13, 1942, the men had been in Poland for less than three weeks. Their commander, Major Wilhelm Trapp, assembled them early that morning and informed them of the very unpleasant task that awaited them: they were to shoot some fifteen hundred Jews in the neighboring town of Jósephów, in large part the women, children, and elderly deemed unfit for work. Visibly upset, he told them that any of the older men among them could opt out of the task if they felt unable to carry it out. Out of a battalion of around five hundred, only a dozen initially declined to participate; in the course of the day, some 10 to 20 percent more asked to be released from a task they found emotionally draining.[43] The same pattern prevailed as the unit carried out further massacres through November of 1943: only a small minority sought to be relieved from participation, even though, as Browning convincingly argues, there is no evidence that any of the recruits would have faced any negative consequences for opting out beyond their own sense of shame at shirking their "duty."

The documentary record of Battalion 101 is unique among sources pertaining to the Holocaust. As Browning puts it, "Never before had I encountered the issue of choice so dramatically framed by the course of events and so openly discussed by at least some of the perpetrators."[44] From the dozens of interrogations, Browning sorts through possible motivations, allowing for the inevitable distortions in the participants' self-reporting. The

42. Christopher Browning, *Ordinary Men: Reserve Battalion 101 and the Final Solution in Poland*, 2nd ed. (New York: HarperCollins, 1998), 47–48.

43. Ibid., chapters 1 and 8.

44. Ibid., xvi.

background of brutal warfare, the perception of German vulnerability to enemies, and a deeply ingrained contempt for Jews all played a part, he concludes, in making this monstrous behavior possible. But Browning in the end locates the decisive factor in the dynamics of the battalion. The 80 to 90 percent of men who carried out mass murder, despite recoiling from the task and having the option of refusing, did so out of conformism, respect for authority, and fear that they would be rejected by their brethren should they refuse to take on their share of an unpleasant duty. They did not especially want to shoot Jews, but they wanted even less to be shunned by the comrades and superiors who at this point made up their entire world.[45] Browning's conclusions are thus less about the "banality of evil" than about the chilling effects of group conformity.

Browning's decision not to foreground anti-Semitic motivation drew the ire of a young Harvard political scientist, Daniel Jonah Goldhagen, who published a scathing review of *Ordinary Men* in the popular press. Browning, he complained, takes the battalion members' statements at face value and thus "reduces the Germans' singular and deep-rooted racist anti-Semitism to little more than one manifestation of a common social psychological phenomenon." These were not "ordinary men" in general, he wrote, but "ordinary members of an extraordinary political culture."[46] Goldhagen, who views zealously murderous anti-Semitism as a centuries-old central component of German culture, published his own book, *Hitler's Willing Executioners*, four years later.

The thesis of Goldhagen's book is blunt and clear: "Germans' anti-Semitic beliefs about Jews were the central causal agent of the Holocaust. . . . The conclusion of this book is that anti-Semitism moved many thousands of 'ordinary Germans'—and would have moved millions more had they been appropriately positioned—to slaughter Jews."[47] The book

45. Ibid., chapter 18. Browning's analysis draws on the famous experiments conducted by Stanley Milgram at Yale in the 1960s, in which unknowing subjects were willing to administer a series of escalating electric shocks to other subjects (who screamed in pain but were in fact actors) just because the investigator, a scientific authority, assured them that there was nothing wrong with doing so.

46. Daniel Jonah Goldhagen, "The Evil of Banality," *New Republic* 207 (July 13–20, 1992), 52.

47. Daniel Jonah Goldhagen, *Hitler's Willing Executioners: Ordinary Germans and the Holocaust* (New York: Knopf, 1996), 9.

locates the source of this widely shared genocidal impulse in what the author describes as a German tradition, unbroken since the Middle Ages, of "eliminationist" anti-Semitism, a view "almost universally shared" through the centuries that Jewish influence was poisonous and that Jews should be removed from German society.[48] Scholars miss the point, he argues, when they agonize over why so many members of a supposedly rational and enlightened culture were able to do what they did. Germans, he maintains, were not "normal," not "people like us"—their culture had been poisoned by anti-Semitism. In the chapters where he delves into the same sources as Browning, Goldhagen comes to the opposite conclusion, namely that the vast majority of Police Battalion 101 who engaged in the killing were motivated not by peer pressure, obedience, or careerism but by an active desire to slaughter Jews, as reflected in accounts of gruesomely callous and cruel behavior. His description highlights horrible instances of German soldiers urinating on Jews, forcing them to crawl on the ground or dig their own graves, of battalion members joking about the splattered brains of their victims, and he discounts numerous men's reports of reluctance and revulsion as postwar self-exculpation.

The works of Browning and Goldhagen add up to a classic instance of two scholars examining the same evidence, asking the same questions, and coming to very different conclusions. Goldhagen's approach to the subject also illustrates the process known generically as historical "revisionism," the project of seeking to overturn established understandings of a period or event. To laypersons the idea that anti-Semitism caused the Holocaust may seem self-evident, but Goldhagen's straightforward thesis actually flies in the face of decades of distinguished scholarship highlighting the complexity of the question. Leading historians in the field mostly agree that the path to genocide was a crooked one involving many contingencies, not a straight line from Jew-hating to extermination, and that the vast majority of Germans were guilty of reprehensible indifference rather than active collusion.[49] Goldhagen's revisionism did not really advance his field of study since his work came under heavy criticism from nearly all of his

48. Ibid., 48.

49. On the current state of the question, see Peter Longerich, *Holocaust: The Nazi Persecution and Murder of the Jews* (Oxford: Oxford University Press, 2010); Peter Kenez, *The Coming of the Holocaust: From Antisemitism to Genocide* (Cambridge: Cambridge University Press, 2013).

fellow scholars, but he articulated his thesis in ways that resonated with a larger public: *Hitler's Willing Executioners* sold over 150,000 copies in the United States.[50] In the end, Browning earned the lion's share of scholarly respect, while Goldhagen walked away with some popular acclaim and a lot more money.

Both the field of Holocaust studies and the terms of this particular debate are accessible to readers with no special historical background, since the issues revolve around clear and compelling moral and social concerns. Browning and Goldhagen agree on the facts of the matter—hundreds of ordinary German recruits agreed to participate in atrocities when they could have refused—but the two scholars are driven by sharply different agendas: Browning wants to understand how some circumstances lead ordinary people to participate in unspeakable crimes, while for Goldhagen the question is not about human motivation in general but about the specific virulence of one society's anti-Semitism. In both cases, these are questions that can easily engage the minds and hearts of a non-academic public.

The historical debate that plays out beyond the ivory tower remains, however, the rare exception. Academic historians' arguments typically stay confined to a specialized field of study, but they are crucial for keeping the scholarship flowing and historical questions alive. For this reason, history students, at both undergraduate and graduate levels of instruction, are trained to present their work in the form of a "thesis" or argument. Just finding and presenting evidence is not enough, aspiring historians are taught; research results must be framed either as a challenge, however respectful, to what someone has said before, or as a supplement that alters, however slightly, the previous picture. As in other disciplines, disagreements among professional historians vary enormously in both scope and

---

50. The book sold even better in Germany, one of many symptoms of that country's postwar culture of atonement, known as *Vergangenheitsbewältigung*. For sales figures, see John Röhl, "Ordinary Germans and Hitler's Willing Executioners: The Goldhagen Controversy," in William Lamont, ed. *Historical Controversies and Historians* (London: UCL Press, 1998), 16. For the German reception of the book, see Robert R. Schandley, ed., *Unwilling Germans? The Goldhagen Debate*, trans. Jeremiah Riemer (Minneapolis: University of Minnesota Press, 1998). For a thorough scholarly critique of Goldhagen's book, see Ruth Bettina Birn, "Revising the Holocaust," *Historical Journal* 40 (1997): 195–215.

tone. Some subfields are collegial and polite, others riven into warring camps, with graduate students enlisted into attacking their mentors' rivals or the students of those rivals. In some cases disagreements map onto ideological convictions or methodological stances (traditionalists versus new social historians in the 1960s and after, everyone else versus postmodernists in the 1990s and beyond). In other cases feuds are driven by individual ambition or professional jealousy. Most often, several of these motives overlap. In the best of cases, though, disagreement can be illuminating or even transformative.

A classic illustration of revisionism leading to transformation is the overhaul, in the 1970s and beyond, of the history of the French Revolution, which has been convincingly described in terms of Thomas Kuhn's model of scientific revolutions (see chapter 3).[51] As in Kuhn's scenario, research in the field had been conducted for a very long time—since the nineteenth century—within a framework so deeply ingrained that it seemed impregnable common sense, like the sun revolving around the earth.[52] "Normal science" amounted in this case to a watered-down version of Marxism, which viewed the Revolution of 1789 as the result of an inevitable collision between, on the one hand, a rising eighteenth-century bourgeoisie—enriched by nascent capitalism, fired up by the ideas of the Enlightenment, but denied access to political power—and, on the other, a decadent aristocracy clinging to its unjust privileges under the protection of a reactionary monarchy. Many of the best-known facts about eighteenth-century France seemed to fit comfortably into this scenario. The French economy was indeed booming, liberal luminaries like Voltaire were lobbing criticism at the aristocracy and monarchy, and political crises culminated in May–June of 1789 in a "national assembly" of middle-class professionals

51. Gerald Kavanaugh, "The Present State of French Revolutionary Historiography: Alfred Cobban and Beyond," *French Historical Studies* 7 (Fall 1972): 587–606, especially 596–97.

52. A classic account of "orthodoxy" and "revisionism" in this field is William Doyle, *Origins of the French Revolution*, 3rd ed, (Oxford: Oxford University Press, 1999); for a more recent survey, see Thomas Kaiser and Dale Van Kley, eds., *From Deficit to Deluge: The Origins of the French Revolution* (Stanford, CA: Stanford University Press, 2010).

loudly clamoring for the rights of the nonprivileged and eventually touching off the Revolution.

It all made perfect sense until, as in Kuhn's scenario, it didn't. In 1964 an iconoclastic British scholar, Alfred Cobban, moved into the Copernicus role when he published *The Social Interpretation of the French Revolution*, a book that argued historians had been getting it all wrong.[53] In a series of sparkling short chapters Cobban posited that, to borrow the phrase of a later historian, "the French Revolution was not a social revolution with political consequences, but a political revolution with social consequences."[54] Soon scholars in the field began to notice all sorts of well known facts, previously overlooked, that did not fit into the reigning paradigm. France may have been a wealthy country, but it remained an overwhelmingly traditional, agrarian economy, to which capitalism of any sort was marginal. Dominant values remained firmly aristocratic: when the odd businessman or banker made a pile of money, his first instinct was to buy a chateau, a royal office, and a fake title and try to pass as a nobleman (Voltaire himself did this). The aristocracy, on the other hand, were anything but uniformly reactionary: the writers of the Enlightenment could barely have survived without the support of nobles who bought their books, protected them from the censors, and fussed over them in their salons. The monarchy lurched between repression and tolerance, but especially under Louis XVI (1770–1789) systematically attempted to carry out enlightened reforms, and far from supporting the aristocracy, conspicuously clashed with them in the political arena.

Eventually the "orthodox" Marxist-inspired view of the French Revolution gave way to the "revisionist" interpretation, which has come to be so widely accepted that it no longer counts as revisionist: most scholars in the field now agree that the 1789 upheaval did not result from the rise of a bourgeois class but from a breakdown of the old regime's political system coupled with major cultural transformations.[55] The French Revolution, in this view, matters less because of its causes, which were mostly accidental

53. Alfred Cobban, *The Social Interpretation of the French Revolution* (Cambridge: Cambridge University Press, 1964).

54. George V. Taylor, "Non-Capitalist Wealth and the Origins of the French Revolution," *American Historical Review* 72 (1967): 491.

55. See, for instance, Suzanne Desan, "What's after Political Culture? Recent French Revolutionary Historiography," *French Historical Studies* 23 (2000): 163–96.

(political dysfunction run amok), than because of its consequences: it provided France, Europe, and the world with powerful models of revolution and democracy well into the twentieth century.

Similar examples of a seemingly commonsense "orthodox" view of a historical question being challenged and replaced by an initially counter-intuitive "revisionist" scenario can be found for many historical fields and questions. The history of the Cold War, for instance, the decades-long armed standoff between the Soviet Union and the United States (1945–1991), has gone through several waves of reinterpretation. Right after World War II American statesmen and historians developed an "orthodox" interpretation of the Cold War's origins, blaming the hostile buildup on the Soviet Union's aggressive designs, especially on Eastern Europe. In the 1960s and 1970s, critical left-wing currents among intellectuals spawned a "revisionist" interpretation that flipped the earlier scenario: now the Americans were often seen as aggressors who cloaked their imperial ambitions under grand statements about "protecting freedom." A third, "post-revisionist" phase tried to find a middle ground by evacuating ideology from the story and taking a clinical view of the great powers as rational actors engaged in realpolitik, and more recently—with the help of newly accessible archives—scholars have disrupted the field in many ways by looking at the Cold War outside the East-West axis: from examining the perspective of the geographic "margins," to emphasizing the role of nonstate actors and organizations such as the United Nations, to recovering the agency of lesser state powers, to reconsidering cultural and ideological factors.[56]

Orthodoxy and revisionism have no inherent political content: in the case of the French Revolution orthodoxy was on the left and revisionism on the right, whereas the opposite was true for Cold War historiography. Nor are challenges to existing views always politically inspired. Goldhagen's attempt at Holocaust revisionism was apparently driven less by a distinctly left- or right-wing agenda than by intense Jewish identification and the acknowledged strong influence of his father, a Holocaust survivor. Not all challenges to established interpretations are driven by politics or

---

56. For recent syntheses, see Melvyn Leffler, "The Cold War: What Do 'We Now Know'"? *American Historical Review* 104 (1999): 501–24; Odd Arne Westad, *Reviewing the Cold War* (London: Frank Cass, 2000); Richard Immerman and Petra Goedde, eds., *The Oxford Handbook of the Cold War* (Oxford: Oxford University Press, 2013).

other passionate beliefs, but the process of revision and reinterpretation always provides the energy and excitement that keep a historical field or question alive.

The renewal of scholarship does not always involve a new wave of historians attacking the work of their predecessors. In fact, trying to demolish the work of an eminence in your field increasingly seems rooted in an old-fashioned, zero-sum view of scholarship which holds that you can only be right by proving someone else wrong. As we have seen in the previous chapters, historical practice has changed in recent decades but in a different way, with new historical actors, new spatial perspectives, and new objects being brought into play: a revolution looks different from the point of view of women, a booming economy from that of slaves; a nation-state seems less inevitable from its borders than from its center. Interpretive change can thus come about "internally," when one mainstream historian disputes another's interpretation, or "externally," when someone proposes a view from the (social, sexual, racial, geographic) margins that reshapes the overall picture.

DO SOURCES AND ARCHIVES MAKE HISTORY?

Readers may at this point be asking themselves an obvious question: doesn't history change when historians find sources that tell them something they did not know before? The short answer to that question is no. Historical research is no more about stumbling across the document that "explains it all" or "changes everything" than archaeology is about Indiana Jones blasting his way to the lost Ark of the Covenant; finding amazing sources is typically the consequence rather than the cause of innovative research. It would certainly be headline news if someone were to come across an actual document in which Hitler ordered the Holocaust, but in the end the field of Holocaust studies would not emerge transformed, since nearly everyone concurs that the genocide depended on a very complex set of causes and changing circumstances. Historians have plenty of "eureka moments" during their research, but these are made possible by a combination of training in the field and immersion in the subject that allows you to recognize the potential of a source. Anyone else reading a document that once made a scholar whoop with excitement would probably walk away mystified, bored, or both. The exceptional source does exist, but it attains exceptional status when an unusually creative historian figures out what can be done with it.

One of the most famous sources in recent North American historiography is the diary kept daily by Martha Ballard, a midwife in Maine, from 1785, when she was fifty, until her death in 1812. Before the 1980s the document was not unknown, cited over the decades by local scholars and historians of childbirth, but even they were inclined to dismiss it as mostly repetitive "trivia."[57] Indeed, if one dips into the diary at random (both the original manuscript and a typed transcription are available online), the quaintly intriguing entries soon become monotonous. June 7, 1791: "Clear frost [this] morning. I [hoed] my Corn and Beens. my [daughters] & Parthena went to mr Hamlins. mrs White & Suky Norcross here. I went to mr Livermores with them." June 8: "Clear. mrs Livermore warp[ed] a web here. mr Shuball Hinklys Lady here. I have been at home, my Children all Dind with me. Jona took Breakfast & Drank Tea. Cyrus went and Brot a Swine home." And so on, day after day, over close to ten thousand brief entries. Dramatic things do happen: children and adults die from disease and in childbirth, Ballard takes harrowing trips across the Kennebec River in all weather to assist birthing women, she attends and describes an autopsy, a judge is accused then acquitted for the rape of a neighbor's wife, someone is murdered. These dramas are recorded, however, in Ballard's unadorned lapidary style, with only an occasional hint of the feelings they evoked: "Mr Savage here. Informs that Mrs Foster has sworn a Rape on a number of men among whom is Judge North. Shocking indeed."[58]

From this unpromising source the historian Laurel Thatcher Ulrich produced a celebrated work in women's history, *A Midwife's Tale*. Working her way through the twenty-seven years' worth of entries, supplementing them with everything from tax rolls to land deeds, court records, other diaries, and even novels, Ulrich performs an extraordinary feat of reconstruction, piecing together the activities of an obscure but impressive woman and the life of her community at the end of the eighteenth century. From the information in thousands of entries, Ulrich teases out the story of a remarkable midwife who delivered 814 children, gave birth to nine of her own, and assisted at an autopsy, but was overshadowed by local male doctors; of a world where husbands and wives worked in separate, parallel economies, each buying, selling, and bartering; where premarital sex was common, children mostly

57. Laurel Thatcher Ulrich, *A Midwife's Tale: The Life of Martha Ballard, Based on Her Diary, 1785–1812* (New York: Knopf, 1990), 8–9.
58. Ulrich, *Midwife's Tale*, 102. The entry is for October 1, 1789.

chose their spouses, and marriages entailed little fuss; where visitors came in a constant stream and women worked together, but close friendships seemed absent.[59] From the daily entries a whole world comes alive, thanks to the historian's grit and patience: "Both the difficulty and the value of the diary lie in its astonishing steadiness," writes Ulrich. "It is powerful in part because it is so difficult to use, so unyielding in its dailiness."[60] Ulrich's book offers a splendid instance of a historian "creating" a source by intuiting its potential. More generally, sources emerge as questions are framed: without the advent of social and women's history, nobody would have thought of spending years scrutinizing the daily record of an obscure eighteenth-century New England woman.

To highlight the role of the historian in the "making" of sources is not to deny that the concrete existence and accessibility of documents does matter: when regimes change, tightening or loosening their rules of access, or when time passes and documentary troves are opened up, or conversely when human or natural disaster leads to the destruction of archives, whole fields of study are decisively affected. And while it is true that historians "make" their evidence by asking some questions and not others, it is equally the case that the existence of sources dictates the terms of history, a proposition that has in recent years given rise to a body of critical thinking. What counts as an "archive" and why? Who decides what documents should be preserved? And what happens to the history of undocumented pasts?

The standard how-to books about writing history often include lists of categories of sources: narratives and memoirs, state and local government archives, newspapers, religious and judicial records, private papers and diaries, images of various sorts, video and audio recordings, and so on.[61] These are often followed by admonitions about the need for critical evaluation of said sources and advice on how to correct for bias or fabrication.[62]

59. Ibid., 32.
60. Ibid., 21, 33.
61. See, for instance, John Tosh, *The Pursuit of History*, 5th ed. (Harlow: Pearson, 2010), chapter 4; Martha Howell and Walter Prevenier, *From Reliable Sources: An Introduction to Historical Methods* (Ithaca, NY: Cornell University Press, 2001), chapter 1.
62. Tosh, *Pursuit of History*, 124–30; Howell and Prevenier, *From Reliable Sources*, 60–68.

The matter of sources ought to be the most unproblematically technical aspect of historical work, since we all agree on the need to locate the best and most sources and use them with utmost diligence, responsibility, and critical caution.

As with many other aspects of the field, matters have become more interestingly complicated in recent decades. The standard view of historical research is of a scholar going to work in a dusty archive; in a majority of cases this is indeed still the scenario, although many archives are no longer dusty (especially those for more recent eras) and the "going to" is increasingly likely to happen online with digitized versions of documents. But what exactly are "archives"? Who created them and decided what would go into them? What we now consider archives have always been generated by groups and individuals who held power in their societies: people with access to literacy and other resources who believed that the record of their past had to be preserved. For centuries, dominant individuals and families, ruling bodies, and religious and educational institutions kept records both for practical reasons—to establish ownership and access to power, to record arbitration and punishment—and out of the belief that their actions and decisions were worth remembering. As with everything else connected to modern history-writing in the West, the "age of revolutions" (1780s to 1850s) marked a decisive turning point, with the founding of national archives to ensure that newly minted nation-states would have repositories for their collective memories. The French National Archives, for instance, were created in 1790, along with the new regime, as "the depository of acts that establish the constitution of the kingdom, the rights of its public, its laws." The foundation of this national institution expressed the ideological tenets of the new order in decreeing principles of both unity (a single repository) and democratic transparency (open access, in theory at least, to government records).[63] Other European nations soon followed suit.

Archives define the modern nation, and states have extraordinary powers to shape their country's past by controlling access: governments decide, on a wide range of grounds, what is classified information and for how long, with significant consequences for accounts of the national past. Archives also, as the Haitian scholar Michel-Rolph Trouillot observes, delineate the

63. Jennifer S. Milligan, "'What Is an Archive?' in the History of Modern France," in Antoinette Burton, ed. *Archive Stories: Facts, Fictions, and the Writing of History* (Durham, NC: Duke University Press, 2005), 161.

modern guild of historians by creating the conditions of possibility for writing history. In so doing, they authenticate historical work: "Archival power determines the difference between a historian, amateur or professional, and a charlatan."[64] Archives are not just passive repositories of documents but, in the words of Antoinette Burton, "full fledged historical actors as well." The latter is conspicuously the case for colonial archives, for instance, in which the keeping of records is inseparable from the project of imposing and maintaining foreign control.[65]

The ways in which documents are gathered and preserved, then, implicitly governs how history should be written. Western national archives, founded in the nineteenth century, are geared to the writing of political and institutional history. Even when the institutions in question are oppositional—a labor, suffrage, or civil-rights organization, for instance—the records generally privilege the activities of leaders and the most deliberate and public aspects of people's lives. Historians looking to reconstruct the lives of ordinary people have to resort to strategies such as painstaking multipronged reconstruction—as in Ulrich's *A Midwife's Tale*—or reading sources against the grain. Accounts by missionaries or explorers encountering "savages," for instance, tell us one side of a story, but by reading between the lines we can try to reconstruct the other side.

Social historians routinely use documents for information unrelated to their original purpose. Judicial records, a classic case in point, have proven a gold mine of information on daily lives and social attitudes among the nonliterate. The judges and inquisitors who generated them sought to establish guilt or innocence, but social historians look for unrelated details revealed around the edges of testimony by defendants or witnesses. In the early fourteenth century, for instance, a bishop named Jacques Fournier set up an inquisitorial office to cross-question the inhabitants of a tiny village in southwestern France, Montaillou, many of whom adhered to a heresy called Catharism. Fournier's court left abundant records that were well known to historians of religion, but in the 1970s a French social historian, Emmanuel Le Roy Ladurie, mined the records not only in search of evidence about religious belief, but to reconstruct, in a way never before attempted, the social life of a medieval village. In spilling the beans about their own and

64. Michel-Rolph Trouillot, *Silencing the Past: Power and the Production of History* (Boston: Beacon Press, 1995), 52.

65. Antoinette Burton, "Introduction," in *Archive Stories*, 7.

their neighbors' religious views, the villagers opened a vista on a lost social world. One woman, for instance, told of two neighbors chatting while "being deloused in the sun by their daughters. . . . All four of them were on the roof of their houses." Bishop Fournier was no doubt interested in the part of the conversation in which the women discuss how people bear the pain of being burned at the stake. ("Ignorant creature! God takes the pain upon himself, of course"), but stories like this provide information about both hygiene and social relations: picking lice out of someone's hair is a process both lengthy and intimate, the occasion for closeness and the exchange of information between lovers, family members, and friends.[66] These and other vignettes form the basis for a vivid reconstruction of everything from village attitudes toward hygiene, sex, and gender roles to the worldview of male teenage shepherds. Social history, in sum, often finds its richest evidence in the margins and "outtakes" of official documents.

Even so, history is built upon silences because, as Trouillot reminds us, every story unfolds at the expense of others left untold or buried under layers of other narratives. Trouillot's *Silencing the Past* opens with a chapter about a set of stories nesting inside each other like Russian dolls.[67] It begins with the description of the ruins of an elegant eighteenth-century palace called Sans-Souci in the hills of northern Haiti, built by Henry Christophe, a hero of the Haitian Revolution who became king of the northern part of the island in 1804 under the name Henry I. Few historians outside of Haiti know of the palace because Caribbean history has for so long been overshadowed by the story of other pasts, and the name Sans-Souci (French for "carefree") evokes Frederick the Great of Prussia, who built a famous rococo palace of that name outside of Berlin in the late 1740s. Western visitors to the island during and right after Henry's death assumed from the name that the Haitian king had modeled his palace on Frederick's; there exists no direct evidence to that effect, but Henry was well versed in European history and acquainted with several German residents of his kingdom. But the presumed Prussian connection has concealed, as Trouillot shows, the existence of a human Sans-Souci, a man probably named after a Haitian rural area or *quartier*. Jean-Baptiste Sans-Souci, a former plantation bondsman, rose to the rank of commander in the rebel slave

66. Emmanuel Le Roy Ladurie, *Montaillou: The Promised Land of Error*, trans. Barbara Bray (New York: George Brazillier, 1978), 141.

67. Trouillot, *Silencing the Past*, 35–69.

army, in which he fought against the French under Henry. By 1802 a "war within the war" had broken out between black creole (Haitian-born) French commanders like Henry and troops led by African-born leaders like Sans-Souci: under pretext of negotiation Henry summoned his former subordinate to a meeting and had him killed. Is it a bizarre coincidence that the king's palace had the same name as an enemy he had murdered? Noting the geographical overlap between the palace and the scene of the killing, Trouillot concludes that coincidence is improbable: "More likely the king was engaged in a transformative ritual to absorb his old enemy."[68]

Each of the Sans-Souci stories conceals another one: the famous German palace obscures the Haitian one; the story of King Henry as Europhile overlays the death of the African Jean-Baptiste Sans-Souci. And just as historians in the West remember Frederick but not Henry, so Haitian historians choose not to recall the war within their glorious war of national liberation, between Haitian-born creoles and African-born "Congos." In the historical record, Trouillot notes, some facts take center stage and others are muffled, "the way a silencer silences a gun."[69] The conspicuous sources, accounts by contemporary European and American visitors, naturally tug the historian toward the story of a Haitian monarch naming his castle after an admired European model. The silenced story requires more ingenuity and digging to bring to light the tale of a murdered African rival.

Extracting the stories hidden under the accepted narratives is not always possible. For many questions to which we seek answers (how did seventeenth-century Iroquois women view their position within their society?) sources are scant or nonexistent. But while it is easy to assume that nonliterate societies and disempowered populations left few or no traces, especially from the distant past, the ingenuity and patience of researchers have regularly proven skeptics wrong. Historians of Central Africa, for instance, have exploded the myth that societies in the rainforests of Equatorial Africa or of the Bantu Great Lakes region did not change for centuries or millennia by resorting to an approach known as historical linguistics.[70] The method consists in working backward from the earliest

68. Ibid., 65.

69. Ibid., 48.

70. Jan Vansina, *Paths in the Rainforests: Toward a History of Political Tradition in Equatorial Africa* (Madison: University of Wisconsin Press, 1990), especially chapter 1; David Schoenbrun, *A Green Place, a Good Place: Agrarian Change,*

eighteenth- or nineteenth-century records, such as the papers of linguists or of missionaries who needed to communicate in local languages. The words documented there delineate social, economic, and political realities at the time they were recorded, but they do more: if two or more distinct languages contain similar terms, these can be traced back to an original root language, allowing historians to piece together earlier patterns of life.[71] If two branches of the Eastern Cushitic language have related words for donkey, for instance, and the languages connect only at the node of the protolanguage, then the historian can assume the presence of donkeys in the society that spoke Proto Eastern Cushitic.[72] The difference between categories of meaning in earlier and later languages has allowed historians of Africa, in particular, to demolish the myth that some people have lived in "lands out of time." The practice of historical linguistics is immensely labor-intensive and its results often forbiddingly technical, but the method strikingly demonstrates the value of imagination and tenacity in historical reconstruction.

Only historians working on very recent periods have a way of directly addressing lacunae in the record by creating their own sources via the approach known as oral history.[73] The method, which consists in capturing the past by systematically interviewing those who lived through it, was long viewed with suspicion by mainstream historians: interviewers, it was claimed, were likely to have an agenda or a bias, interviewees' memory and motives could not be trusted, and the spoken word in general was unreliable and subjective, far inferior to the written document. As late as 2001 a guide to the practice of history cautioned that "historians can place trust in oral sources only to the extent that they can be verified by other means" and that an interview "is in itself an interpretation, a source that must be analyzed with extreme care."[74]

Gender, and Social Identity in the Great Lakes Region to the Fifteenth Century (Portsmouth, NH: Heinemann, 1998), 3–61; Christopher Ehret, "Linguistic Archaeology," *African Archaeological Review* 29 (September 2012): 109–30.

71. An accessory technique forbiddingly named "glottochronology" allows researchers to establish average time spans for linguistic change to establish the rough dates of a language. Vansina, *Paths in the Rainforests*, 16.

72. Ehret, "Linguistic Archaeology," 24.

73. For the nuts and bolts of the method, see Donald A. Ritchie, *Doing Oral History*, 3rd ed. (Oxford: Oxford University Press, 2014).

74. Howell and Prevenier, *From Reliable Sources*, 26–27.

Many historians now resist the idea that written sources are "better" than oral sources as an instance of implicit bias against illiterate groups in the past. Whole categories of written documents are in fact transcriptions of oral events such as speeches, assembly debates, and courtroom depositions. But practitioners of oral history also embrace the ways in which interviews, with all of their distortions and subjectivity, give the historian access not so much to some elusive "truth" about the past, but to the meaning of that past for those who lived through it. Even mistakes and distortions in testimonies are telling, and the peculiarities of recorded speech—pace, pauses, hesitations, and so on—provide clues about feelings and attitudes. As a leading practitioner of the genre has put it, "The unique and precious element that oral sources force upon the historian . . . is the speaker's subjectivity."[75]

The practice of oral history also stands out from other approaches as the only instance of historians creating their sources even as they carry out their research. Historian-interviewers typically approach their role self-consciously, fully aware that their presence and lines of questioning will most likely inflect the material. Gail Hershatter, who spent many years, along with a Chinese colleague, interviewing women in remote villages in Shaanxi Province about their experience of revolution and collectivization in the 1950s, was disconcerted at the attention she attracted as a foreign scholar—all the more when she returned to previously visited homes to find framed photographs of herself displayed alongside cherished family portraits.[76] Navigating her own conspicuousness as best she could, Hershatter put oral history in the service of upending the accepted narrative of what the Chinese Revolution did for women.

After the Communist Party took over in 1949, it claimed to have freed women from hidden "inner" work and introduced them as equals to the public, paid, and recognized work of men and to participation in political

75. Alessandro Portelli, "The Peculiarities of Oral History," *History Workshop Journal* 12 (Fall 1981): 99. See also chapter 9, "Oral History," in Anna Green and Kathleen Troup, eds., *The Houses of History: A Critical Reader in Twentieth-Century History and Theory* (New York: New York University Press, 1999), 230–52, and Gwyn Prins, "Oral History," in Peter Burke, ed. *New Perspectives on Historical Writing* (University Park: Penn State University Press, 1991), 114–39.

76. Gail Hershatter, *The Gender of Memory: Rural Women and China's Collective Past* (Berkeley: University of California Press, 2011), 19.

life: women now plowed the fields alongside their husbands, and some threw themselves into leadership as "labor models."[77] For many these were positive developments, but talking to elderly village women Hershatter uncovered many a darker side to revolutionary "progress." Alongside the public fieldwork as equal partners to their men, women had to keep up a second shift of more traditional domestic duties, including endless nighttime sewing to keep their families clothed, "inner" labor that was granted no official existence: "When there was no electricity, I lit a lamp and did needlework. When my sons woke up, I held them up to pee and then put them down. I worked past midnight making clothes for my sons. I worked in the collective during the day. I never slept. I was so pitiful."[78] These words from a woman named Xiao Gaiye are echoed by many others who describe snatching every spare moment—a party meeting, a break during fieldwork—to complete their needlework, and the resulting exhaustion from work on two fronts. Many features of the women's lives run counter to the state-sanctioned narrative of progress: reduction of infant mortality was a success for the revolution but a problem for mothers, who had more children to raise with already insufficient resources. Women's very patterns of memory diverged from those of men, with recollections tied not to the official "before" and "after" of the Great Leap Forward but to the birth years of children, identified via the animals of the Chinese zodiac. Without Hershatter's interviews, the experience of these women and their remote communities at a time of immense political transformation would be lost, and our understanding of the social effects of the 1949 Revolution considerably poorer, skewed to elite, male, and urban experiences of political change.

As subject matter, history toggles between description and explanation, the latter often shaped by debate. History as "just a story" survives in some forms of popular historical writing, although even best-selling biographies and military chronicles cannot help but embrace a point of view or value judgment, and frequently put forth an explicit argument. The production of books, documentaries, and museum exhibits inevitably involves more or less visible choices, and the most "public" forms of history—museums, heritage sites—occasionally find themselves embroiled in bitter dispute. Academic history openly embraces debate as the motor that drives research

77. Ibid., 287–88.
78. Ibid., 192.

and interpretation: the ambition of every scholar, undergraduate to emeritus, is to enter the conversation by saying something new. In most cases, the questions historians ask drive the search for sources (rather than the source creating the project). Historical research involves much persistence, patience, and creative ingenuity, with sometimes a stroke of dumb luck: most of the time it takes years of training to "bump into" a terrific source, and what you find flows from the questions you ask. In the unusual case of oral history, researchers are able to take this proposition to its logical extreme by actually creating the sources they need. For many questions, however, there will never be sources, and the stories of those whose lives were deemed unworthy of record will forever remain untold.

CAUSES OR MEANINGS?

5

CAUSALITY AND HISTORY

E. H. Carr's *What Is History?*, first published in 1961 and still one of the most widely read introductions to the discipline, includes the memorably pithy pronouncement: "The study of history is a study of causes."[1] This statement makes sense to most people intuitively: the story of "what happened" must be inseparable from considerations of "why it happened." You cannot describe a general losing a battle, strikers defeating their bosses, or malcontents overthrowing a government without introducing some consideration of causality. From this commonsense point of view, the theme and subtitle of a 2015 forum in the leading history journal in the United States may come as a surprise: "Explaining Historical Change, or: The Lost History of Causes." On the opening page, the editor of the *American Historical Review* frames the exchange among a panel of distinguished specialists by noting that "not long ago it was common for historians to think about 'cause' as an element of historical analysis." Scholarly books and articles once wrestled with the causes of the Protestant Reformation, of European imperialism, the rise of capitalism, or the French Revolution, he continues, but "it has been a long time since mainstream historians have thought in terms of 'causes' and causality."[2] To those outside the field of academic history the fact that the word "causes" arrives crowned with quotation marks will probably be puzzling: how did the study of causes in history get so discredited that the word must be used in a defensive "we know we don't do this anymore" manner? What is the problem with causes, and if historians are no longer in the business of locating and describing them, what has replaced that pursuit?

1. Edward Hallett Carr, *What Is History?* (New York: Random House, 1961), 113.
2. Robert Schneider, "Explaining Historical Change, or: The Lost History of Causes," *American Historical Review* 120, no. 4 (October 2015): 1370.

In response to those questions, this chapter discusses the ways in which the project of historical interpretation has always been tugged in two directions. This bifurcation is variously identified as description versus interpretation, synchronic description (how things relate to each other at the same moment) versus diachronic analysis (how things change over time), or, as in this chapter's title, meaning versus causality. Anyone who writes history will tell you that these things cannot be separated in practice: the diachronic, causal, blow-by-blow story of how the battle was lost, the strike won, or the government overthrown will not make much sense to readers unless the writer pauses at some point in the narrative for a synchronic description of the numbers and training of the soldiers, the leaders and goals of the labor union, or the social composition and ideology of the regime's opposition. Most historians, most of the time, provide in their prose a mix of description, narrative, and interpretation, and in the best of cases these are woven together so skillfully that readers will not experience awkward lurches between the various intellectual tasks. But analytically separating these components is important, this chapter argues, because it helps us understand the historical enterprise. Causal analysis was indeed the backbone of historical work when Carr wrote *What Is History?* In subsequent decades, new trends appeared that put the spotlight elsewhere: less on the origins of the great event and more on what the people involved believed they were doing, within their own frame of reference; less on how large numbers of people in the past got from point A to point B, and more on how people experienced their world, first at point A and later at point B. These more recent approaches come with labels such as "microhistory" or "cultural history"; some of the historians who practice them reject considerations of causality on principle, more simply ignore them in practice, while still others struggle to reconcile change and meaning. Nor is it clear that the two strategies—focusing on causes or on meanings—are incompatible, either in theory or in fact. The rise of cultural history in the 1980s and after was one sign of an emerging discomfort with historians' classic preoccupation with finding and ordering the causes of great events, but not the only one. To what extent is thinking of history in terms of causality bound up with traditional nation-centered, Western agendas? How does causality play out, if it does, in the new world of transnational and global history?

Historians have always been preoccupied with establishing the causes of the events they narrate. Nearly three millennia ago Homer traced the outbreak of the Trojan Wars back to the anger of two goddesses, Hera and

Athena, toward the Trojan mortal Paris, who picked their rival Aphrodite in a contest maliciously set up by the goddess of discord. In the fifth century BC the Greek historian Herodotus attributed the Greco-Persian wars to a mix of human motivations, chief among them the overweening ambition of the Persian king Xerxes. His near contemporary Thucydides explained the outbreak of the Peloponnesian wars by distinguishing, as historians still do, between underlying causes (the growth of Athenian power) and triggering events (larger powers being sucked into a struggle over the city-state of Epidamnus). Events in the ancient world prompted historians to reflect on the causes and nature of political change. The second-century BC historian Polybius devised a cyclical pattern of political change whereby states evolve from despotism to monarchy, then to tyranny, aristocracy, democracy, mob rule, and back to despotism, with each change rooted in psychological dynamics among rulers and ruled: monarchy evolves into tyranny, for instance, when the king's descendants develop an ingrained sense of superiority, which leads to arbitrary and self-serving behavior and alienates the governed.[3]

As long as history was not conceived of as a story of open-ended "progress," individual character and behavior loomed large as causal factors. Historians in late-republican Rome, anxious about the decline of their political system, looked to the past to provide *exempla*, models of good or bad conduct that could exert a sort of gravitational force on contemporaries, drawing them to virtue and warning them away from its opposite. Writing in the first century BC, historians like Sallust or Livy hoped that readers might thus become exemplary citizens and save the republic from encroaching rot.[4] For a very long time, and in many different contexts worldwide, history was understood as a compendium of useful stories about famous people who happened to live in the past but whose world was imagined as no different from that of the historian.

The view of history as a trove of past events and characters analogous to those of the historian's present and available to serve as models or warnings

3. Ernst Breisach, *Historiography: Ancient, Medieval, and Modern* (Chicago: University of Chicago Press, 2007), 15–16, 46–48.

4. J. E. Lendon, "Historical Thought in Ancient Rome," in Lloyd Kramer and Sarah Maza, eds., *A Companion to Western Historical Thought* (London: Blackwell, 2002), 60–77; Clayton Roberts, *The Logic of Historical Explanation* (University Park: Penn State University Press, 1996), 274.

survived in the West well into the eighteenth century. The Age of Enlightenment and the national revolutions that capped it, however, decisively changed writing about the past into the form of "history" familiar to most of the world today. Eighteenth-century thinkers like Giambattista Vico in Italy, Charles de Montesquieu in France, and William Robertson in Scotland developed new theories of "stadial" history that divided the past into a succession of "stages" with distinct characteristics: theocratic, aristocratic, democratic, anarchic; hunter-gatherer, pastoral, agricultural, commercial; savage, barbaric, civilized.[5] These schemes were more conjectural than empirical, but combined with the late-century democratic revolutions and the appearance of modern nationalism, they contributed to the birth of what is usually referred to as "historicist" thinking, initially formulated by German writers like Johann Gottfried Herder (1744–1803): the assumption that the past is radically different from the present, and that history deals with events in their unique rather than generic aspect. In contrast to modes of history in which the chronicle of a ruler's courage or weakness could easily be transposed and applied to another setting, in a historicist account the development of Germany, for instance, would be seen as incommensurate with that of Britain or France.[6]

As we saw in chapter 2, the genesis of modern historical thinking in the West coincided with the birth of Euro-American nationalism in the late eighteenth and nineteenth centuries. Emerging national histories coalesced, as they still do, around highly significant events. Some of these are heavily symbolic (the battle of Agincourt for the English, the siege of Stalingrad for the Russians, the victories and martyrdom of Joan of Arc for the French), some traumatic and transformative (revolutions, major wars, anticolonial struggles), others more protracted, such as Spain's conquest of the "new world" or North American settlers' westward expansion. Carr made his confident pronouncement that history consists in "the study of causes" at a time when the most self-evidently important and prestigious areas of inquiry for historians were topics such as the causes of the German

5. Johnson Kent Wright, "Historical Thought in the Era of the Enlightenment," in Kramer and Maza, *Companion to Western Historical Thought*, 123–42.

6. Roberts, *Logic of Historical Explanation*, 274–75; Peter Reill, *The German Enlightenment and the Rise of Historicism* (Berkeley: University of California Press, 1975).

Reformation, the origins of the French Revolution, or the reasons behind World War I.

Causality has not disappeared from historical inquiry, far from it. For one thing, sorting out and prioritizing causes remains one of the most useful ways of teaching students about historical analysis. Of all the causes of the Russian Revolution of October 1917, which matter most and least? Did it result from drastic inflation, rapid industrialization, increasingly harsh labor and living conditions for the swelling urban working class? Would the upheaval have happened had Russia not entered World War I, and how did the decision to join that conflict relate to the Russians' defeat by the Japanese in 1905? How much weight should we give the fact that Lenin was an unusually effective leader, or Tsar Nicholas II a particularly inept one? Where do worsening conditions for the peasantry fit into this web of causes? How about the spread of Marxist ideas and the example of Western European socialism? Did Empress Alexandra's obsession with the mystical con artist Rasputin, or the fact that the heir to the throne was a fragile hemophiliac child, matter in any way at all? Working back from a major event, sorting through and classifying the constellation of factors that contributed to it, makes for excellent training in weighing the general against the particular, direct triggers against remote origins against everything in between, what actually happened against its counterfactual alternative. What students, scholars, or readers learn in the process about understanding the present as well as the past still constitutes one of the most powerful arguments for the study of history.

IN SEARCH OF LAWS AND PATTERNS: SOCIAL SCIENCE HISTORY AND COMPARISON

What students and others do *not* learn through this kind of exercise is anything one might call the "laws of history." Since the nineteenth century, the heyday of deterministic causal thinking, various intellectual currents have sought to enshrine history as a science.[7] Although historians have in the past been eager to confer prestige on their discipline by arguing that their work is as rigorous and as concretely useful as that of their colleagues across campus, analogies between the natural sciences and history are never

---

7. On nineteenth-century causal determinism and its subsequent decline, see Stephen Kern, *A Cultural History of Causality: Science, Murder Novels, and Systems of Thought* (Princeton, NJ: Princeton University Press, 2004), 1–26.

very convincing. Scientists formulate causal laws for predictive purposes (cause A will lead to effect B), while historians must determine the causes of events retrospectively (effect B must have had cause A); working with more manageable sets of variables, scientists seek to establish replicability, while historians deal with events that are inherently nonreproducible.[8] History offers no universally applicable laws, no rules that invariably lead to the same outcome. At best, philosophers of history and social scientists point to probabilistic laws, such the proposition, first formulated by Alexis de Tocqueville in the nineteenth century, that revolutions tend to break out when repressive regimes begin to engage in reforms. But like psychology, history allows at best for induction rather than deduction: human behavior in a specific place and time is much too messy to be pressed into universal laws.[9]

While parallels between the physical sciences and history have never gained much traction, historical research has often contributed to, and drawn inspiration from, the social sciences. Since the eighteenth century, traditions of wide-ranging scholarship have made use of historical evidence to provide general explanations of the different evolution of societies over time. Montesquieu is often credited with writing the first major work of comparative social science, *The Spirit of the Laws* (1748), which accounted for the emergence of republican, monarchical, and despotic governments in different parts of the world by pointing to geographical, historical, cultural, and legal determinants. More recent classics in the fields of historical sociology and comparative politics have dealt in bold comparisons between different historical situations in search of recurring patterns across time that point to the essence of phenomena such as "dictatorship" or "revolution."

Two classic works of historical sociology appeared in the middle decades of the twentieth century, Barrington Moore Jr.'s *Social Origins of Dictatorship and Democracy* (1966) and Theda Skocpol's *States and Social Revolutions* (1979). Taking for granted the inevitable modernization of societies worldwide, Moore looked to history for an explanation of why the transition to economic and political modernity (industrialization and mass politics) had taken different political forms—democracy, fascism, or communism—in different European and Asian countries. The reason for

8. I wish to thank Indira Raman for this formulation of the difference between disciplines.

9. Roberts, *Logic of Historical Explanation*, 3–15.

these varying outcomes, Moore argued, could be found in the balance of forces and resulting alliances between social groups. In the classic instance of "bourgeois revolution," societies such as Britain, France, and the United States included numerous and wealthy members of the middle classes who took advantage of incipient industrialization to neutralize the older agrarian elite and institute democracies (Moore believed that this had taken place in the United States in the wake of the Civil War). Fascism, by contrast, resulted from the endurance of a traditional landed elite that was able, as in Germany and Japan, to co-opt industrial leaders while defeating popular movements. Where the balance of social forces in a modernizing nation instead tilted to a revolutionary peasantry, communism would result, as in Russia and China.[10] Moore's is a classic instance of a social scientist drawing on historical sources to illuminate not a country's particular trajectory but a general proposition about political outcomes.

A dozen years later, the political scientist Theda Skocpol, a student of Moore's, published an ambitious comparative analysis of the French, Russian, and Chinese revolutions, *States and Social Revolutions*.[11] Unlike most previous scholars, who saw revolutions as the outcome of class conflict, Skocpol located the origins of these "classic" revolutions primarily in the internal contradictions, and eventual breakdown of, old regime states—in all cases, hastened by the demands of international competition and the pressure on resources from expensive foreign wars. Revolutions broke out when the state's structural weaknesses, exacerbated by foreign competition, came under pressure from a peasantry angered by government's inability to protect them from the exploitative behavior of their landlords. Skocpol thus argued that the state is the principal actor in the origins and outcomes of successful revolutionary dynamics. Moore's and Skocpol's classic works are examples of the ways in which social science history, as practiced by sociologists and political scientists, differs from what (mostly) goes on in history departments. The purpose of projects like Moore's and

---

10. Barrington Moore Jr., *Social Origins of Dictatorship and Democracy: Lord and Peasant in the Making of the Modern World* (Boston: Beacon Press, 1966); for a helpful discussion of the book and its reception, see Jonathan Weiner, "The Barrington Moore Thesis and Its Critics," *Theory and Society* 2 (Autumn 1975): 301–30.

11. Theda Skocpol, *States and Social Revolutions: A Comparative Analysis of France, Russia, and China* (Cambridge: Cambridge University Press, 1979).

Skocpol's is not to tease out the particularities of a historical situation but to bring several comparable events together and sort out similarities and differences so as to formulate a general proposition applicable to multiple instances of the same phenomenon: "Fascism results from the persistence of traditional elites in a modernizing economy," or "Revolutions have happened when dysfunctional states are subject to sharp financial pressure, usually as a consequence of expensive wars."

Social scientists engaged in comparative historical work may be thorough and attentive to details, but the nature of their projects demands that they sort out the wheat of essential and comparable information from the chaff of particular and idiosyncratic facts in order to make a general statement. There is no place in their approach for a fragile hemophiliac Russian prince. Historians, on the other hand, typically love the particular details of their fields of study. As Clayton Roberts puts it, "Historians study the battle of the Marne, not battles in general; they seek the causes of the Enlightenment, not of enlightenments in general; they study the rise of Hitler, not of dictators in general. Things in general they leave to the sociologists."[12] That is not to say that historians are not rigorous thinkers, but their thinking proceeds in a different way: their project is to order, and make sense of, a complicated set of events at a particular point in the past. Their purpose is not to extract from one historical situation a generalization that can be applied to another.

Some historians research and write something called comparative history, which on the face of it can seem rather similar to historical sociology. Notable explorations of similar historical phenomena in different geographical settings have included studies of race relations in the American South and in South Africa, fascism in Germany and Italy, the development of welfare states in France and Britain, and slavery in North and South America and the Caribbean.[13] But where historical sociologists resort to comparison in

12. Roberts, *Logic of Historical Explanation*, 8.

13. George Frederickson, *White Supremacy: A Comparative Study in American and South African History* (Oxford: Oxford University Press, 1981); Susan Pedersen, *Family, Dependence and the Origins of the Welfare State: Britain and France, 1914–1945* (New York: Cambridge University Press, 1993); Jonathan Steinberg, *All or Nothing: The Axis and the Holocaust 1941–1943* (London: Routledge, 1990). For an overview of the comparative slavery literature, see Enrico Dal Lago, "Comparative Slavery," in Mark M. Smith and Robert L. Parnelle, eds., *The Oxford*

search of a sort of Platonic essence of fascism or slavery, historians do so with a very different goal. In most cases they limit their comparison to two settings that they explore in detail, the better to illuminate the particulars of both. The benefits of historical comparison are the same as those of any deep cross-cultural immersion: by forcing us to look at a familiar situation in unfamiliar ways, it sharpens our understanding and compels us to explain things we might otherwise take for granted.[14]

One of the most successful examples of this strategy is Peter Kolchin's *Unfree Labor: American Slavery and Russian Serfdom* (1987), which compares two forms of personal bondage that flourished in the eighteenth and nineteenth centuries and were abolished around the same time: Tsar Alexander II decreed the end of serfdom in 1861, and the American Congress outlawed slavery in 1865.[15] Why, Kolchin asks, has the legacy of slavery remained an enduringly difficult issue in United States history to this day, while serfdom left little trace on Russian society after its abolition? He notes some structural similarities between the two systems: both originated in the sixteenth and seventeenth centuries, in areas peripheral to the European "core" where land was plentiful but labor scarce; both were forcibly terminated "from above." In both systems masters had full control over the labor and lives of their bondsmen.

The differences between serfdom and slavery in Kolchin's account, however, are more revealing than the similarities. Serfs worked on huge estates, typically for absentee landlords who rarely knew them individually; while personally unfree, they belonged to self-regulating village communities and to families that landlords had no interest in breaking up. American slaves inhabited much smaller plantations, and most were personally known to their masters, who in the name of paternal "duty" or personal interest brutally interfered in their lives, imposing religious norms and practices, whipping

---

Handbook of Slavery in the Americas (Oxford: Oxford University Press, 2010), 664–84.

14. Peter Baldwin, "Comparing and Generalizing: Why All History Is Comparative, Yet No History Is Sociology," in Deborah Cohen and Maura O'Connor, eds., *Comparison and History: Europe in Cross-National Perspective* (London: Routledge, 2004), 1–22; George Fredrickson, *The Comparative Imagination: On the History of Racism, Nationalism, and Social Movements* (Berkeley: University of California Press, 2004).

15. Peter Kolchin, *Unfree Labor: American Slavery and Russian Serfdom* (Cambridge, MA: Harvard University Press, 1987).

them into submission, outlawing their marriages, sexually exploiting female slaves, and tearing families apart. Race made for a big difference between the two systems, but so did the fact that the lives of serfs took place within a pattern of long-term sociocultural continuity, while those of African-born slaves and their progeny were marked by violent cultural disruption.

Most revealing, perhaps, is Kolchin's comparison of how the two systems ended. In the traditionally autocratic and hierarchical context of Russia, landlords long conditioned to obey the tsar did not oppose the 1861 decree, whereas in the more democratic, pluralistic culture of the United States, Southern masters went to war to preserve their way of life: it proved harder, paradoxically, to eradicate slavery from a "freer" society. While the painful legacy of African-Americans' original exclusion from the nation plays out in the United States to this day, Russian serfs were quickly reintegrated into a peasantry from which they had never been wholly separate.

As the example of Kolchin's book suggests, a well-informed comparison illuminates two comparable but different cases because it demands a consistently high level of analysis. While many accounts of the past are driven by the straightforward urge to document and describe, comparative history forces its practitioners to systematically ask *why* something happened one way in one place and differently in another. Their goal is not, in sum, to formulate a law applicable to cases they have not studied but to provide the deepest understanding of the specificities of two or more comparable but distinct historical phenomena.

MARXISM AND THE ANNALES SCHOOL

If historians work very differently from social theorists, delving deep into one or more particular contexts in the past rather than seeking essences, they have also relied for generations on the models provided by social scientists—economists, sociologists, political theorists, anthropologists, and others—as guides for their analyses. No theory has been more influential in modern historical analysis than Marxism, even though the number of historians who explicitly claim to be Marxists has always been small. Marx's analysis of history as powered by class struggle and of societies as shaped by a sequence of evolving modes of production has indelibly imprinted the work of all modern historians, whatever their political or methodological beliefs (see chapters 1 and 2). Marxist history attained the height of its influence worldwide from around the 1960s to the 1980s, providing a major impetus for the developments we have seen in earlier chapters, including social, global, and postcolonial history. Today Marxism is far less conspicuous, ironically because many its premises have been so completely absorbed: even many scholars with a conservative bent unquestioningly accept that material factors are central to historical change and that relations between unequal social groups are in essence antagonistic. All over the world, for instance, including in staunchly anticommunist countries, high school and college students have been taught for many decades the standard Marxist view that the French Revolution happened because an increasingly wealthy protocapitalist "bourgeoisie" grabbed political power from a decadent aristocracy whose time had passed: not even Cold War Americans were immune to the power of the bushy-bearded German's ideas.

Naturally, academics have argued for many decades over the specifics of Marx's thought and its application to historical analysis. There is much room for disagreement since Marx did not set out a definitive theory of history in any of his works, and also changed his mind and equivocated on central issues, most notably the extent to which humans' fate is strictly determined by economic factors. Marx and his collaborator Friedrich Engels conceived of their project as "materialist" history, in reaction against the then-dominant views of the philosopher G. W. F. Hegel, who explained history as the unfolding of a world-historical spirit or *Geist*. Marx's philosophy of history enshrined at its center the productive forces of mankind rather than a transcendent spirit. Where Marxists all view the forces and relations of economic production as the motor of history, they have disagreed sharply among themselves on the role of human consciousness in the process of change. Marx's writings provide plenty of fuel for interpretive dispute since he himself was tugged in two different theoretical directions with respect to the matter that preoccupied him most centrally, the future political defeat of capitalism: he sometimes wrote as if the impersonal forces of history doomed the capitalist mode of production regardless of human activity, while in other accounts he granted plenty of room to the conscious agency of workers.[16] One of his most frequently quoted passages, the dramatic lines near the beginning of *The Eighteenth Brumaire of Louis Bonaparte*, bears witness to this tension in his thinking: "Men make their own history, but they do not make it just as they please; they do not

16. Walter L. Adamson, "Marxism and Historical Thought," in Kramer and Maza, *Companion to Western Historical Thought*, 209–16.

make it under circumstances chosen by themselves; rather they make it in present circumstances, given and inherited. Tradition from all the dead generations weighs like a nightmare on the brain of the living."[17] Readers under the sway of Marx's hallucinatory metaphors of historical determinism can easily forget the five simple words that begin those famous lines: "Men make their own history."

The central program of the influential school of British Marxist history epitomized by E. P. Thompson in the mid-twentieth century was to resist deterministic, workers-as-puppets accounts by describing the ways in which working men and women processed economic change through the experience of their own lives, cultures, and consciousness.[18] Laborers were not the hapless victims of industrialization but agents of resistance to a brutal new world, which they opposed with deep-rooted traditional norms of community and justice; the working class, as Thompson famously put it, "was present at its own making."[19] More generally, working out the relation between the economic "base" and the legal, political, and cultural "superstructure," and moving away from the kind of mechanical determinism Marx espoused in his more polemical statements, are issues that have occupied the minds of several generations of sophisticated historical thinkers. Where ultimate causes—of misery for the poor, of resistance, of political change—are concerned, however, there was no dispute: in the famous phrase of a twentieth-century American presidential campaign, "It's the economy, stupid."

In the second half of the twentieth century, every major school of historical interpretation shared with Marxists the assumption that the important forces in history were socioeconomic. The most influential new movement in historical studies after World War II was the French Annales school, named after their journal, whose original title translates as *Annals of Economic and Social History*.[20] The journal was founded in 1929 by two

17. Mark Cowling and James Martin, eds., *Marx's "Eighteenth Brumaire": (Post) modern Interpretations*, trans. Terrell Carver (London: Pluto Press, 2002), 19.

18. Harvey J. Kaye, *The British Marxist Historians: An Introductory Analysis*, (Cambridge: Polity Press, 1984).

19. E. P. Thompson, *The Making of the English Working Class* (New York: Vintage, 1963), 9.

20. Traian Stoianovich, *French Historical Method: The Annales Paradigm* (Ithaca, NY: Cornell University Press, 1976); Peter Burke, *The French Historical Revolu-*

young historians based in Strasbourg, Lucien Febvre and Marc Bloch, who set about challenging the primacy of political history by opening the discipline up to methods borrowed from a wide range of social sciences, such as economics, geography, and anthropology. In the 1930s Bloch and Febvre moved their journal to Paris. Bloch was executed by the Gestapo for Resistance activities in 1944. Nonetheless, the interdisciplinary historical method known as the Annales School flourished from the 1940s to the 1970s as the single most important new historical school, not only in France but worldwide.[21]

The Annales historians shared neither the Marxists' interest in the dynamics of historical change, nor traditional historians' focus on personalities and events. Instead, they looked to other disciplines such as economics, geography, and anthropology for ways of describing, with unprecedented complexity and depth, the ways in which all aspects of a society in the past interlocked: they sometimes wrote of their ideal as "total history," *histoire totale*. The school's most enduringly famous work is the two-volume, thousand-page study *The Mediterranean and the Mediterranean World in the Age of Philip II* (1949), some of it drafted in a German POW camp, whose author, Fernand Braudel, went on to postwar fame and power as the journal's editor and one of the world's most celebrated historians.[22] An epic account of a time and place, the work has been compared to Tolstoy's *War and Peace*, not just because of its length, ambition, and evocative power but because of Braudel's view of the futility of human action within the immensity of historical time and space.[23] Braudel's magnum opus lays out a vision of different aspects of past societies, tiered like a wedding cake, each evolving within a different time frame. At the base of the cake is the

---

tion: *The* Annales *School, 1929–1989* (Cambridge: Polity Press, 1990); Georg G. Iggers, *Historiography in the Twentieth Century: From Scientific Objectivity to the Postmodern Challenge* (Hanover, NH: Wesleyan University Press, 1997), chapter 5.

21. Lynn Hunt notes that an *International Handbook of Historical Studies* published in 1979, with articles on historical studies in Eastern and Western Europe, India, Latin America, Japan, and Africa, includes "more entries for the *Annales* than for any other subject except Marx and Marxism": Hunt, "French History in the Last Twenty Years: The Rise and Fall of the *Annales* Paradigm," *Journal of Contemporary History* 21 (1986): 210.

22. Fernand Braudel, *The Mediterranean and the Mediterranean World in the Age of Philip II*, 2 vols. (New York: Harper and Row, 1972–1973).

23. Burke, *French Historical Revolution*, 42.

geohistory of soil, climate, and land and sea routes, which shapes people's lives but evolves with glacial slowness (Braudel gave it the oxymoronic label "immobile history"); in the middle is the layer of social and economic activity, which goes through permutations in a matter of decades; at the top is the fast-moving realm of political and other events. Braudel prized the big picture, the geohistory of dusty, sun-baked lands around the Mediterranean with their centuries-old lifeways; least important were events in the top layer—diplomacy, war, government—which he described in a later work as "surface disturbances, crests of foam which the tides of history carry on their strong backs."[24]

Later Annales historians in France shared Braudel's interest in the physical environment of history but turned increasingly to social and economic studies, often based upon masses of quantified data—birth and death records, for instance, or price or trade patterns. The Annales school produced landmark cultural studies too, inspired by anthropology and psychology: long-range histories of religious observance, or classic studies of attitudes toward childhood, fear, or death.[25] But for Annales historians and their followers the hierarchy of past realities was clear: the bedrock worlds of economy and society trumped the more evanescent realms of culture and "events." While a few *annalistes* identified with Marxism, most of them kept a distance from what they saw as the straitjacket of Marxian ideology. But though their purpose was different, their agenda intellectual rather than political, their analyses often static rather than dynamic, they shared with Marxist historians a firm belief in the overriding importance of social and economic determinants in the past: what was (or wasn't) on people's plates always took precedence over what was in their minds.[26] Like Marxists, they also tended toward "big history": longer time spans, massive data, historical casts of thousands.

24. Cited ibid., 35.

25. Some representative titles are Philippe Ariès, *L'enfant et la vie familiale sous l'Ancien Régime* (Paris: Plon, 1960); Ariès, *L'homme devant la mort* (Paris: Le Seuil, 1977); Jean Delumeau, *La peur en Occident, XIVe–XVIIIe siècles* (Paris: Fayard, 1978); Michel Vovelle, *La mort et l' Occident de 1300 à nos jours* (Paris: Gallimard, 1983).

26. Hunt, "French History," 213–14.

MULTICAUSAL HISTORY AND THE RETURN OF THE EVENT

Owing to the influence of schools such as Marxism and the Annales, many historians in the mid-twentieth century tended to privilege deep-rooted social and economic causal factors over the accidents of personality, psychology, belief, or behavior. When E. H. Carr wrote in 1961 that "every historical argument revolves around the question of the priority of causes," he was alluding to the fact that approaches to historical causality then tended to align with political conviction: conservative "idealists" stressed personalities, ideas, and the role of chance, as against "determinists" like Carr himself, who were influenced by Marxian ideas about the inevitability of certain historical processes.[27]

In *What Is History?* Carr famously offered an everyday puzzle as an illustration of his views on historical causation. One night a man named Jones is driving home from a party somewhat inebriated, in a car with defective brakes; rounding a corner where visibility is poor, he knocks over and kills another man, Robinson, who happened to be crossing the road to buy cigarettes. What is the cause of Robinson's death? In Carr's view, history "is a process of selection in terms of historical significance," and only generalizable causes are historically significant.[28] Drunk driving, faulty brakes, and blind corners, all known to cause accidents, are, in his view, "rational and real" causes because they lend themselves to generalization ("blind corners are hazardous to pedestrians") and also to remedy; such factors are historically significant because we can learn lessons from them about sobriety at the wheel, vehicle safety, and street lighting. They give history a moral purpose. Robinson's urge to get a pack of smokes, on the other hand, did not "cause" his death any more than the length of Cleopatra's nose, in the canonical example of counterfactual trivia, determined the fate of Rome: one cannot build historical generalization on the basis of one person's sudden decision to run an errand or the lust of another (Marc Antony) for a beguiling woman. Carr, a "strong determinist" influenced by Marxism, held that vesting importance in accidental or "contingent"

27. Carr, *What Is History?*, 117; Niall Ferguson, ed., *Virtual History: Alternatives and Counterfactuals* (New York: Basic Books, 1999), 44–56.

28. Carr, *What Is History?*, 137–38.

causes was both logically and ethically flawed, a stance that robbed history of moral purpose.[29]

The fatal encounter between Jones and Robinson is such an engagingly simple parable that it endured for decades as fuel for classroom debate. But Carr's blunt distinction between rational and accidental causes, and his view that the only causes that matter in history are those which allow for lessons or predictions have been roundly criticized by later historians and philosophers of history as a severely restrictive view of causality.[30] A more popular, ecumenical position holds that surely *all* causes in history matter in some way, even if they don't have equal weight: however likely it was that an accident would someday take place on that stretch of road, Robinson's pursuit of a nicotine fix was necessary for that *particular* fatal crash to occur. If all identifiable causes of a major event matter in some way, the historian's task is not to declare some of them out of bounds but to decide how to sort out and prioritize them.

Even before the sorting out begins, the historian has to decide where to draw the line, since every event connects back to a bottomless abyss of potential causes. As John Lewis Gaddis puts it, nobody is going to trace the bombing of Pearl Harbor back to the time when "the first Japanese island rose up, in great billowing clouds of smoke, from what was to become the Pacific Ocean."[31] Whether a historian reaches back five months, five years, five decades, or more, might result from their philosophical or methodological convictions, though often it simply depends on their subject matter: in search of the causes of the French Revolution of 1789, an economic historian will look back over a century of rising prices; an intellectual historian may reach back a few decades to describe the corrosive impact of Enlightenment ideas; and a practitioner of traditional political history will focus on the personal shortcomings and failed policies of Louis XVI and his ministers in the years or months immediately before the upheaval. Most of the time, historians work away happily in their various silos, connecting what they find to some already existing causal interpretation,

29. Ibid., 137–43.

30. Mark Hewitson, *History and Causality* (London: Palgrave, 2014), 87–93; Ferguson, *Virtual History*, 54–55; Richard Evans, *In Defense of History* (New York: W. W. Norton, 1999), chapter 5; John Lewis Gaddis, *The Landscape of History: How Historians Map the Past* (Oxford: Oxford University Press, 2002), 93–95.

31. Gaddis, *Landscape of History*, 96.

which their work will modify or complete. Only when writing a synthesis or lecturing to a class do they have to confront the hard questions about which causes matter more, and why.

Historians often avoid putting their money on one type of cause over another, instead explaining how various factors accumulate over time to a point of no return. Lawrence Stone, a distinguished historian of early modern Britain, did this several decades ago in a short and popular synthesis entitled *The Causes of the English Revolution, 1529–1642*, an account of how the English came to overthrow their monarchy, go to war against, and eventually execute King Charles I.[32] Rather than separate out economic, social, ideological, and political causes, Stone draws on theorists of revolution to set up a three-tiered explanatory scheme of "preconditions" stretching back a century; "precipitants" covering the decade 1629–1639; and "triggers" in the two years before Parliament deposed Charles. "Preconditions" include mostly broad structural changes in England's economy and society, such as the growth of the landed gentry and the professional classes, but also government instability and dysfunction; as "precipitants," Stone emphasizes repeating political factors, namely the monarchy's systematic intransigence on religious and fiscal matters in the 1630s; and finally, the "triggers" that turned the probability of an upheaval into a certainty include a series of foolhardy decisions by Charles and his advisors in 1640–1642, such as plotting to secure Scottish support against Parliament and an attempted arrest of five leading members of the House of Commons.

Considering the origins of revolutions in general, Stone proposes a distinction between conditions that make a revolution possible (a major change in society such as rapid economic development), those that render it probable (an inflexibly reactionary elite), and the short-term events, decisions, or personalities (a foolishly provocative move by the ruler, the rise of an exceptionally charismatic leader in the opposition) that make the crisis inevitable.[33] How can we describe the change in circumstances that shift an event from possible or probable to inevitable? Gaddis suggests that we borrow from the discipline of physics the concept of "phase transitions," the points where a stable system becomes unstable and transforms—when water boils or freezes, for instance, or fault lines fracture. Typically, such

32. Lawrence Stone, *The Causes of the English Revolution, 1529–1642* (New York: Harper & Row, 1972).

33. Ibid., 9–10.

transitions are located in an event's recent rather than more distant past: in the case of Pearl Harbor, this would be, for Gaddis, the 1941 American oil embargo against Japan, rather than the prior Japanese takeover of French Indochina or France's 1940 defeat by the Germans, which made the latter possible.[34]

Gaddis's commonsense stance—it all matters, but more recent events bear more causal weight—reflects the intellectual temper of recent times. In the early twenty-first century, stark philosophical and methodological commitments among historians are waning: it is now increasingly rare to come across Marxists who insist that it's all about modes of production, idealist believers in the pure power of ideas, determinists who hold that this or that historical event was absolutely fated to happen, or contingency buffs who rattle on about things like Cleopatra's nose. If pressed, many would adhere to a historian's version of chaos theory: there are laws out there, but they encompass such complex variables that no outcome can be neatly deduced from a set of preexisting conditions.[35] Clayton Roberts proposes the term "colligation" to describe historians' explanatory process: the tracing of multiple factors and events as they feed into a given outcome, an approach that combines narrative and analysis.[36] Historians' current discomfort with grand causal schemes parallels the evolution of science in the last few decades, away from linear thinking and toward the forking and branching of fractal geometry and chaos theory.[37] History writing, in short, has moved away from overarching causal frameworks, even as the discipline's practice has been enduringly enriched by Marx's insights about power and historical change and Braudel's creative interdisciplinarity.

Historians' traditional preoccupation with causal hierarchies presupposes a certain view of what matters in the past, and how it matters. The frequency with which revolutions have been mentioned in the previous pages—with wars a close second—reflects Eurocentric nationalist preoccupations with traumatic founding events and turning points. But the tradi-

---

34. Gaddis, *Landscape of History*, 95–100. Roberts makes this argument too, pointing out that it coincides with legal standards for establishing individual guilt; Roberts, *Logic of Historical Explanation*, 123.

35. Ferguson, *Virtual History*, 71–90.

36. Roberts, *Logic of Historical Explanation*, especially chapter 2.

37. John Holte, ed., *Chaos: The New Science* (Lanham, MD: University Press of America, 1993).

tional focus on causes in history also implies a sharp dividing line between cause and event, with the latter getting far less academic respect. In the workshop of history, the conventional division of labor has the professors analyzing and debating the causes and consequences of wars and revolutions while "popular historians" write the blow-by-blow narratives of battles and barricades—and often laugh all the way to the bank.

The cause/event dichotomy maps onto a similar opposition, commonly invoked by social scientists, of structures to events. Even specialists have a hard time defining a "structure," finding it easier to give examples—in Roberts's case "the organization of church and state, of society and the economy, of the county and the parish, of the schools and universities, of ideas and beliefs." Structures—whether concrete, such as a bureaucracy, or ideological, such as a theology—theoretically allow societies to endure in a steady state since they "lead to lawful acts, to customary behavior, to rule- and role-governed activities, and to standardized events."[38] Social and cultural structures, in short, inform the predictable repetition of certain kinds of behavior and occurrences. Structures are never really stable, of course, and their perpetuation regularly comes under threat from combinations of systemic dysfunction and human agency, whether by Martin Luther, Martin Luther King, or an army of anonymous Martins. Exceptional "events," in this standard view—someone nailing a denunciation of clerical practices to the door of a Wittenberg church or marching on Selma—are the outcome of structural dysfunction. Their consequences are understandable in relation to their causes.

But as William H. Sewell has argued, events themselves, rather than their causes, can have transformative effects. Drawing on the work of the anthropologist Marshall Sahlins, Sewell offers the example of a famous event in global history, the British captain James Cook's 1779 arrival in Hawaii and subsequent murder.[39] Cook's arrival in Kealekekua bay in January

38. Roberts, *Logic of Historical Explanation*, 135, 137. For an illuminating discussion of the difficulty of defining structure, see William H. Sewell Jr., *Logics of History: Social Theory and Social Transformation* (Chicago: University of Chicago Press, 2005), chapter 4.

39. Sewell, *Logics of History*, chapter 7; Marshall Sahlins, *Islands of History* (Chicago: University of Chicago Press, 1985), chapters 1, 3, 4. As Sewell notes, Sahlins's interpretation of the events surrounding and following Cook's arrival were sharply attacked by Gananath Obeyesekere in *The Apotheosis of Captain Cook:*

1779 happened to coincide with a winter festival celebrating Lono, the god of reproduction who returns to the islands every year with the fertilizing rains of winter. Cook not only showed up at exactly the right time; he also left a few days later, just as Lono should, invested with mana, or spiritual power. But a broken mast forced an unexpected return to the island, which the local ruler interpreted as a threat to his power, and a series of aggressions on both sides led to Cook being stabbed to death by the king's subjects. While the British ceremonially disposed of what they could find of Cook's body in the sea, some of the Hawaiians, followers of Lono, integrated what they claimed were his remains into a tradition of venerating deceased monarchs. Cook's mana, they believed, had been transferred to the rising king Kamehameha, who worshipped Cook's memory and initiated a policy of friendship with the British. Both the spiritual powers he drew from Cook's death and the new alliances that followed allowed Kamehameha to acquire the resources—ships, guns, strategic advice—to perform the unprecedented feat of conquering the whole Hawaiian archipelago.

Sewell uses the anthropologist's analysis of this classic historical encounter to propose a new understanding of the ways in which events function in history. The story of Cook's arrival in Hawaii, he points out, is not just a matter of Europeans overpowering a "native" culture, bending it to their technologically superior will. Rather, Hawaiians integrated the events of the British arrival into the categories of their own culture. Absorbing Cook into their religious traditions made the arrival of threateningly powerful and different outsiders conceptually manageable: the Hawaiians "domesticated European mana through the person of Captain Cook."[40] But in adopting Cook as a personal god, Kanehameha and his followers also broadened the Hawaiian concept of mana, which emerged from this episode transformed: no previous ruler had amassed power on the scale of Kanehameha's.[41] Cook's "apotheosis" durably altered cultural-political categories for the Polynesians. The arrival of Cook in Hawaii thus presents an instance of

---

European Mythmaking in the Pacific (Princeton, NJ: Princeton University Press, 1992). Obeyesekere argues that the idea that Hawaiians translated Cook's arrival into their religious categories is a European projection, based on European sources.

40. Ibid., 202.

41. Marshall Sahlins, *Historical Metaphors and Mythical Realities: Structure in the Early History of the Sandwich Islands Kingdom* (Ann Arbor: University of Michigan Press, 1981), 22–26.

the general process Sewell calls "events as transformations of structures."[42] Often framed as the dramatic but conceptually irrelevant outcomes of Really Important Causes, what we call "events" are actually complicated occurrences, extended in time and space, that can radically alter preexisting structures. Viewed in this way, events do not seem sharply distinct from causes, and no longer deserve the second-class status academic historians have often conferred on them.

Sewell's argument about the transformative power of the event is one symptom of historians' recent uneasiness with a sharp distinction between deep, significant causes and shallow, derivative events. This, in turn, harks back to the development mentioned at the start of this chapter, a wider discomfort with traditional questions of causality in historical writing today. Many of the reasons for the eclipse of causality are those we previously saw in chapter 2: the waning of national histories and of the grand interpretive schemes known as "metanarratives," as well as the rise of global history. Ongoing challenges to national history as the dominant framework of inquiry—and, as we will see shortly, the rise of cultural history in the 1990s—have meant a corresponding drop of interest in debates around the causes of those great anchor-events, wars and revolutions. (The exception might be the history of the Holocaust, which is often held to transcend the national context and to raise issues that are as much moral and philosophical as strictly historical.) While decolonization and its consequences did much, in the long term, to chip away at Eurocentric nationalist history, the end of the Cold War similarly weakened Marxist metahistory and its capitalist mirror image, modernization theory. Twentieth-century developments have, over the course of decades, undermined teleological understandings of history as a linear narrative unfolding toward some hoped-for or dreaded future: the fulfillment of national destiny, the triumph or demise of capitalism.

Absent a story with a clear imagined endpoint, anchored around dramatic way stations, traditional inquiry into "causes" has come to seem less compelling. The rise of transnational and global history has accentuated the process, since the complex subjects they address—the Atlantic slave trade, for instance—do not easily lend themselves to what William H. Sewell calls

---

42. Sewell applies this phrase to another example he analyzes, the storming of the Bastille at the start of the French Revolution; Sewell, *Logics of History*, chapter 8.

the "billiard-ball" model of causality.[43] This not to say that historians ignore questions of change over time, far from it. But now that units of historical study are more likely to involve local communities in global context, explanations of change have become more complex, more empirical, more site-specific.[44] As we have noted before, history is a slow-moving and capacious craft whose practitioners are loath to toss out their older tools, even the outmoded ones: undergraduates are still taught to sort out the origins of the American Revolution, graduate students still required to get a handle on the old debates on the causes of the English Civil War or World War I for their comprehensive exams. But historians are less likely today to cluster their inquiries around a small number of Big Questions or to build careers by shooting down each other's causal schemes. Where causality is concerned, productive chaos now reigns.

IN SEARCH OF MEANING: MICROHISTORY

In 1976 a young Italian scholar named Carlo Ginzburg, already known for his work on sixteenth-century witchcraft, published a short book with an intriguingly odd title. *The Cheese and the Worms* tells the story of an obscure man named Domenico Scandella, known as Menocchio, a miller in the Friuli region of northeastern Italy, who was hauled before the Inquisition in 1584 for questioning about his heretical beliefs. Menocchio had alarmed his neighbors in the town of Montereale by sharing incendiary ideas, which he stoutly repeated to the inquisitors: his heresies included the beliefs that "anyone who has studied [can] become a priest without being ordained," that "Hell was invented by the priests," and most explosively that Jesus "was a man like the rest of us, but with more dignity."[45] Oblivious to the book of Genesis, he shared with his ecclesiastical questioners his theory about the world's origin. From a chaos of the

---

43. William H. Sewell, in Schneider, "Explaining Historical Change, or: The Lost History of Causes," 1380. As the title of the conversation suggests, all of the participants stress the enduring importance of "change" in the agenda of historians, even as traditional approaches to causality are on the wane.

44. R. Bin Wong, "Causality," in Ulinka Rublack, ed., *A Concise Companion to History* (Oxford: Oxford University Press, 2011), 27–56, especially p. 40.

45. Carlo Ginzburg, *The Cheese and the Worms: The Cosmos of a Sixteenth-Century Miller*, trans. John and Anne Tedeschi (Baltimore: Johns Hopkins University Press, 1980), 6, 10, 76.

four elements, he said, a bulk mass formed, just as cheese is made out of milk; and in this mass angels appeared, as worms do in cheese, and among those angels was God ("he too having been created out of that mass at the same time") as well as Lucifer and the other archangels.[46] The inquisitors heard Menocchio out and went easy on him: he was ordered to abjure his errors and spent three years in prison. Fifteen years later, however, after someone again reported him for blasphemy, he was tried, repeated some of his heresies, and this time was sentenced to death.

In the course of his questioning, Menocchio, who was poor but literate, revealed that he got some of his ideas from books; he owned a few, and appears to have borrowed others from various people in the area: the Bible in vernacular, religious works, travel books, possibly even a version of the Koran. Ginzburg does impressive detective work connecting the miller's utterances with books he was known to, or may, have encountered. But the historian also shows that Menocchio combined his idiosyncratic reading of learned sources with ideas and experiences drawn straight from his peasant environment. Centuries-old pre-Christian notions, rooted in rural lore, about the material origins of the world, combined with everyday sights like that of maggots spontaneously appearing in lumps of moldy *formaggio*.

The Cheese and the Worms made a splash by reframing the question of how culture circulated between elite and popular classes in early modern Europe. While most scholars at the time believed either that the worlds of the learned and the populace were hermetically separate, or that elite culture "trickled down" to the poor, Ginzburg was able, though patient and imaginative work, to document a case in which a man of the lower classes not only absorbed the ideas of his "betters" but took what he wanted from them, combined his book-learning with the daily experiences and oral traditions of his rural culture, and created his own cosmology and theology. Menocchio may have been a reckless crank—that sort of person's life is more likely to make the record—but his story tells us something suggestive about the interaction of "high" and "low" culture in sixteenth-century Italy.

The Cheese and the Worms was not just hailed as a particularly thought-provoking contribution to debates about early modern European elite and popular cultures. More importantly, this was the first time a major historian

46. Ibid., 5–6.

had written an entire book about a totally obscure person from the past. The "new social history" was well established by the mid-1970s, but it was taken for granted that "social" always meant "plural"; even as studies inspired by E. P. Thompson increasingly turned away from quantification, and even if individual plebeian actors played important roles along the way, the very essence of "the people" was to exist in the aggregate. The singular biography, on the other hand, had always been a genre reserved for the exceptional member of the upper classes.[47] Ginzburg's book broke through those conventions by suggesting that you could derive historical significance from studying the life of a single obscure individual.

Ginzburg's chronicle of the humble but dramatic life of Menocchio was the first notable book in the genre known as "microhistory," which originated in the 1970s among a group of young leftist Italian historians disillusioned with Marxism.[48] With the appearance of several widely read books similar to Ginzburg's in the 1980s and 1990s, microhistory quickly became a standard item in the historical repertoire, with instances appearing in almost every field: successful examples have included the stories of a woman captured by Native Americans in seventeenth-century New England, of a sixteenth-century French peasant who fraudulently took on the identity of a missing man, of a Chinese translator interned in an insane asylum in eighteenth-century Paris, of the murder of a prostitute in nineteenth-century New York, and of the young American black men wrongly accused of raping two white women in Tennessee in 1931.[49] Several of the books discussed in the previous chapters fall within the category: James Sweet's biography of

47. A thought-provoking discussion of the matter is Jill Lepore, "Historians Who Love Too Much: Reflections on Microhistory and Biography," *Journal of American History* 88 (2001): 129–44.

48. For an introduction to the first generation of Italian microhistorians, with representative essays, see Edward Muir and Guido Ruggiero, eds., *Microhistory and the Lost Peoples of Europe*, trans. Eren Branch (Baltimore: Johns Hopkins University Press, 1991).

49. John Demos, *The Unredeemed Captive: A Family Story from Early America* (New York: Knopf, 1994); Natalie Zemon Davis, *The Return of Martin Guerre* (Cambridge, MA: Harvard University Press, 1983); Jonathan Spence, *The Question of Hu* (New York: Vintage, 1988); Patricia Cline Cohen, *The Murder of Helen Jewett: the Life and Death of a Prostitute in Nineteenth Century New York* (New York: Vintage, 1998); James E. Goodman, *Stories of Scottsboro* (New York: Pantheon, 1994).

the globe-trotting Domingos Álvares, Emmanuel Le Roy Ladurie's reconstruction of the medieval village of Montaillou and its heretical inhabitants,
Laurel Thatcher Ulrich's chronicle of Martha Ballard and her world, all of
them fine-grained accounts of the lives of history's "lost people."

Practitioners and commentators have differed sharply as to what can
and should constitute a microhistory: even the small group of Italian historians who pioneered the genre disagreed as to the overall program of the
movement, with some of Ginzburg's colleagues complaining that he paid
too much attention to Menocchio's cultural universe and not enough to
the social world of Montereale. Some microhistories, especially within the
Italian tradition, focus on a whole community rather than a single individual.[50] The genre's most thoughtful practitioners emphasize the simple importance of scale: by getting in very close, tightening your focus to a single
person or a tiny corner of the world, you can operate on a level, the nitty-
gritty of social history, invisible to historians who work in a more general
register.[51] In this sense, microhistory can be viewed as a sort of historical
laboratory, a microscope trained on the past. But in its best-known guise, as
pioneered by Ginzburg and reproduced by countless imitators, microhistory has three defining traits: it concerns a nonfamous person or group of
people; it centers on a crisis; and the author uses the story to make a point
about some broader historical question such as, in Ginzburg's case, the
relation between elite and popular culture. In addition, microhistory, with
its dramatic incidents and texture-of-life details, lends itself to evocative
writing and good storytelling; the most successful instances of the genre
have gained fame on course syllabi or even best-seller lists.

In the 1970s and 1980s microhistory offered historians a revolutionary
new perspective: the focus of a book like Ginzburg's was not on explaining
historical change but on showing what the world looked like to a specific

50. On divergences within the original group of Italian microhistorians, see
David Bell, "Total History and Microhistory: The French and Italian Paradigms,"
in Kramer and Maza, *Companion to Western Historical Thought*, 269–73; Fran-
cesca Trivellato, "Is There a Future for Italian Microhistory in the Age of Global
History?," *California Italian History* 2 (2011): 5–6; Sigurður Gylfi Magnússon
and István M. Szijártó, eds., *What Is Microhistory? Theory and Practice* (London:
Routledge, 2013), chapter 1.

51. Giovanni Levi, "On Microhistory," in Peter Burke, ed., *New Perspectives on
Historical Writing* (University Park: Penn State University Press, 1991), 95–98;
Trivellato, "Is There a Future?," 5.

person at a single moment in time. Ginzburg did not suggest that people like Menocchio were advancing subversive ideas that would have this or that effect over time; instead, starting with the miller's apparently eccentric beliefs, he went looking for all of the different elements Menocchio drew upon—religion, learned culture, local lore—and the meanings he derived from them. His purpose, in short, was not to interpret Menocchio's role within some larger linear historical narrative, but to explain how the heretical miller understood the world around him.

That same focus on patterns of meaning informs what may be to this day the most widely read microhistory, not a book but an essay published in 1984 by a leading cultural historian of early modern France. Robert Darnton's "Workers Revolt: The Great Cat Massacre of the Rue Saint-Séverin" explores the meaning of an incident that happened in a printer's shop in Paris in the late 1730s, as reported twenty years later by one of the participants.[52] The story revolved around the hardships suffered by two of the printer's apprentices, Jerome and Léveillé, poorly fed and housed and also sleep-deprived because of the nightly racket from alley cats on the roof over the shop. Adding insult to feline injury was the fact that the master's wife kept a pet cat, which she adored and reportedly fed much better than her husband did his workers. One night the teenage apprentices vented their frustrations: one of them climbed onto the roof over the master's bedroom and loudly imitated the cats' yowling, whereupon the boss ordered the boys to get rid of the animals—but with special instructions to spare the mistress's pet *la grise*. The apprentices went on a rampage, rounding up and bludgeoning every cat in the neighborhood, including *la grise*. Then, along with the other workers, they improvised a mock trial for the dead and dying animals, "complete with guards, a confessor, and a public executioner." As they strung the cats up from an improvised gallows, their mistress appeared and shrieked with horror until the boys assured her (falsely) that her cat was not among the victims. The men were racked with laughter that night, and over the course of the following weeks Léveillé reenacted the whole story for his mates "at least twenty times," in each instance sending them into gales of laughter.

---

52. Robert Darnton, "Workers Revolt: The Great Cat Massacre of the Rue Saint-Séverin," in *The Great Cat Massacre and Other Episodes in French Cultural History* (New York: Basic Books, 1984), 75–104.

Darnton's point of entry into the story is to note that what seemed so hilarious to the printers is a joke lost on most modern readers: why was it funny to torture cats, try and execute them, and repeat this scene over and over? It is precisely, he argues, when you fail to get the point of something that seems replete with meaning to insiders that you have located a point of access to an alien culture.[53] Darnton proceeds to build up around this bizarre incident the many layers of contextual references that, he argues, gave it the explosive emotional force it had for the print-shop workers. Some of the tensions behind the episode were social, the degradation of journeymen and apprentice printers' status in the eighteenth century with the contraction of a trade that offered fewer and fewer workers the hope of attaining independence and a good living; all of the tensions, old and new, in the lives of these workers would be experienced and expressed in the cultural categories of the world they lived in. These included meanings borrowed from the language of carnival, the period before Lent when carnal appetites for food and sex could be freely expressed and role reversal was licit, a season whose festivities sometimes included the torture of cats. Carnivals included mock trials, and so did the ceremonies particular to each craft, which took place a various times of year. Cats figured everywhere in the cultural repertoire of early modern Europe, usually associated with the darker forces of sex (the French *chatte* means the same as the English "pussy"), magic, and witchcraft. The cat massacre and its periodic reenactments thus allowed the printers to express many things: their social frustration as workers, their want of food and material comfort, their lack of access to sex as unmarried men, their desire to get back at their masters and turn the world upside down. The explosive laughter this elicited underscored their understanding of an act of violence whose meaning was obvious without being explicit, in a situation where overt resistance was unthinkable.

Darnton makes gestures toward the broader, more conventional historical framework ("A half-century later, the artisans of Paris would run riot in a similar manner, combining indiscriminate slaughter with improvised popular tribunals"[54]), but his purpose is not to say something about the origins of the French Revolution. The point of this microhistorical exercise is to explain what the cat massacre may have meant to those who did

53. Ibid., 77–78.
54. Ibid., 98.

it, at the time they did it—not what it might signify to a scholar surveying the broader sweep of history. Both Darnton and Ginzburg start with an incident or detail that seems baffling (why was the killing of cats so hilarious? why would someone believe that the world originally took shape in the same way as a lump of cheese?) and use it as a key to unlock an alien culture. Instead of asking how these stories fit into a narrative driving toward the modern world—workers gearing up for the French Revolution, peasants absorbing the new ideas of the Protestant Reformation—microhistory highlights the utter strangeness of actions and beliefs that puzzle us but made sense to specific actors in their own context.

One issue has dogged the practice of microhistory from the start, the problem of representativeness. Unlike traditional biography, which traces the singular destiny of an exceptional individual, microhistory strives for exemplariness—its purpose is to suggest that any given story it tells is not, within the terms of the surrounding culture, unique.[55] Ginzburg closes *The Cheese and the Worms* with a rhetorical flourish to this effect. Around the time Menocchio was executed, he writes, the authorities picked up rumors of another man in the area, named Marco or Marcato, who was said to believe that the soul died with the body: "About Menocchio we know many things. About this Marco or Marcato—and so many others like him who lived and died without leaving a trace—we know nothing."[56] Maybe there were other Menocchios out there spewing heresy, but how can we be sure that Scandella was not just an eccentric crank? As Edward Muir, a leading practitioner of the genre, puts it, "How can historians concerned with trifles avoid producing trivial history?"[57]

The neatest answer to this quandary is the one Darnton provides as a methodological framework for his essays on cultural history. His approach begins, he writes, "from the premise that individual expression takes place within a cultural idiom, that we learn to classify sensations and make sense of things by thinking within a framework provided by our culture."[58] Microhistorical incidents, in this view, are utterances that take on meaning in the context of a broader grammar—they serves as clues that point us toward a

55. Lepore, "Historians Who Love Too Much," 133.
56. Ginzburg, *The Cheese and the Worms*, 128.
57. Muir and Ruggiero, *Microhistory*, xiv.
58. Darnton, *Great Cat Massacre*, 6.

society's "culture," its interlocking system of meanings.[59] Darnton repeatedly compares his approach to the past to an anthropologist's elucidation of an alien culture, and in doing so acknowledges the influence of his Princeton colleague, the celebrated anthropologist Clifford Geertz, whose writings became one of the touchstones, in the 1980s and beyond, for new culture-centered approaches to history.

CLIFFORD GEERTZ, MICHEL FOUCAULT, AND THE "NEW CULTURAL HISTORY"

Clifford Geertz was a cultural anthropologist, a specialist in the study of Indonesia whose case studies offered models of what he called, in a famous methodological essay, "thick description."[60] The practice consists, as Geertz explains in his most widely quoted essay on the subject, in restoring as many layers of meaning as possible to a chosen event or action. As a mundane illustration, he offers the example, borrowed from the philosopher Gilbert Ryle, of one boy winking at another. A "thin description" of the event would record that the boy is "rapidly contracting his right eyelids," which accounts for physical fact but does not address the possible sociocultural meanings of this facial movement: the boy could be twitching involuntarily or acting out the cultural meaning of this gesture in our society, which is to convey a conspiratorial understanding between two people. For that matter, another boy could wink as a parody of the first boy, doing so laboriously and clumsily, drawing on other cultural codes. The central object of ethnography, according to Geertz, is not the mere recording of the wink but the reconstruction of "a stratified hierarchy of meaningful structures" in terms of which winks and parodies of winks are performed and understood: anthropologists engage in thick description when they restore to a given form of human expression its richest possible layering of meanings.[61] Those patterns of meaning make up a culture, the ethnographer's ultimate quarry. Geertz defines culture as the man-made "webs of signification" woven for and through public communication: culture does not exist in people's heads but is instantiated in interpersonal gestures and practices

59. Ibid., 260.
60. Clifford Geertz, "Thick Description: Toward an Interpretive Theory of Culture," in *The Interpretation of Cultures: Selected Essays* (New York: HarperCollins, 1973), 3–30.
61. Ibid., 6–7.

ranging from the mundane (a wink) to the elaborate (Balinese cockfights involving complex patterns of betting).[62]

Geertz's writings provided one source of inspiration for the constellation of new historical scholarship that by the late 1980s was becoming known in the United States as the "new cultural history."[63] In the past historians had approached "culture" as an object of study, either the "high culture" of the elites or the "popular culture" of the plebs. "Culture" was the content of a library, a set of folk festivals, a cycle of religious rituals, a school curriculum: it could be itemized, described, sometimes even quantified, but it was an object, not a context. The new cultural historians, in contrast, embraced an abstract, anthropologically inflected definition of culture along the lines of Geertz's "webs of meaning": their project was to track systems of signs, recurrent cultural reflexes, and patterns in order to describe those webs. Lynn Hunt's widely read books on the political culture of the French Revolution, for instance, took the form of a series of essays that explored such questions as Why were rhetoric and the command of language so central to the culture of the Revolution? Why was it important to *dress* like a patriot? What cultural factors lay behind the revolutionaries' visceral hatred of Marie-Antoinette? What meanings were embedded in the cult of revolutionary "brotherhood"? What, in short, were the unspoken assumptions about politics and public life that undergirded the Revolution's new political practices, and how were these expressed through the creation and manipulation of symbols?[64]

Not all practitioners of the new style of history signed on to the Geertz-Darnton model of cultural analysis. Italian microhistorians, for instance, generally dismissed Geertz's "webs of meaning" as a straitjacket for the historical actors tangled up in them: they complained that Geertz's method

62. Geertz's much quoted definition of culture is: "Believing, with Max Weber, that man is an animal suspended in webs of significance he himself has spun, I take culture to be those webs, and the analysis of it to be therefore not an experimental science in search of law but an interpretive one in search of meaning." Ibid., 5. For Balinese cockfighting, see ibid., chapter 15.

63. This new trend took on its label with the publication of an influential collection, Lynn Hunt, ed., *The New Cultural History* (Berkeley: University of California Press, 1989).

64. Lynn Hunt, *Politics, Culture and Class in the French Revolution* (Berkeley: University of California Press, 1984); Hunt, *The Family Romance of the French Revolution* (Berkeley: University of California Press, 1992).

erased social differences and tensions by assuming that a coronation ceremony or a cockfight means roughly the same thing to all those who participate in it. Other scholars similarly objected that Darnton's view of his character's actions as the expression of a general idiom was just *too* neat to account for the complexity of the real world and the multiplicity of people's experiences.[65] For all of the criticism, though, the project of cultural analysis offered an immensely compelling way of gaining access to past subjectivities, especially those of the nonliterate: deciphering the gestures and rare utterances of the poor in the context of a broader culture is still, for historians, the best way of getting inside the heads of people who were denied the formal means of expression afforded to the elites.

The new cultural history, at its most influential in the 1990s, proposed a profound and controversial revolution in approaches to the past. As we have seen, the major historical schools of the twentieth century, Marxism and the Annales school among them, took for granted the primacy of the "hard facts" of social and economic history; most historians assumed that the realm of culture, while a worthwhile object of study, was secondary and derivative, a "reflection of" socioeconomic dynamics. Practitioners of cultural history challenged this long-standing hierarchy, pointing out that all human activities, from tilling a field to voting to getting married, are shaped by, and enacted through, cultural codes: far from tossing out "the social," they proposed a new, less rigid way of linking culture to society.[66] The point was not that "culture" should take precedence over material conditions and experiences, but that the two cannot be disentangled: no aspect of the world, they argued, exists prior to, or separate from, its cultural construction. For new cultural historians, deciphering the codes that frame human activity, and especially the actions of the poor, became an agenda for renewing the discipline.

A focus on meaning, cultural historians insist, does not entail neglecting human agency. The best cultural history has always taken the view that people are not trapped in cultural codes but choose ways to act within and through them. Examples going back to the 1960s and 1970s include

---

65. Levi, "On Microhistory," 108–9; Magnússon and Szijártó, *What Is Microhistory?*, 19; Roger Chartier, "Text, Symbols and Frenchness," *Journal of Modern History* 57 (1985): 689–94.

66. Lynn Hunt, "Introduction," in *New Cultural History*, 1–6; Peter Burke, *What Is Cultural History?* 2nd ed. (Cambridge: Polity Press, 2008), 41.

studies of early modern crowd behavior, such as E. P. Thompson's famous essay on the "moral economy" of eighteenth-century English crowds (see chapter 1). Cultural historians soon developed a set of concepts to describe the central role of human activity within their analyses: they wrote of "practice," "performance," "appropriation," terms that have now entered mainstream historical vocabulary. Carlo Ginzburg did not use the word "appropriation" with respect to Menocchio, but what he describes falls under that rubric: the miller read books written by the learned class and appropriated them by lifting out the elements that interested him and combining these with other elements from his culture and his own opinions. He was not, any more than any other reader, an empty vessel waiting to be filled with a book's pristine original meaning.

The history of books and reading offers, in fact, an excellent example of the shift from traditional cultural history to new approaches that highlight human agency. Traditional intellectual history focuses on the content of books, and sociocultural historians have long been interested in the book as a countable and trackable cultural item: excellent histories of the book have long been and still are dedicated to locating and counting titles, lists of books owned by individuals and institutions, books produced by publishers and disseminated by booksellers, or volumes banned by censors and seized by the authorities.[67] In the last few decades, however, cultural historians have developed a complementary line of inquiry, the history of reading—a quintessential "cultural practice." How, they ask, over time and across space, have readers approached written and printed matter? Historians of both Europe and North America have argued, for instance, that because, over the course of the eighteenth century, the availability of print exploded, reading shifted from an "intensive" to an "extensive" mode. Rather than reading the same texts—usually devotional ones—closely over and over, readers began to peruse more superficially a much broader range of materials, including novels and periodicals; reading something only once turns out to be a radically modern experience.[68] Until the comparatively recent past, most reading was oral and collective, and books, as Robert Darnton

67. For overviews of this immense field, see David Finkelstein and Alistair Mc-Creary, *The Book History Reader*, 2nd ed. (London: Routledge, 2006); Alexis Weedon et al., eds, *The History of the Book in the West: A Library of Critical Essays*, 5 vols. (Burlington, VT: Ashgate, 2010).

68. Robert Darnton, "History of Reading," in Burke, *New Perspectives*, 148–49.

puts it, "had audiences rather than readers"; only in the last two centuries or so has solitary reading (which at first was sometimes considered as alarming as masturbation) become the norm.[69] How do readers experience books differently when standing in a frigid sixteenth-century German library reading at a wooden counter as opposed to sitting alone on a sofa in a Victorian living room? What difference did it make to the experience of the word when individual readers, as one scholar shows, stopped mouthing the words aloud and began to read silently?[70] What is a historian to make of readers' deeply emotional, somatic responses to texts, whether eighteenth-century sentimental fiction or twentieth-century romance literature?[71] How, in short, has the audience for books over the centuries appropriated and performed the content of their reading matter? All of this new history of reading highlights the activity of humans as they encounter cultural products, showing them to be anything but passive recipients.

From Geertz's winkers to Thompson's crowds to the readers bending the contents of books to their wills and desires, humans act out culture: foregrounding agency is therefore not usually a major problem for cultural historians. A much bigger problem, and one that has at times made cultural history controversial, is the issue of change over time. The founding works of cultural history discussed so far—by Darnton, Hunt, Ginzburg, and other widely read microhistorians like Natalie Davis—all take the form of essays or short books. Even notable full-length books in this mode—such as Judith Walkowitz's study of the culture of sexual danger in late-Victorian London—often resemble collections of thematically linked

69. Ibid., 160. On the connection between solitary reading and masturbation, see Thomas Laqueur, *Solitary Sex: A Cultural History of Masturbation* (New York: Zone Books, 2003).

70. Roger Chartier, ed. *Pratiques de la lecture* (Marseille: Rivages, 1985); various essays in Chartier and Henri-Jean Martin, eds., *Histoire de l'édition française* 4 vols. (Paris: Promodis, 1982–1986); Guglielmo Cavallo and Chartier, eds., *A History of Reading in the West* (Amherst: University of Massachusetts Press, 2003); Paul Saenger, *Space between Words: The Origins of Silent Reading* (Stanford, CA: Stanford University Press, 1997).

71. Darnton, "Readers Respond to Rousseau: The Fabrication of Romantic Sensitivity," in *Great Cat Massacre*, 215–56; Janice A. Radway, *Reading the Romance: Women, Patriarchy and Popular Culture* (Chapel Hill: University of California Press, 1984).

essays.[72] The brevity of the typical cultural history offering is telling: in its purest form cultural history aims to make synchronic connections, bringing together around a central core—a person, an event, a practice—a wide variety of contextual factors that elucidate its meaning *at that point in time*. While it may contain or revolve around a story, the analytical mode of a classic "new" cultural history is analogous to a snapshot, not a film.

Many cultural historians have found both inspiration and an intellectual rationale for their synchronic approach in the work of a celebrated and controversial French thinker, Michel Foucault.[73] Along with E. P. Thompson and Fernand Braudel, Foucault is among the most influential figures in recent Western historiography. But while even their critics express respect for Thompson's and Braudel's achievements, Foucault is a thinker many historians love to hate, if only because he was not a member of the discipline but a philosopher who wrote books based on historical sources. A mythical figure even in his relatively short lifetime (he died in 1984, aged fifty-eight), Foucault was a brilliant intellectual polymath who, although formally trained in philosophy, developed an early interest in the history of psychiatry and produced as his doctoral thesis a thousand-page study of madness in early modern Europe. His many books include philosophical histories of the knowledge-systems of early modern and modern Europe, *The Order of Things* and *The Archaeology of Knowledge*, a multivolume meditation on the history of sexuality, and the book many consider his masterpiece, *Discipline and Punish*, a study of the shift in Western societies from physical punishment to imprisonment as the standard response to crime.

Starting with his doctoral thesis on madness, Foucault delighted in going against the grain of conventional wisdom to point out the historically contingent nature of "scientific" knowledge. "Madness only exists in soci-

---

72. Judith R. Walkowitz, *City of Dreadful Delight: Narratives of Sexual Danger in Late-Victorian London* (Chicago: University of Chicago Press, 1992).

73. Academic commentary on Foucault is abundant and often very difficult. The best initial approach to the development of his thought is through biographies, notably Didier Eribon, *Michel Foucault*, trans. Betsy Wing (Cambridge, MA: Harvard University Press, 1991), and James Miller, *The Passion of Michel Foucault* (New York: Simon and Schuster, 1993). See also Allan Megill, "The Reception of Foucault by Historians," *Journal of the History of Ideas* 48 (1987): 117–41; Jan Goldstein, ed., *Foucault and the Writing of History* (Oxford: Blackwell, 1994).

ety," he told a journalist in 1961. "It does not exist outside of the forms of sensibility that isolate it, and the forms of repulsion that expel it or capture it."[74] Decades before the notion became ubiquitous in academia and beyond, Foucault made the case in his early work that mental illness was "culturally constructed" in different ways over time. Tracking the logic of such cultural constructions led him to work on identifying general systems of knowledge in the past, for which he coined the word "episteme." In *The Order of Things*, for instance, he contrasted an early modern episteme in which knowledge was organized as a system of correspondences and reflections (for instance, between the political system and the human body), to later approaches based on exhaustive classificatory schemes that capture and isolate the elements of human knowledge, as in the modern "disciplines" of biology and political economy.

Even more influential than Foucault's notion of episteme was his borrowing of the term "discourse" from linguistics. Discourses are systems of signs that give meaning to language internally, and also externally as the various "texts" circulating in a culture merge into broader "discursive formations." The intellectual historian John Toews describes discourses as "impersonal formal structures operating anonymously behind the backs of speakers and actors, constituting the world of objective reality and subjective agency by making certain types of speech and behavior possible and others impossible."[75] For instance, when a slaveholder in nineteenth-century America referred to slaves as his "children," the word referred back to a wider discourse of paternalism that governed the way social relations were understood among the elite, made up of interrelated understandings such as "African-Americans are intrinsically childlike," "masters are responsible for the moral guidance of their bondsmen," "masters can and should apply physical punishment to slaves," and so on. Among the master class, this discourse was so pervasive that, while it governed the daily actions of slaveholders, most of the time people did not need to articulate its basic tenets, even to themselves. Now widely and often carelessly used, the term "discourse" serves a purpose for cultural historians very close to that of Geertz's "webs of meaning"; it invites the interpretation of any form of

74. Miller, *Passion*, 98.

75. John Toews, "Linguistic Turn and Discourse Analysis in History," in Neil Smelser and Paul Baltes, eds., *International Encyclopedia of the Social and Behavioral Sciences*, vol. 13 (Amsterdam: Elsevier, 2001), 8917.

expression, linguistic or other, as an utterance whose meaning may be determined within a broader system of signification.

At the core of Foucault's inquiry into systems of knowledge are questions about the nature of power in modern society, and specifically about how power acts upon the human soul. Explicitly rejecting Marxism, Foucault argued in a series of brilliantly counterintuitive intellectual moves that power is not concentrated in society but dispersed (he wrote of "microtechnologies of power"), and that its effects are not repressive but productive.[76] Power operates everywhere, at every level, even the most intimate, to impose identities upon us, to *create* us: "power" is not the state or the ruling class forbidding you to do something; it is your teacher, doctor, or psychiatrist telling you who you are. Foucault made this point most vividly in *Discipline and Punish*, whose argument revolves around a contrast between the elaborate systems of physical punishment used in early modern Europe and the rise of the modern penitentiary. Whipping, branding, mutilation, and theatrical public executions are reviled in the modern world as barbaric, but, Foucault argues, in the past these served a cathartic communal purpose, ridding the world of evil by "inscribing" it on the body in a ritual that brought together the sovereign, the spectators, and the condemned. Modern punishment, on the other hand, overwhelmingly prison-based, is founded on the perpetual observation of individual inmates and designed to work on the soul rather than the body via the rhetoric of "reform." Foucault memorably illustrated the essence of modern punishment by describing a plan for an ideal prison elaborated by the nineteenth-century British thinker Jeremy Bentham, a system in which a single guard located in a central tower could at every moment observe every prisoner in his cell. Bentham called his scheme the Panopticon, and for Foucault "panopticism" (another neologism) served as a metaphor for all forms of modern power at its most insidious: eventually the prisoners in the Panopticon would internalize the guard's constant surveillance and become the wardens of their own souls.

For decades now, some historians have found Foucault's work profoundly inspiring, while others denounce it as wrongheaded and even morally objectionable. Some have attacked him on what they consider a misuse

---

76. For an especially lucid discussion, see Patricia O'Brien, "Foucault's History of Culture," in Hunt, *New Cultural History*, 25–46, esp. 34–36.

of sources and overall lack of historical competence.[77] For others, however, the problem lies deeper, in what they view as Foucault's irresponsible relativism and anti-teleology. A central purpose of a book like *Discipline and Punish* is to dismiss the conventional narrative of liberal humanitarian progress as a self-congratulatory stance that looks down on earlier cultures, and by the same token to dispute the beneficial impact of modern "humanitarian" solutions. For a quintessentially liberal historian like Lawrence Stone, "The central challenge of the Foucault model is to the humanitarian values and achievements of the eighteenth-century Enlightenment." While conceding that Foucault's insights had "set the agenda for the last fifteen years of research" on madness in history, Stone worried that the Frenchman's work had had "an enormous and disturbing influence upon traditional views of recent Western history."[78]

A central feature of Foucault's work that many historians have found disconcerting is his deliberate shunning of causality. His sweeping surveys of the history of madness, psychiatry, penal practices, and the social sciences move from one broad cultural configuration to the next without explaining the sources of transformation. This dismissal of causality was utterly deliberate; Foucault once derided the scramble to locate the causes of this and the origins of that as "harmless enough amusements for historians who refuse to grow up."[79] In the place of traditional theories of causality, he offered an alternative view of historical change that he labeled "genealogy."[80] As in the familiar case of a family tree, the concept of "genealogy" implies that any given occurrence, just like the birth of a human being, has not a single central cause but many different, random and ramifying, "beginnings." In place of a vision of history as a stream of uninterrupted continuities,

77. See, for instance, George Huppert, "*Divinatio et Eruditio*: Thoughts on Foucault," *History and Theory* 13 (1974): 191–207; H. C. Erik Midelfort, "Madness and Civilization in Early Modern Europe: A Reappraisal of Michel Foucault," in Barbara C. Malament, ed., *After the Reformation: Essays in Honor of J. H. Hexter* (Philadelphia: University of Pennsylvania Press, 1980), 247–65.

78. Lawrence Stone, "Madness," *New York Review of Books* 29, no. 20 (December 16, 1982).

79. Michel Foucault, *The Archaeology of Knowledge*, trans. Alan Sheridan (New York: Pantheon, 1972), 144.

80. The term is borrowed from the philosopher who most influenced Foucault, F. W. Nietzsche; see Alan Sheridan, *Michel Foucault: The Will to Truth* (London: Tavistock, 1980), 115–20.

Foucault proposed an account of the past that privileged "the categories of discontinuity and difference, notions of threshold, rupture, and transformation."[81] His approach was a gauntlet thrown down to conventional history: looking for causes amounts to a form of narcissism, he implied, a way of organizing the past around the historian's present.

Foucault's writings have not given birth to a school of history properly speaking. While E. P. Thompson and the Annales historians have had plenty of imitators, no historian so far has courted ridicule by trying to replicate Foucault's unique blend of theoretical brilliance, idiosyncratic erudition, and intellectual provocation: it is unclear, as Patricia O'Brien has put it, that his is "a game that more than one can play."[82] As someone who opened up new areas of research and new ways of looking at old problems, however, his influence has been immense: the entire field of the history of sexuality and sexual identities, for instance, bears his founding imprint. Beyond the introduction of new topics and the upending of old ones, Foucault has been important in legitimating forms of history writing that, if they do not renounce causality as explicitly as he did, are comfortable politely ignoring it.

An instance of a major historical work inspired by Foucault is Thomas Laqueur's *Making Sex: Body and Gender from the Greeks to Freud* (1990).[83] The book is a survey of how Europeans over the course of several centuries understood the biological and psychological differences between men and women. In classic microhistorical fashion, it begins by foregrounding a detail that is baffling to the modern reader: early modern Europeans believed that female orgasm was necessary for conception to take place. Surely, we want to protest, there must have been plenty of evidence to the contrary. Weren't lots of women available to testify that they had gotten pregnant without experiencing sexual pleasure? What about victims of rape? If recent work in the history of science has taught us anything, though, it is that scientific "facts" exist within dominant frameworks of knowledge, and that, as Steven Shapin has most notably argued, scientific credibility is profoundly enmeshed with social status and gender (see chapter 3).

81. Ibid., 89–110, quote p. 93 (from *The Archaeology of Knowledge*).

82. O'Brien, "Foucault's History of Culture," 44.

83. Thomas Laqueur, *Making Sex: Body and Gender from the Greeks to Freud* (Cambridge, MA: Harvard University Press, 1990).

Making Sex advances the surprising argument that around the eigh-teenth century, Europeans shifted from a "one-sex" to a "two-sex" model of the biological difference between men and women. Most readers are startled by the part of Laqueur's argument which proposes that Europeans once thought of men and women as a single sex. By "one sex" Laqueur means that ancient, medieval, and early modern societies in the West viewed women as creatures essentially identical to men in nature, but infe-rior. Women's genital organs, for instance, were represented in sixteenth-century anatomical illustrations as the same as men's but turned outside-in, with the vagina as a penis and the ovaries as testicles. The sixteenth-century French surgeon Ambroise Paré reported on the case of a young peasant girl who, in the heat of puberty, jumped across a ditch, causing ligaments to rupture in her nether parts and male organs to appear; in one moment, the girl Marie became the boy Germain. Women, Paré explained, "have as much hidden within the body as men have exposed."[84] Women were understood to function sexually in the same way as men, and while writers differed as to whether females produced something equivalent to sperm during sexual congress, they all agreed that female "heat" was indispens-able for conception. As the familiar canon of bawdy sixteenth-century lit-erature suggests, women were assumed to be more lustful than men since their sex stood closer to the base realm of matter.[85] Over the course of the eighteenth century, new ideas and understandings coalesced, over-turning these assumptions: by the nineteenth century a "two-sex" model prevailed, in which male and female anatomies were viewed as radically dif-ferent; the ideal woman was now a spiritual creature, and women's innate sexual passivity was enshrined as an article of faith.

On the matter of *why* such a huge shift in perceptions of sexual differ-ence emerged, Laqueur makes it clear that social and political changes cannot in themselves account for the reinterpretation of bodies: neither the Enlightenment, nor new scientific ideas, nor the cultural consequences of the French Revolution, nor the conservative backlash against the Revo-lution, nor incipient feminism can be said to have "*caused* the making of a new sexed body."[86] The remaking of the body, he argues, was intrinsic to all of these developments, but neither their cause nor their consequence;

84. Ibid., 127.
85. Ibid., chapter 2.
86. Ibid., 11.

while he identifies a host of major changes in the era he writes about, he pinpoints none of them as causal. Like Foucault's books and unlike the typical microhistory, *Making Sex* covers a vast swath of time, though its argument and most of its evidence cluster around the period from around 1600 to 1850. Despite its broad temporal scope, however, and in keeping with the practice of cultural history, this is a book that sidesteps questions of causality: the point is to uncover assumptions about human sexual difference, not to explain why those meanings changed.

Cultural historians' indifference to causal explanation has on occasion drawn the ire of historians who see in Geertzian or Foucauldian cultural analysis an abdication of history's moral or political responsibility akin to the corrosive effects of postmodernism (see chapter 6).[87] What is the point, they ask, of showing us that people viewed the world differently three centuries ago, if accounts of cat killers, heretical millers, and strange early modern attitudes toward judicial punishment or female anatomy aren't made part of a story that explains how we got from there to here? What is the purpose of a history that mostly invites us to understand and accept the past's radical otherness? Critics complain that by focusing solely on the *meaning* of something like judicial amputation, cultural analysis introduces a dangerous relativism into academic practice. Cultural historians, on the other hand, believe that their approach respects the integrity of past societies and that it has moral value as a counter to the arrogance of those who believe that only modern understandings and solutions are worthwhile.

For many historians and their readers, the ethical purpose of the discipline is the construction a narrative that, causally linking the past to the present, invites us to act upon that story to further or change it. Causes matter, they argue, because causes link the past to the present, directing us to the future. For cultural historians, on the other hand, exploring and accepting the strangeness of the past on its own terms is a lesson in tolerant relativism and an invitation to critique the present: we may be able, for instance, to challenge the idea that women are less interested in sex than are men if we know that three centuries ago nobody assumed this was the case. Clifford Geertz himself acknowledged that cultural analysis does not address humanity's overarching questions; what it provides, he wrote, is a humanistic perspective nourished by knowledge of the many ways those

87. See, for instance, Evans, *In Defense of History*, chapters 6 and 7.

interrogations have been answered across time and space. The purpose of cultural anthropology, he wrote, "is not to answer our deepest questions, but to make available to us answers that others, guarding other sheep in other valleys, have given, and thus to include them in the consultable record of what man has said."[88]

In the heyday of cultural history, some scholars worried that the new approaches amounted, as one of them put it, to a terrible Faustian bargain, "an offer of the entire world as a domain of meaning, but at the cost of our historical souls."[89] Today, the loud sounding of alarm about cultural history has all but ceased and historians are reassured that they can practice cultural analysis without signing over their lives to Foucault-as-Mephistopheles. The stark choice between grand causal narrative, on the one hand, and fine-grained, culturally inflected microhistory, on the other, seems to have blurred in recent years, as historians opt for more eclectic approaches, with anthropology and discourse analysis as just more weapons in their arsenal. While a majority of popular histories remain wedded to traditional narrative form, most academic works engage, analytically, in a little of this and a little of that. A historian writing a study in, say, nineteenth-century Native American history might frame her story with broad causal developments such as industrial and ecological changes, while resorting to Geertzian analysis to explain how these developments played out in local worldviews. These two approaches might be incompatible in theory, but not in practice. Unlike historical sociologists who like to tidy up their research into distinct propositions, historians tacitly accept the need for a degree of methodological fuzziness in pursuit of the messy reality of any given area of the past.

Advocates of sweeping causal schemes and enthusiasts for the new cultural history and microhistories were once at loggerheads. As we shall see in the next chapter, related disputes in the 1980s and 1990s around the trend known as "postmodernism" could get even nastier. Nowadays—but for how long?—historians have backed away from methodological slugfests into a stance that Lynn Hunt has dubbed "mindful eclecticism": "Different

88. Geertz, *Interpretation of Cultures*, 30.

89. Keith Michael Baker, "On the Problem of the Ideological Origins of the French Revolution," in Dominick LaCapra and Steven Kaplan, eds., *Modern European Intellectual History: Reappraisals and New Perspectives* (Ithaca, NY: Cornell University Press, 1982), 200. Baker himself was sympathetic to cultural history.

problems often require different methods of approach, and no one method can answer every question we might have." In the early twenty-first century, innovation in the field is driven by the call to "globalize" history, which as she notes is not a method or a theory but a process.[90] Some historians worry that the discipline is currently too pacific for its own good, that the reigning eclecticism in methods amounts to the "domestication" of theory in history, a loss of the field's critical and analytical edge.[91] It is to be hoped that such is not the case, or not for long. Vigorous debates over methods and approaches are vital to history, as to any discipline: arguing about the primacy of causes versus meanings, or about any aspect of how we approach the past, is crucial to clarifying what we are doing and why we are doing it.

90. Lynn Hunt, "Where Have All the Theories Gone?," *Perspectives on History* (March 2002), 5.

91. For instance, Joan Scott, "History-Writing as Critique," in Keith Jenkins, Sue Morgan, and Alun Munslow, eds., *Manifestos for History* (New York: Routledge, 2007), 19–38; Gary Wilder, "From Optic to Topic: The Foreclosure Effect of Historiographic Turns," *American Historical Review* 117 (June 2012): 723–45.

6

FACTS OR FICTIONS?

THE RISE AND FALL OF OBJECTIVITY

If you ask historians whether they consider themselves "social scientists" or "humanists" you will get various responses, the most common of which will likely be "both." The ultimate hybrid discipline, rooted in the real and framed by storytelling, history straddles the "harder" and "softer" disciplines at the "arts" end of the curriculum. On the one hand, historians are quintessentially hard-nosed empiricists, digging endlessly in archives until they get all their information lined up, cowing colleagues in other disciplines with the depth of their command of "the facts." On the other hand, history books are most often built around stories, and the most successful histories, the ones that are widely read and endure for years, usually have some of the same qualities as a good novel. The discipline's essential hybridity is one main reason for recurrent debates among historians about the line between "fact" and "fiction" in the reconstruction of the past.[1]

On the face of it, the question of whether history is fact or fiction should be easy to answer just by drawing a bright line: history cannot be fiction since the most basic ground rule for the discipline—in its modern form, at least—is that you are not allowed to make things up. But if modern professional norms tell us that history must be grounded in verifiable facts, postmodern sensibilities make us inescapably aware that all historical accounts are the products of choices and that different accounts of the same thing can be equally valid as long as a historian respects professional protocols and standards. Few people, even among members of the public with little exposure to academic debates, nowadays believe that writing history is just a matter of lining up all the evidence and letting the facts "speak for themselves." Even within the context of wide agreement that accounts of the

1. On the deep roots of history's quintessential "doubleness," see Ann Curthoys and John Docker, *Is History Fiction?* (Ann Arbor: University of Michigan Press, 2005), chapters 1–6.

past are inevitably shaped by the historian's political, aesthetic, or other predilections, however, there remains a vast amount of room for debate.

And debate there has been, especially around the end of the last century, when the trend known as "postmodernism" hit the academy, engulfing many disciplines in various forms of radical skepticism and touching off especially bitter disputes among historians. But the crisis around postmodernism was merely the final stage in a longer evolution away from an earlier belief that a stance of complete objectivity toward their material was, for historians, both possible and the ultimate professional goal. While postmodernism is no longer the hot-button issue it was twenty years ago, its legacy endures, both as an intellectual trend that has shaped certain aspects of historical writing and as a theoretical challenge that brought up important issues about the practice of historians and their relation to the "past" they track in the archives. It raised in their most acute forms questions that perennially surround the practice of historical research and writing: How can we reconstruct the past accurately and responsibly, even as we acknowledge that we come to our material with specific identities and experiences, and with various intellectual, emotional, and political agendas? How much invention does and should go into connecting the dots between our documents? To what extent is writing history a literary enterprise? And how can historians square skepticism about ultimate truth and objectivity with the goal of writing politically engaged history?

As we have seen (chapter 4), the newly formed historical professions in Europe and the United States in the late nineteenth century modeled themselves on the scientific disciplines, which were then at the peak of their prestige: for academic historians in the decades after 1880, gaining credibility and status for their work depended on establishing truths as unquestionable as those wielded by their colleagues in physics, chemistry, and biology. Firmly rejecting history as "literature" or "art," American historians of the later nineteenth century defined their project as the rigorous and exhaustive mastery of facts. Historian Edward Potts Cheyney, for instance, declared in a 1901 report to the American Historical Association that the task of the historian was "to collect facts, view them objectively, and arrange them as the facts themselves demanded."[2] Just as a revered scientist like Isaac Newton

2. Peter Novick, *That Noble Dream: The "Objectivity Question" and the American Historical Profession* (Cambridge: Cambridge University Press, 1988), 21–40,

was said to have "held a mirror to nature," historians were enjoined to hold a mirror to the past. Their goal should be to line up all the facts through the critical study of original documents; scholars assumed that a scientifically examined source could yield only one meaning, and they sometimes spelled out the implicit corollary that history was an exhaustible discipline. As a leading French guide to historical studies published in 1898 bluntly put it, "History has at its disposal a limited stock of documents; this very circumstance limits the possible progress of historical science. When all the documents are known, and have gone through the operations which fit them for use, the work of critical scholarship will be finished."[3]

Underlying this scientific ideal of the professional study of the past was the ideal of "historical objectivity," which Peter Novick defines as "a commitment to the reality of the past, and to truth as correspondence to that reality; a sharp separation between knower and known, between fact and value, and, above all, between history and fiction."[4] From the 1880s until the mid-twentieth century, many, perhaps most, Euro-American historians were convinced that the study of the past wholly free of the distortions of personal bias or belief was both desirable and possible. It was easy to subscribe to that ideal at a time when nobody was around to challenge it plausibly. For decades, the near consensus about historical objectivity was linked to the fact that history departments were extremely homogeneous workplaces peopled by white male Protestant scholars from upper-class backgrounds.

In the United States in the late nineteenth and early twentieth centuries most history professors came from the upper-middle and upper classes. When the profession began to open up between the wars to young men from a slightly wider range of backgrounds, including non-Protestants, this caused concern within the WASP establishment. It was acceptable at the time for Jews, for instance, to enter the sciences or even the newer social sciences, but not a discipline like history, which, despite its scientific ideals, was assumed to require a humanistic background, a certain sort of

---

quote 38–39; Joyce Appleby, Lynn Hunt, and Margaret Jacob, *Telling the Truth about History* (New York: W. W. Norton, 1994), chapter 2.

3. Charles-Victor Langlois and Charles Seignobos, *Introduction aux études historiques* (1898), as cited in Novick, *That Noble Dream*, 39.

4. Novick, *That Noble Dream*, 1–2.

"culture"—leaders of the profession fretted about a potential decline in "taste" or "aesthetic sense." Confidential letters of recommendation written in the 1920s and 1930s for brilliant young Jewish scholars like Oscar Handlin, Daniel Boorstin, or Richard Leopold, who went on to become major historians, include a stream of defensive reassurances that the candidate "has none of the offensive traits which some people associate with his race," "is a Jew, though not the kind to which one takes exception," or, because a Princeton graduate, "is not of the offensive type [of Jew]." Catholic historians most frequently taught at institutions specific to their faith or in seminaries, and the few women who got doctorates were usually sent on to positions at all-female colleges.[5] The ideal of a value-free, dispassionate approach to the past flourished in part because historians at leading institutions in the United States belonged to a largely uniform sociocultural universe.[6]

The dominant ideal of historical objectivity did not, however, go unchallenged in the first half of the twentieth century, even from within this homogeneous group. Even before World War I, American "Progressive" historians launched an assault on the ideal of impartial and consensual history. Most famously, Charles Beard's provocative *An Economic History of the U.S. Constitution* (1913) courted controversy by interpreting the nation's founding document as a protocapitalist tract whose authors were seeking to protect their interests as property owners. World War I delivered conceptual shocks as well, as historians witnessed governments and the scholars who supported them shaping historical evidence to suit the agendas of wartime propaganda; that this occurred most egregiously in Germany dealt a serious blow to the traditional reverence for Teutonic scholarly standards. Finally, a range of intellectual developments between the wars, from the advent of the a new area of studies, the sociology of knowledge, to the "legal realism" of writers like Oliver Wendell Holmes, to the cumulative impact and growing prestige since the 1880s of cultural anthropology, all contributed to the growth of a relativistic ethos in the social sciences and to burgeoning skepticism about the possibility of value-neutral scholarship.[7]

---

5. Ibid., 63–68, 169–75, 491; quotes 172–73.
6. Appleby, Hunt, and Jacob, *Telling the Truth*, 129–30.
7. Ibid., chapter 4; Novick, *That Noble Dream*, chapters 4–6.

A more fundamental challenge to the ideal of historical objectivity in the American profession was brought on by the massive transformation of academia in the decades after World War II. The GI Bill, which provided education benefits for over two million war veterans—its effects amplified a generation later by the postwar baby boom—created an unprecedented demand for higher education and many new jobs for professors. In the 1930s about 150 history doctorates were awarded annually; by the late 1960s that number was over a thousand. Meanwhile, membership in the American Historical Association grew by over 60 percent in the 1950s, then by 90 percent in the 1960s. The ranks of history professors now included young men (and a few young women) from a much wider range of social, ethnic and religious backgrounds. In 1957 the chairman of Yale's history department fretted that while "the subject of English still draws [graduate students] from the cultivated, professional, and well-to-do classes . . . the subject of history seems to appeal on the whole to a lower social stratum." The sons of janitors, salesmen, clerks, and mechanics were applying to study history at the Ivy League, using the profession, he worried, as a social "elevator."[8] Such students made up the midcentury generations, alert to the experiences of the non-elite, who would revolutionize the discipline by pioneering such topics and approaches as labor history and "history from below" (see chapter 1).

While the younger generations of the 1950s through 1970s introduced perspectives and agendas sharply different from those of their elders, however, they did not usually question the presumed scientific and objective nature of historical inquiry. Their work featured different actors and different stories but did not challenge the status of historical facts. While the more patrician senior faculty pursued the "truths" of political, military, or diplomatic history, the younger generation countered with another set of "truths" about labor movements, working-class life, or slavery. As the Cold War, McCarthyism, the Vietnam War, and the Watergate scandal engulfed campuses in political turmoil, each side accused the other imposing an ideological agenda on the past, but each side also believed staunchly in the reality of its version of what mattered. The conflicts of the 1960s, in sum, productively destabilized the discipline by introducing sharply differing

8. Novick, *That Noble Dream*, 362–66, quote p. 366.

perspectives, but stopped short of mounting a philosophical challenge to the truth-claims of historical narratives.[9]

Far more disruptive to the epistemology of the discipline was the arrival in history departments, starting in the 1970s, of small but vocal minorities of women and African-American scholars. These groups introduced new approaches to the past that for the first time demanded that the historian's identity be an openly acknowledged component of scholarship. The number of women in the historical profession had actually declined in the socially conservative postwar years—from about 20 percent of new doctorates in the 1940s to 12 percent in the 1960s—but "second-wave" feminism, starting in the 1970s, brought them back in even greater numbers; by the 1980s women accounted for about a third of history dissertations (in 2008 that proportion stood at 42 percent).[10] Unlike left-wing male colleagues of their generation whose Jewish, Italian, or Irish ethnic identities bore only implicitly, if at all, on their scholarship—Jewish scholars, for instance, did not typically work on Jewish history—many female scholars explicitly connected who they were to what they studied and how they studied it. Following the lead of feminist social scientists like J. D. Winnicott, Eleanor Maccoby, and Carol Gilligan, who portrayed women's affective and cognitive styles as radically different from those of men, women scholars who espoused feminism (not all of them did, of course) began to argue that because of their differing experiences, women could and should write history differently than their male colleagues. This led some female historians to acknowledge explicitly their "subjectivity" as women, and eventually to explore radical new methodologies, including gender theory, psychoanalysis, and postmodernism.[11]

Around the same time, radical African-American scholars started to make a similar case that the content of historical scholarship could not, and should not, be separated from the identities and experiences of those who produced it. The most radical among them challenged the ability of white

9. Ibid., chapter 13.

10. Ibid., 366–67, 491–93. Robert B. Townsend, "The Status of Women and Minorities in the History Profession, 2008," *Perspectives on History*, September 2008. From 1961 to 1980 women made up around 20 percent of faculty hired in history departments, in subsequent decades 30 to 35 percent, and from 2000 to 2008, 47 percent.

11. Novick, *That Noble Dream*, 491–93.

historians to speak to the experiences of African-American slaves and other historically subjugated people of color. In the early, more militant days of Black Power movements in the academy, in the 1960s and early 1970s, such concerns sometimes led to white scholars at conferences on slavery being booed and shouted down, to black scholars ostentatiously walking out of white colleagues' talks, or to demands that black studies programs accept no nonblack instructors. While much of the tension around the identity politics of African-American and other minority history eventually abated, questions about who could credibly and legitimately convey the historical experience of ethnic and racial minorities left their mark on the profession and the practice of history.[12]

Through the end of the twentieth century, then, the ideal of historical objectivity in the United States was undermined from within the historical community: scholars practicing "history from below" insisted that the stories of the poor mattered as much as, or more than, those of the powerful, while some historians of women and nonwhites argued that the experience of marginalized groups was so different as to be incompatible with the "master narrative." Only the most radical argued for embracing "subjectivity," but the more different perspectives on history accumulated, the harder it became to believe that any historian, however honest and well-intentioned, could tell the story of the past from a position of Olympian detachment, untainted by class, gender, racial, national, and other biases.

Current global perspectives have dealt a final blow to the ideals of earlier generations where objectivity is concerned. The very form in which we write history today, whether from above, below, or the margins, is itself, we are increasingly aware, the outcome of a historical process that resulted in Western conventions for recording the past overpowering other traditions. It is almost impossible nowadays to escape imagining "history" as a single giant time line into which all of the world's events, as documented by written records, can be fitted. But as Daniel Woolf and others have shown, what is now universally deemed "history" really amounts to a set of Western codes and practices for remembering and narrating the past, which

---

12. August Meier and Elliott Rudwick, *Black History and the Historical Profession, 1915–1980* (Urbana: University of Illinois Press, 1986), 289–93; Novick, *That Noble Dream*, 472–79. From the 1960s to the 2000s the proportion of minority faculty hired in history departments has stagnated around 15 percent; Townsend, "Status of Women and Minorities."

colonized the mental landscapes of other societies only when and because Europe, and later America, became economically and geopolitically dominant a couple of centuries ago.[13]

All societies have ways of representing collective pasts, though these take many forms, oral and written, including myths, legends, epics, genealogies, chronologies, and ethnographies. In African and American societies, memories and traditions were transmitted orally, while Asians and Europeans have for centuries kept written records. Asian historiographical traditions predated Western ones: "No civilization in the world," writes Woolf, "has consistently and continuously placed as high a priority on the recording and understanding of its past as the Chinese."[14] Ancient Chinese approaches to historical time differed from those that prevailed in the West, with histories based on a succession of different eras rather than a single time line "since the founding of Rome" or "since the birth of Christ," but historical writing also developed earlier and more elaborately, with official rules, practices, and positions for historians. As early as 90 BC the historian Sima Qian completed a major historical enterprise begun by his father, the *Shiji* (Records of the Grand Historian), a complex work in five sections comprising annals of the major dynasties, chronological tables, treatises on the branches of knowledge, chronicles of the great houses, and biographies. (So devoted was Sima to the project's completion that when he fell out of favor with the emperor he submitted to the degrading penalty of castration rather than honorably committing suicide and leaving his task unfinished.)[15]

In Mughal India, as in contemporary Persia and the Ottoman Empire, historical writing flourished at the same time and in similar ways as in the courts of early modern Europe, as a support for princely, royal, and religious authority. Contemporary Europeans recognized the sophistication of other traditions, just as they would later celebrate the fourteenth-century

13. The best synthetic discussion is Daniel Woolf, *A Global History of History* (Cambridge: Cambridge University Press, 2011). See also Prasenjit Duara, Viren Murthy, and Andrew Sartori, eds., *A Companion to Global Historical Thought* (Oxford: Wiley Blackwell, 2014), and many essays in *The Oxford History of Historical Writing*, 5 vols. (Oxford: Oxford University Press, 2011–2015).

14. Woolf, *Global History*, 51–52.

15. Ibid., 53–66; Burton Watson, *Ssu-Ma Ch'ien, Grand Historian of China* (New York: Columbia University Press, 1958), biographical details in chapter 2.

Islamic scholar Ibn Khaldūn as a forerunner of sociological history in the tradition of Giambattista Vico or Charles de Montesquieu.[16] While early modern Europeans acknowledged the written historical traditions of Asian and Islamic cultures, however, they begrudged a past to societies where history took other forms. The sixteenth-century historian Garcilaso de la Vega was unique in that his mestizo heritage allowed him to weave the oral traditions of his Inca ancestors into his Spanish-language histories of Peru; most of his predecessors and contemporaries dismissed indigenous accounts of the past as untrustworthy and "barbarian" because based on oral traditions.[17] Africa, a continent where the written word was much scarcer, was simply considered a place without history, a view that many clung to well into the twentieth century. As late as 1963 the eminent British historian Hugh Trevor-Roper notoriously declared, "Perhaps, in the future, there will be some African history to teach. But at present there is none, or very little: there is only the history of the Europeans in Africa. The rest is largely darkness, like the history of pre-European, pre-Columbian America. And darkness is not a subject for history."[18] Absent the specific materials for writing Western-style history, a whole continent's past could be summarily dismissed.

Even as Europeans "discovered" and laid claim to far-flung lands, they devised, by the eighteenth century, the concept of a single, "universal," linear history as an umbrella for the previously plural histories of regions, dynasties, and religions: the concept of capital-H History encouraged a vision of the past in which societies were more or less advanced on a single highway to civilization. At the same time, confronted with other modes of historicity, Western historians sought to codify their own scholarship more rigorously by contrasting their ways of recovering and describing the past to the lesser practices of other societies. Thus, while the French historian Joseph de Guignes (1721–1800) showed a commendable interest in Middle Eastern and Asian history, he disparaged Chinese historiography as arid and boring, and "the Arab" as "no more than a chronicler." Major figures of the European Enlightenment dismissed pictorial and oral sources as fatally flawed—conveniently forgetting the reliance of some of their own

16. Woolf, *Global History*, 127–29, 211–25.

17. Ibid., chapter 5.

18. Cited ibid., 16; see also Frederick Cooper, "Africa's Pasts and Africa's Historians," *Canadian Journal of African Studies* 34 (2000): 298–336.

past luminaries, such as Thucydides, on oral traditions. "The frail memories of men," wrote David Hume in the eighteenth century, "their love of exaggeration, their supine carelessness; these principles, if not corrected by books and writing, soon pervert the account of historical events."[19]

In the heyday of Euro-American imperialism, the nineteenth and early twentieth centuries, the canons and conventions of Western historical scholarship were implanted in universities all over the world, where the elites of colonized countries had little choice but to adopt them.[20] While it has become by now just about impossible to think outside the box of modern Western historical norms, we are at least aware of the historically contingent process that made them inescapable. Viewed in global context, the objectivity long prized by Euro-American scholars amounts to the cherry on the cake of a centuries-long process of Western erasure of competing historical traditions, an ideal linked to underlying convictions about the value of written ("objective") documents as sources and of history as a unitary, linear process.

Since around the 1950s, then, a succession of shocks have rattled the once optimistic (or complacent) conviction that a historian could arrive at the ultimate truth: a previous generation's standard of "objectivity" has been challenged by dissenters within and outside academia as the particular perspective of the white upper-class men at the helm of Western historical professions. In this process of erosion, methodological and sociological developments have been inseparable: scholars from non-elite ethnic backgrounds challenged the primacy of elite political history, women and people of color told white male scholars "your truth is not ours," the globalization of world culture and academia allowed for radical new perspectives on Western historical norms.

Alongside these shifts in the identities and perspectives of scholars there appeared in the 1980s a set of philosophical challenges to traditional understandings of history, broadly labeled "postmodernism," which for a while roiled the profession and continue to this day to cause expressions of alarm in some quarters.

19. Jennifer Pitts, "The Global in Enlightenment Historical Thought," in Duara, Murthy, and Sartori, *Companion to Global Historical Thought*, 184–96; Woolf, *Global History*, 281–340, quotes 283 (Hume), 317 (Guignes).

20. Ibid., chapter 8.

POSTMODERNISM AND HISTORY: RADICAL SKEPTICISM AND NEW METHODS

"Postmodernism" is a catchall term frequently used to describe the intellectual tsunami that hit the humanistic end of the academy with full force in the 1980s, originating in the fields of linguistics, philosophy, and literary studies, associated with the names of difficult and controversial thinkers such as Jacques Derrida, Jacques Lacan, and Paul de Man. For our purposes, the most important aspect of postmodernism, as it came to affect historical work and nourish controversy, is its emphasis on language and "text." Prominent in the genealogy of academic postmodernity are the twentieth-century French intellectual movements known as structuralism and poststructuralism.[21] Structuralism goes back to the early twentieth-century work of the linguist Ferdinand de Saussure, who carved out a new path in his field by arguing, in his 1916 *Course in General Linguistics,* that every language is a closed system in which words derive meaning not from their connection with the things they designate (signifieds), but in relation to other words, or signifiers. The word "cat," for instance, has nothing intrinsic to do with a four-legged furry animal; it means something to an English speaker because we understand it to be different from "cap" or "bat." Structural linguistics, in other words, departs from a traditional diachronic approach to language (how did it evolve over time?) to consider it instead as a complex synchronic grid in which meaning arises not from a coincidence between word and thing, but from the differences between words within a given system.

Saussure's approach, structural linguistics, became influential as a way of understanding, not just language, but culture in general when it was embraced by anthropologists, most notably the celebrated French ethnographer Claude Lévi-Strauss. As Saussure had done for language, Lévi-Strauss sought to analyze cultures as grids in which meaning derives from codes—kinship patterns, myths, totemic systems—made up of contrasting binary terms. Any item within a culture, Lévi-Strauss argued, is intelligible only in relation to its opposite: the idea of "raw" food has meaning only in relation to its "cooked" opposite, just as ideas such as "male" and "female" or "light" and "dark" are

---

21. The following discussion relies on the exceptionally lucid accounts of structuralism and poststructuralism in Terry Eagleton, *Literary Theory: An Introduction,* 3rd ed. (Oxford: Blackwell, 2008), chapters 3 and 4.

understandable only in opposition to each other. (Examples extend into the recent past: we didn't know that our clocks were analog until digital ones appeared, or what it meant to be a cisgender person until transgender identities became conspicuous.)

Structural linguistics and structural anthropology introduced into the nexus of twentieth-century Western thought influential ideas whose offshoots we have already encountered in other contexts. Structuralism posits that meaning is not immanent in the "real world" but rather comes to exist in and through autonomous linguistic or cultural codes, and in particular through the operation of difference within those codes. Because of its emphasis either on language itself (linguistics) or on concepts expressed linguistically (cultural anthropology), structural analysis is primarily concerned with the importance of words and texts rather than with the "real world," with "signifiers" rather than "signifieds." By the same token, structuralism brackets off the human subject.[22] Structures, not people, generate meaning, and humans are therefore not the causes but the effects of linguistic and cultural structures: we can think, speak—in short, exist—only through preexisting grids of collective meaning. Structuralism is therefore "antihumanist," in the technical sense that it discounts individual human behavior and experience, which it views as subordinate to systems of signs.

While structuralism, highly influential in the 1950s and 1960s, rejects the humanistic notion that men and women can be the autonomous authors of their own destinies, its method allows for the possibility of ultimately decoding a system of signs such as a language or a culture. Far more radically skeptical were the theories that grew out of and superseded structuralism starting in the 1970s, known as poststructuralism or deconstruction. Poststructuralists (Jacques Derrida was the most famous) pushed structuralist insights to their most radical conclusion. While thinkers like Saussure or Lévi-Strauss were confident that they could tease out meaning from the semiotic structures—systems of signs—that govern human existence in any given place or time, poststructuralists took matters to the edge of a theoretical abyss. Rejecting the stable antinomies of structuralism, they argued that the ultimate meaning of any given term can never be apprehended since meaning is predicated on absence, and entails the rejection of not just one opposing term ("cat" is not "bat") but an unlimited number

22. Ibid., 98–99. See also Appleby, Hunt, and Jacob, *Telling the Truth*, 215–16.

of terms. To be a "man," for instance, is to be "not a woman," but also to be not an infinite number of other things; any given concept, such as masculinity, contains and is constantly threatened by all of the potential opposing terms that go into defining it. Meaning, then, is endlessly "deferred," since a term is "always already" engaged in the process of pushing away this infinity of potential opposites.[23]

This sort of high theory sounds remote from the preoccupations of most historians, and indeed only a tiny number of them engaged firsthand with the writings of theorists like Derrida. Within academia, however, structuralism and poststructuralism helped create, by the 1980s, a broad intellectual climate known as postmodernism whose implications translated into controversial propositions regarding historians' approaches to the past. We have already encountered, in previous chapters, some of the writers and movements influential with historians that fall into the broader "postmodern" category. Structuralism had a big influence, for instance, on thinkers like Michel Foucault and Clifford Geertz, whose work bypassed "man" in favor of the "discourses" or "webs of signification" in which humans are ensnared. More generally, the 1980s saw the advent in Western historical studies of approaches to the past in which sources were viewed not as transparent windows onto a past reality but as "texts."

The emphasis on "texts," which came to be known as the "linguistic turn," was a change in perspective whereby historians sympathetic to movements like postmodernism and the new cultural history started reading sources as patterns of words and stories, as forms of "fiction" in the broadest sense, rather than as documentary evidence.[24] (In its original sense, "fiction" does not mean "something untrue" but "something created and shaped," an important distinction.) One popular application of this strategy, for instance, involves judicial sources.

A traditional historian, faced with the records of criminal law institutions in a past society, would use these to determine, say, the incidence of various types of criminality or patterns of judicial repression: who committed what crimes, how often, and how were they punished? In the context of the linguistic turn, however, cultural historians approached the courtroom

23. Ibid., 110–16.
24. John Toews, "Linguistic Turn and Discourse Analysis in History," in Neil Smelser and Paul Baltes, eds., *International Encyclopedia of the Social and Behavioral Sciences*, vol. 13 (Amsterdam: Elsevier, 2001), 8916–22.

not in search of evidence of crime and punishment but as an institutional setting that generates words, and especially narratives. Prosecutors, defendants, and lawyers have always crafted the details of what happened into a story that will (they hope) prove persuasive to the jury, judge, or other authorities because it connects with stories and cultural categories with which the listener is familiar or fits into widespread stereotypes and popular narratives.

Natalie Davis's *Fiction in the Archives* (1987), for instance, a study of judicial petitions addressed to the king in early modern France by petitioners who had committed serious crimes, argues that defendants who sought royal mercy shaped their accounts of their crimes so that they conformed with familiar contemporary narratives. In the opening pages of her book, Davis explains her methodological premise. When she was a student, she writes, "we were ordinarily taught as scientific historians to peel away the fictive elements in our documents so as to get at the real facts."[25] In her study, she proposes to do just the opposite, to show how the "fictional" dimensions of pardon tales, the ways in which they were molded into stories that echoed other stories, made them effective within their culture. Petitioners' tales fell into specific types, including plots and details keyed to different social classes and settings. A frequent "peasant's tale," for instance, takes place at a wedding in which young men from another village intrude. They bother the women, and one of them defies and maybe slaps the petitioner, who in a fit of "hot anger" (*chaude colle*) kills the intruder. Such stories were effective (a large majority of petitioners were pardoned), Davis suggests, because the situations and motivations they portrayed corresponded to familiar tales of justified anger.[26]

Whether in the courtroom or in the press, crime stories have provided fodder for many classic works of cultural history influenced by postmodernism. Judith Walkowitz's *City of Dreadful Delight*, for instance, revolves around "narratives of sexual danger" in 1880s London.[27] One such set of stories has remained famous, the gruesome newspaper accounts of the crimes of the serial prostitute-killer known as Jack the Ripper. Less well

25. Natalie Zemon Davis, *Fiction in the Archives: Pardon Tales and Their Tellers in Sixteenth-Century France* (Stanford, CA: Polity Press, 1987), 3.

26. Ibid., 36–43, 51.

27. Judith Walkowitz, *City of Dreadful Delight: Narratives of Sexual Danger in Late-Victorian London* (Chicago: University of Chicago Press, 1992).

known now but equally electrifying at the time were the exposés of child prostitution penned in 1885 by W. T. Stead, the editor of the popular *Pall Mall Gazette*, under the melodramatic title "The Maiden Tribute of Modern Babylon" (Stead's accounts frequently alluded to the legend of the Minotaur, with the journalist as the modern Theseus rescuing young girls from the monster); the first installment described in lurid detail how Stead, posing as a customer, negotiated for five pounds the purchase from her mother of the virginity of a thirteen-year-old working-class girl. Walkowitz shows how, in order to make the "Maiden Tribute" stories resonate with his readers, Stead drew upon familiar contemporary genres such as stage melodrama, gothic romance, pornography, and the writings of urban social reformers. The book situates Stead's voyeuristic journalism—his paper also prominently covered Jack the Ripper—in many overlapping social contexts: traditions of upper-class male spectatorship, the new activities and occupations of women in urban space, the role of feminists in abetting and addressing these sexual alarms, and much else. At the heart of the inquiry, however, is this question: why did this particular setting produce, and respond so strongly to, horrifying accounts of defiled children and murdered prostitutes? *City of Dreadful Delight* belongs to a genre of historical inquiry that is fact-based but organized around fictions, and whose purpose it is to show why certain stories resonated, and to what effect, in a given place and time.

Most historical sources, of course, do not come in narrative form: the storylike nature of a political or judicial speech is a lot easier to grasp than that of a tax roll, a commercial invoice, or a parish register. But stories can also lurk behind ostensibly nonnarrative sources: the constitutions of modern democracies, for instance, all hark back to the story of the "social contract," a dramatic tale of how men (but not women) in a hypothetical state of nature came close to killing each other before deciding that it was a better idea to survive by inventing laws and government.[28] A rigorously postmodern approach entails the assumption that all documents, even the most abstract—sets of numbers, for instance—are not windows onto a past reality but expressions of the mental categories and cultural conventions of the world that produced them. Prior to the postmodern "moment,"

28. Carole Pateman, *The Sexual Contract* (Stanford, CA: Stanford University Press, 1988). Pateman's classic in feminist political theory "denaturalizes" contractual theory by highlighting its storied components.

historians examining a census would use it to establish a country's population, or critique it to show how and why it under- or overrepresented the numbers, looking to reconstruct the past "reality" beyond the documents. A postmodern approach, by contrast, would focus on the census as a "text" that reveals assumptions about such things as social categories and hierarchies, or how people carved up social space, and would consider its relation to some past demographic reality either irrelevant or unknowable.

The linguistic turn invited historians to think of all of their sources not as unproblematic reflections of a past reality but as culturally configured texts: a sixteenth-century map, in this perspective, does not tell you about the geography of a physical place but about the mental universe of the cartographers. But the premium that postmodernists placed upon "texts" and "fictions" (again, in the broad sense) also extended to the writings of historians themselves: at the same time that they drew attention to the fictional nature of historical sources, scholars began to attend to the ways in which historical writing, past and present, is shaped by literary conventions. The most famous proponent of this agenda has been the literary theorist Hayden White, who gained fame with the 1973 publication of *Metahistory: The Historical Imagination in Nineteenth-Century Europe*, and remained influential through a large corpus of writings about the theory of history.[29]

All historical writing, White argues, is a form of fiction-making. He does not thereby suggest that historians invent documents or sources, but that at least in the modern Western mode, historical writing invariably adheres to one of several types of narrative plots drawn from, in the broadest sense, literary culture. White does not deny the existence of historical evidence in the form of facts, but he maintains that for a historical account to be intelligible those facts have to be organized around a recognizable plot. (A historian could theoretically choose just to line up information in chronological order, but that would amount to a "chronicle," a form that in contemporary culture is devoid of meaning.)[30] Evidence about the past does not come to us in the form of a story: we impose narrative upon it. The "facts" of history do not themselves contain interpretive elements;

---

29. Hayden White, *Metahistory: The Historical Imagination in Nineteenth-Century Europe* (Baltimore: Johns Hopkins University Press, 1993).

30. Hayden White, *The Content of the Form: Narrative Discourse and Historical Representation* (Baltimore: Johns Hopkins University Press, 1987), 42–43.

they are not like pieces of a jigsaw puzzle waiting to be fitted together. Rather, the facts are available in what Alun Munslow calls a "pre-jigsawed" state, and historians shape them so that they can fit a pattern: "Historical facts do not ordain interpretations," writes Munslow, "only plot structures do that."[31]

In *Metahistory*, White identifies Western culture's four basic modes of emplotment as romance, comedy, tragedy, and satire.[32] While it is not usually a conscious choice, historians organize their stories to fit these plot types: E. P. Thompson, for instance, tells the story of the British Industrial Revolution as a tragedy in which beleaguered artisans are doomed to exploitation and poverty; another historian might cast it in the classical mode of comedy, in which, despite setbacks and misunderstandings, reconciliation prevails in the end (the standard of living rises for everyone!). Marxist and nationalist historians often write in the mode of romance, which tells of heroes prevailing in the face of adversity.[33] White does not claim universal valence for these plots: they work for Western historians because they draw on their culture's most familiar literary forms.[34]

White argues that this "fictional" dimension of historical writing is the historian's most powerful tool, since historians do not share a common technical language: "The historian's characteristic instrument of encodation, communication and exchange is ordinary educated speech." As a result, historians must draw on widely accepted forms of figurative language to accomplish their goal "of rendering the strange familiar and, of rendering the mysterious past comprehensible."[35] To point to the ways in which historians fictionalize the past does not mean, White insists, that we cannot distinguish between good and bad history based on thoroughness of research, logical consistency, responsible use of evidence, and the like. Nor, it bears repeating, does saying that historical writing adheres to

31. Alun Munslow, *Deconstructing History* (London: Routledge, 1997), 149. See also Keith Jenkins, *On "What Is History?"* (London: Routledge, 1995), 134–35.

32. White, *Metahistory*, 7–30.

33. White does believe that two or more of these plot types can coexist in tension within the works of historians and, indeed, that this is characteristic of the greatest among them. White, *Tropics of Discourse: Essays in Cultural Criticism* (Baltimore: Johns Hopkins University Press, 1978), 94.

34. Ibid., 58.

35. Ibid., 94.

familiar plots in any way imply that historians invent their material. Rather than undermining the historical enterprise, White argues, recognition of what history owes to fiction will allow historians to be more lucid and honest about their own practice, and to make use of what has always been the discipline's greatest strength, its ability to connect with lay readers.[36] As with the attention to the storied nature of sources, White's writings are symptomatic of a moment in which scholars became highly conscious of the process of fabrication that goes into all "texts," whether the documents we use as primary material, or the secondary accounts written by historians.

EVERYTHING IS CONSTRUCTED

The postmodern "moment" in historical writing, which crested in the early 1990s, decisively recast approaches to many questions, most notably those about social groups and identities. The earliest and most momentous such transformations occurred, as we saw in chapter 1, in the 1980s, when some feminist historians made the case for a shift from "women's" to "gender" history. Historians like Joan Scott drew upon structuralist and poststructuralist methods in order to recast the history of women (a biologically determined category of persons) as gender history, or the history of the linguistically and culturally defined relationship between the sexes. Scott's famous essay "Gender: A Useful Category of Historical Analysis" opens with the observation that "words, like the ideas and things they are meant to signify, have a history." "Gender," a grammatical term transposed to social categories, has been not just useful but crucial to all historians in pointing to the arbitrariness of verbal codes, thereby leading us to ponder the similarly variable nature of the sexual differences we take for granted. Some languages have gender classifications, many do not (or have more than two), and within those that do the ascription of gender appears mostly arbitrary: there seems to be no reason why a bed is masculine in French and feminine in Spanish, or why the German word for young girl, *Mädchen*, is neuter. Gender in grammar, writes Scott, is "a socially agreed upon system of distinction rather than an objective description of inherent traits."

36. Ibid., 97–99. For a helpful analysis of White's role within the "linguistic turn," see Lloyd Kramer, "Literature, Criticism, and Historical Imagination: The Literary Challenge of Hayden White and Dominick LaCapra," in Lynn Hunt, ed. *The New Cultural History* (Berkeley: University of California Press, 1989), 97–128.

Moreover, the difference between masculine and feminine has varied with time and place. Just as linguistic terms—following the likes of Saussure—have meaning only in relation to one another, so "gender legitimizes and constructs social relationships" by organizing the way we talk about oppositions and hierarchies in the social world. Men can only be "men"—powerful, competent, rational, and so on—because they are "not women" in ways that are constructed by, and reflected in, language.[37]

Gender theory applied to history performed a crucial role in denaturalizing social categories: as historians stopped thinking of the difference between men and women as grounded in timeless biological fact, they extended this insight to other sorts of seemingly natural social distinctions. What could be more natural, more blatantly visible than the difference between the skin colors and other physical features of various human groups? "Race" has been noteworthy for as long as humans from different places have encountered one another, and in nineteenth-century Europe and America it became the object of intense scientific scrutiny. In the United States, the tragic legacy of slavery and persistent discrimination against black Americans, as well as the vexed history of other groups, including Native Americans, Asians, and Hispanics, have generated, since the mid-twentieth century, a large and sophisticated body of historical studies of the origins and meaning of racial prejudice.[38]

Until the 1980s, however, most scholars took for granted the existence of race as a physical reality that stood as ground zero for their inquiries: people *were* black, white, brown, or yellow, and the project of progressive scholars was to analyze critically how and why various negative traits came to be associated with skin color and other racial features. One of the first historians to challenge the seemingly obvious biological nature of what we call race was Barbara Fields, in an essay entitled "Race and Ideology in American History" (1982). Fields pointed to well-known facts routinely ignored because they did not fit with dominant assumptions, in this case

37. Joan Wallach Scott, "Gender: A Useful Category of Historical Analysis," in *Gender and the Politics of History* (New York: Columbia University Press, 1988), 29, 46. See chapter 1.

38. Pioneering works on the subject include George Fredrickson, *The Black Image in the White Mind: The Debate on Afro-American Character and Destiny* (New York: Harper & Row, 1971), and David Brion Davis, *The Problem of Slavery in the Age of Revolution, 1770–1823* (Ithaca, NY: Cornell University Press, 1975).

about the physicality of race. If blackness and whiteness are skin colors, why so many exceptions? Why did nineteenth-century Europeans always describe light-skinned North Africans as black? Why have there always been American "blacks" who looked white? Why the one-drop rule? Why was it a staple of American racial thought that a white woman could give birth to a black child, but a black woman could not give birth to a white child? The answers to all of these questions are not biological, of course, but political, and Fields called for an inquiry into those politics starting from the premise that "the view that race is a biological fact, a physical attribute of individuals, is no longer tenable."[39]

Race, Fields posited, is a form of belief, an ideology that people hold, often in the face of massive contrary evidence, like those antebellum planters certain that their slaves were physically incapable of surviving without their white masters even as they saw many free blacks doing just that. Fields urges historians to stop looking at race in American history as a transcendent, metaphysical problem, and attend instead to the specific historical circumstances in which divisions and prejudices took root or were abetted—most notably the tragic sociopolitical dynamic of Reconstruction. Although Fields was not drawing on postmodern thinkers, her conclusion about race is strikingly similar to Scott's about gender: "Race became the ideological medium through which people posed and apprehended basic questions of power and dominance, sovereignty and citizenship, justice and right." Race is an ideology, Fields argues, but that does not make its consequences any less tragically real: "Once acted upon, a delusion can be as murderous as a fact."[40]

In historical perspective, then, blackness is in the eye of the beholder; but so, historians have shown, is whiteness. Until not long ago it was common to view whiteness either as a nonrace or as the "default" race from which others constituted abnormal departures, and to assume that most white people have always inhabited a single category. Far more complicated stories have emerged from recent research; the experience of the United States, with its waves of successive European immigrants encountering African and Native American minorities, has allowed historians to

39. Barbara Fields, "Ideology and Race in American History," in J. Morgan Kousser and James McPherson, eds., *Region, Race and Reconstruction: Essays in Honor of C. Vann Woodward* (Oxford: Oxford University Press, 1982), 149.

40. Ibid., 162, 159.

show that "whiteness" is no more a straightforward physical characteristic than any other racial label. Two centuries ago Irish workers in Britain and the United States were represented with dark skin and simian features, and the whiteness of other immigrant groups in America—Italians or Jews, for instance—was not always taken for granted.[41]

Workers in industrializing America, as David Roediger argued in an influential book, invoked their own whiteness as a way of warding off their fears of dependency. As more and more of them lost their actual independence to wage labor in the early nineteenth century, losing their workshops and entering factories, they constructed an idealized identity as autonomous white workers in contrast to the degraded status of black slaves; they insisted on being called "hired men" instead of "servants," and adopted for their employers the term "boss" instead of "master." Whiteness became crucial to the identity of early industrial workers as a way of saying "I am not a slave," a psychic compensation for their actual loss of control over their labor: to be white in the early nineteenth century, Roediger suggests, was to be "not black," and for that matter, "not Indian," in the same way gender historians posit that men throughout history have been in different ways "not women."[42] In America, as in any multiethnic society, whiteness was never a simple or stable category: in the era of mass arrivals from Europe from the 1840s to the 1920s, the Anglo-Saxon elite viewed themselves as at the top of a hierarchy of whitish races that included Teutons, Celts, Slavs, Hebrews, and others. Only after the spigot of immigration was turned off in the 1920s did race in America jell into primarily a dichotomy of "Caucasian" and black.[43] Outside of the Western world race has never taken the form of simple biological binaries either: recent work by African historians, for instance, has uncovered the complexity of racial categories, prejudices, and struggles in places like nineteenth-century Egypt and Zanzibar, inviting us to move away from the—literally and metaphorically—black and white categories of Western societies.[44]

41. Noel Ignatiev, *How the Irish Became White* (New York: Routledge, 1995).

42. David Roediger, *The Wages of Whiteness: Race and the Making of the American Working Class*, 2nd ed. (1991; New York: Verso, 1999).

43. Matthew Frye Jacobson, *Whiteness of a Different Color: European Immigrants and the Alchemy of Race* (Cambridge, MA: Harvard University Press, 1998).

44. See, for instance, Jonathon Glassman, "Slower Than a Massacre: The Multiple Sources of Racial Thought in Colonial Africa," *American Historical Review*

BARBARIANS AT THE GATES

In the 1980s and 1990s, then, leading historians of gender and race pioneered a line of inquiry known as "cultural constructionism," which holds that even those identities that seem to us the most self-evidently biological are defined by the way people speak, write, and think about them. (We have seen in previous chapters instances of this approach applied to issues of sexuality, as historians like Thomas Laqueur and George Chauncey have shown how infinitely variable both homo- and heterosexual relationships and identities have been in past societies.) Such inquiries typically emphasized "texts," using every sort of descriptive source—pamphlets, treatises, medical texts, news media, plays, novels, and more—to reconstruct the ways in which people imagined, understood, and represented women, gays, members of racial minorities, and others: identities, these works argued, are inseparable from the discourse about them. As in the case of studies that emphasized the fictional or "storied" aspects of sources, this approach owed much to the general influence of postmodernism. As a result, all of these approaches became the target of much criticism, in forms ranging from reasoned objections to vitriolic tirades.

Some of the most eloquent and extreme opponents of the influence of postmodernism on historical work have been British historians seizing the chance to vent traditional Francophobia by denouncing the corrupt Gallic roots of these menacing theories. "The absurd always sounds better in French," sniffed the politically and intellectually conservative Cambridge don Sir Geoffrey Elton, one of the last prominent historians to proudly define his professional ideal as "the search for truth."[45] The late Elton, famous for heated rhetoric when he pronounced on matters of historical method, delivered in the early 1990s a set of lectures that described poststructural theories variously as an infectious disease, a diabolical seducer,

109, no. 3 (June 2004): 720–54; Glassman, *War of Words, War of Stones: Racial Thought and Violence in Colonial Zanzibar* (Bloomington: Indiana University Press, 2011); Eve Troutt Powell, *A Different Shade of Colonialism: Egypt, Great Britain and the Mastery of the Sudan* (Berkeley: University of California Press, 2003); Bruce Hall, *A History of Race in Muslim West Africa, 1600–1960* (Cambridge: Cambridge University Press, 2011).

45. G. R. Elton, *Return to Essentials: Some Reflections on the Present State of Historical Studies* (Cambridge: Cambridge University Press, 1991), 27, 48.

and a form of substance abuse. Postmodernism was "a virus," more threatening than Marxism "because it took its origin from characteristically charismatic Frenchmen." He and his allies were fighting, he thundered, not only for their own survival as historians but "for the lives of innocent young people beset by devilish tempters who claim to offer higher forms of thought and deeper truths and insights—the intellectual equivalent of crack, in fact." Among those tempters where "fanatical feminists" like Joan Scott, whose alleged blend of Marxism and deconstruction was "like spiking vodka with LSD."[46] A few years later Elton's younger colleague at Cambridge Richard Evans—his successor in the prestigious Regius Chair in modern European history—produced a much more balanced but still alarmist statement, a book titled *In Defense of History*, which described postmodernism as an "irresistible" intellectual trend and its adherents as "intellectual barbarians at the disciplinary gates . . . loitering there with distinctly hostile intent."[47]

What was it about postmodern approaches to history that these and many other scholars found so deeply alarming? A rigorously postmodern position does indeed present a serious philosophical challenge to the way most people think of history in that it suggests we can never be assured that the past really happened. All we historians have, a postmodernist would argue, are words and "texts" (including oral testimony, images, and physical artifacts), whose relationship to a "real past" can never be known. Textuality, in the words of the historical theorist Keith Jenkins, is "the only game in town."[48] Since history therefore consists of the interpretation of those texts, the process of making history is inevitably subjective— for a theorist like Hayden White, as we have seen, writing about the past is akin to emplotting a work of fiction: however respectful of their evidence, historians are always writing, in the widest sense, a literary account. To Elton, a historian's acknowledgment of his or her subjectivity and of an agenda rooted in present-day concerns constitutes an act of egregious narcissism—it amounts to selfishly putting oneself over and above "the authority of our sources."[49]

46. Ibid., 27–29, 41.
47. Richard J. Evans, *In Defense of History* (New York: W. W. Norton, 1999), 7, 11.
48. Jenkins, *On "What Is History?"* 32.
49. Elton, *Return to Essentials*, 36, 42–43, 49.

Evans does not share his predecessor's old-fashioned views about truth and objectivity; his objections are of the sort widely shared in the 1990s by middle-of-the road historians. A majority, perhaps, of academic historians at the time and since have worried that the postmodern position, bracketing past "reality," undercut the central moral and political rationales for writing history, the reconstruction of a credible narrative that illuminates the present and points to the future. How, they ask, can a past whose existence we question provide us with enlightenment and guidance? Furthermore, such critics argue, the new theories' agnosticism about the reality of past experience is an insult to all those who have suffered in history. Indeed, as many critics of postmodernism have pointed out, there are many instances in which a community finds it morally exigent to state their belief in a past that actually happened. Evans, a historian of modern Germany, points as many others have done to the Holocaust: "Auschwitz was not a discourse. It trivializes mass murder to see it as a text. The gas chambers were not a piece of rhetoric. Auschwitz was indeed inherently a tragedy and cannot be seen as either a comedy or a farce."[50]

More generally, Evans charges that a postmodern focus on words and texts privileges the self-absorbed preoccupations of present-day academics over the reality of suffering and oppression in the past.[51] Nor were conservatives the only ones to attack postmodernism; many left-leaning historians joined them in denouncing what they saw as a dangerous development in the profession. To the most orthodox Marxists postmodernism was anathema in that it inverted the materialist relation between base and superstructure, ignoring the bedrock of socioeconomic life in favor of the abstract and derivative realm of words.[52] More generally, many left-leaning historians were hostile to theories that located the operation of power in discursive formations rather than in the blood and sweat of actual social relations. Leading feminist historians entered into high-profile arguments with Joan Scott, charging that her emphasis on textuality obscured the realities of women's actual experiences of violence and exploitation in the

50. Evans, *In Defense of History*, 107.

51. Ibid., 159.

52. See, for instance, Bryan D. Palmer, *Descent into Discourse: The Reification of Language and the Writing of Social History* (Philadelphia: Temple University Press, 1990); Alex Callinicos, *Against Postmodernism: A Marxist Critique* (New York: St. Martin's Press, 1990).

past. As the title of one landmark critical article put it: "If 'Woman' is Just an Empty Category, Then Why Am I Afraid to Walk Alone at Night?"[53] While postmodernists always insisted that theirs was a critical political project that exposed the ways in which power works through discourses to define and trap people, their opponents countered that for history to be politically significant and effective it must rest on a belief in the reality of past suffering and injustice. Many left-leaning academics shared with their conservative colleagues the suspicion that postmodernism was a self-indulgent and politically irresponsible intellectual game.

Most historians in the 1990s and after fell somewhere between these warring camps, borrowing some of the insights of postmodernists but rejecting their more radical premises. For all of the loud clanging of alarm bells—Evans claimed, writing in 1997, that postmodernism was "espoused by the majority" of historians—no major scholars actually wrote postmodern works of history; they merely borrowed insights from the trend, while experimental and theoretical work remained confined to the margins of the discipline.[54] Many creative historians took the "linguistic turn" in the 1980s and 1990s, looking to stories or representations, but almost none of them professed disbelief in the reality of the past. Why, then, did postmodernism cause such a major hubbub? Maybe because its most fundamental premise—that, in the famous words of Jacques Derrida, "there is nothing outside the text"—is indeed very hard to dispute: the existence of the past is highly plausible but not, in the end, provable. In response to the postmodern philosophical challenge, those historians who worry about such

53. Laura Lee Downs, "If Woman Is Just an Empty Category, Then Why Am I Afraid to Walk Alone at Night?" *Comparative Studies in Society and History* 35, no. 2 (April 1993): 414–37; see in the same issue the response by Joan Scott (438–43) and rebuttal by Downs (444–51).

54. Evans, *In Defense of History*, 12. The targets of Evans's onslaught—written quite late in the game, in 1997—are mostly theorists like Keith Jenkins, Frank Ankersmit, Alun Munslow, and Elizabeth Deeds Ermarth. The actual historians he names are few—Patrick Joyce and Diane Purkiss, notably—and not especially influential. But Evans also wrongly identifies as "postmodernists" some leading cultural and microhistorians, such as Natalie Davis, Robert Darnton, Simon Schama, and Carlo Ginzburg, for whose work he expresses admiration. Lawrence Stone also noted in 1992 that "it is impossible to think of a major historical work written from a thoroughly postmodern perspective." Stone, "History and Postmodernism," *Past & Present* 135 (1992): 191.

things usually find themselves emulating the eighteenth-century British writer Samuel Johnson, who, when asked to rebut the theory of a thinker who denied the existence of matter, famously landed a mighty kick into a large stone and said, "I refute it *thus*."[55]

The best-known historians' script for Johnsonian stone-kicking is laid out in a book published 1994 by a trio of leading historians, Joyce Appleby, Lynn Hunt, and Margaret Jacob. Their widely read *Telling the Truth about History* seeks to carve out a middle way between the skeptical relativism of postmodernists and other cultural constructionists, on the one hand, and outmoded beliefs in the objective pursuit of historical truth, on the other. Reviewing twentieth-century challenges to absolutist truth in science and history, the authors cheerfully conclude that these have been positive developments, symptomatic of the opening up of American higher education to different voices and perspectives, and that "a democratic practice of history . . . encourages skepticism about dominant views."[56] The sense of crisis in the academic world of the early 1990s, in this view, was due to the collapse of "absolutist" beliefs in the infallibility of science, the inevitability of progress, and the goal of perfect objectivity; increasing doubt about these verities stemmed from a healthy spirit of democratic challenge. But the authors draw the line at caving in to the "cynicism and nihilism" of complete relativity or the lure of multicultural fragmentation. Rejecting postmodern doubts about the existence of any objective reality, they espouse a stance they call "qualified objectivity," which acknowledges both the subjectivity of those who study history and the existence of objective traces of the past that constrain what the historian can say: the past is indeed present in texts and material remains, though it cannot dictate "history," which is inevitably shaped by those who write it. "Qualified objectivity," then, amounts to an interactive relationship between an inevitably subjective historian and the materials that limit and shape her inquiry. But historians are also trained and constrained sociologically, by the institutions in which they operate, and an ideally democratic society will generate norms of scholarship and learning that encourage dissent and skepticism while also subjecting scholars to the rules and standards set by the intellectual community. The authors, in sum, pragmatically locate

55. James Boswell, *The Life of Samuel Johnson* (New York: Penguin Classics, 1986), 122.
56. Appleby, Hunt, and Jacob, *Telling the Truth*, 3, 11.

224

the solution to the postmodernist dilemma in the operation of democratic scholarly institutions.[57]

DISTORTION OR IMAGINATION: WHERE DO WE DRAW THE LINE?

Appleby, Hunt, and Jacob's compromise position—that we are inevitably subjective, but constrained by the traces of the past and the norms of our intellectual communities—is most likely palatable to most historians working today. In any event, social and cultural historians have moved away from focusing on texts and representations and toward concentrating not on how culture shapes people but on what people *do* with culture: concepts of "practice" and "performance" have become productively ubiquitous in recent years.[58] But issues of truth and fiction, questions about the historian's subjectivity and freedom with respect to past materials, are not about to disappear. A major reason the passions aroused by the postmodernist "threat" among historians have been so intense is no doubt that the allegedly sharp line between history and fiction so easily gets blurred: historians are particularly sensitive to encroachments from the fictional end of the writing spectrum precisely because they are more like novelists than any other group in the scholarly world. Agreement reigns in principle that historians are bound by the facts and obey a strict embargo on invention. But the historian's task also consists in assembling scattered sources and connecting the dots between them, and superior historical work involves the ability to imagine the past and recreate it in vivid prose. Disagreement often arises, often contentiously, as to which forms of dot-connecting and imagination are licit and which are not.

Over the years the historical profession has been rocked at regular intervals by scandals that involve the alleged fabrication or distortion of sources, with historians either united in their indignation or painfully divided. Sometimes wide agreement prevails in the profession about a case of egregious "historical malpractice." In the early 2000s, for instance, a scandal erupted around a rising star in the American historical profession, Michael Bellesiles, a professor at Emory University, eventually forcing him out of the

57. Ibid., chapters 7–8, especially pp. 254–61.
58. For a good overview, see Gabrielle M. Spiegel, "Introduction," in Spiegel, ed. *Practicing History: New Directions in Historical Writing after the Linguistic Turn* (New York: Routledge, 2005), especially 11–26.

academy.[59] In 2000 Bellesiles was in a position most academic historians can only dream of as the author of a politically important book glowingly reviewed in the popular press, which had already snagged one of the profession's biggest awards, the Bancroft Prize in American history. In addition, he had gained respect and sympathy from his liberal fellow academics for coming under attack from one of their greatest foes, the National Rifle Association. Bellesiles's *Arming America: The Origins of a National Gun Culture* (2000), a study of guns in America from colonial times to the Civil War, centered on a surprising set of findings whose political import was immediately obvious. *Arming America* overturned the standard image of colonial America as a land of proudly gun-toting individuals. From his research into probate sources—wills and inventories—Bellesiles had discovered that in the period 1765–1790 only an average of 14.7 percent of all households owned guns. By the mid-nineteenth century, when the spread of interchangeable parts allowed the industrialized production of arms to surge, the proportion rose to 31 percent, but not until the Civil War, he argued, did gun culture truly overtake the nation. Gun culture in America was rooted, it seemed, in capitalism rather than the Constitution.

Academic reviewers were predictably ecstatic about the implications for Second Amendment–based arguments that grounded gun ownership and its alleged constitutional sanction in the culture of the Revolutionary generation, and the NRA was just as predictably furious, with Charlton Heston himself entering the fray to denounce the book and its author. Wishful thinking and wagon-circling on the part of academics may have delayed serious examination of Bellesiles's sources and methods, but eventually specialists scrutinized his numerical tables and raised serious issues in a forum published in a leading journal in 2002: the crucial table providing the low percentage for the eighteenth century, for instance, did not indicate

59. The following account is based on Peter Charles Hoffer, *Past Imperfect: Facts, Fictions, Fraud—American History from Bancroft and Parkman to Ambrose, Bellesiles, Ellis and Goodwin* (New York: Public Affairs, 2004), chapter 5, and Jon Wiener, *Historians in Trouble: Plagiarism, Fraud and Politics in the Ivory Tower* (New York: New Press, 2005), chapter 4. Wiener's very partisan book argues that cases of academic fraud emerge mainly when historians are targeted by right-wing political interests and media, and that Bellesiles's errors were not all that egregious. The committee hired by Emory that issued the damning 2002 report, however, was made up of three liberal academics.

the base number of cases, the percentage computations seemed to be faulty, and there was troubling vagueness in the identification of actual counties where records were consulted.[60] On the defensive, Bellesiles piled up excuses: he had not kept a log of his travels to archives, the yellow legal pads where he noted his findings were destroyed in an office flood, and in any case, he protested, his argument rested on far more than those tables. In the end, an outside committee hired by Bellesiles's own department found, after a three-month investigation, evidence of serious professional violations in the conduct of his research, including outright falsification. Within a year Bellesiles resigned his tenured position, his prize was rescinded, and his publisher discontinued printing the book.

The Bellesiles case caused huge embarrassment—all manner of presses, reviewers, and academic committees emerged with egg on their faces—and most professors were chagrined that the outcome played into the hands of the gun lobby. But once Bellesiles's guilt in playing fast and loose with his sources had been established, the case was not especially divisive as he found no prominent defenders.[61] Even less divisive is what many consider the ultimate instance of the dishonestly tendentious manipulation of sources, Holocaust denial. Historians of modern Germany and others refuse as a rule to engage in debates with Holocaust deniers both on the moral grounds that doing so would publicize the deniers' positions and grant them spurious legitimacy, and on the intellectual grounds that it would be a waste of time and energy to go after propositions so far outside the pale of sound scholarly knowledge: would scientists spend time, they ask, arguing with someone who claims that the earth is flat? A debate of sorts was forced upon the public in the late 1990s, however, when a prominent Holocaust denier named David Irving took historian Deborah Lipstadt to court in London, charging that she had defamed him in a book she wrote chronicling the history of those who dispute the Final Solution. Irving in the end lost his suit, but one of the experts called upon for the trial was Richard Evans, who subsequently wrote a book systematically demolishing Irving's work. Evans overcame his field's reluctance to engage with an

60. Hoffer, *Past Imperfect*, 146–51.

61. Jon Wiener, however, argues that Bellesiles was unfairly targeted for "errors in a tiny portion of the documentation," and writes that several prominent historians whom he names agreed with this assessment in phone conversations. Wiener, *Historians in Trouble*, 91–93.

abhorrent thesis to do the hard and dispiriting work of demonstrating that Irving's claims were based on research rife with tendentious selections, misrepresentations of documents, and deliberate omissions.[62]

It is easy for professional historians and others to unite in their rejection of the clearly fraudulent manipulation or invention of sources, especially in the case of Holocaust denial, when dishonesty is put in the service of a widely reviled agenda. But the lines between tendentiousness, carelessness, and dishonesty can be a lot harder to draw, as the controversial and wrenching case of a young academic named David Abraham demonstrated in the mid-1980s.[63] Abraham, a junior faculty member at Princeton, published a book in 1981 about the relation between the German business community and the rise of the Nazis, *The Collapse of the Weimar Republic*. This specialized study presented a rather abstract Marxian argument about systemic strains on the political economy of Germany in the 1920s and 1930s, but it was published by a major press and favorably reviewed. The higher administration at Princeton declined to award Abraham tenure, despite his department's support, but his future on the job market looked good.

Around the time of his tenure denial, however, Abraham became the target of attacks by two senior historians in his field, Henry Turner at Yale and Gerald Feldman at Berkeley. Abraham had posited the existence of an objective convergence of interests between German big business and the Nazis; Turner had been laboring for years at his own research, which argued, roughly speaking, the opposite. Scrutinizing Abraham's book, Turner embarked on a campaign of letter-writing to the *American Historical Review* and to every major historian in the field in America and Europe, claiming that Abraham's arguments were based on fraudulent research, including the outright fabrication of nonexistent documents. When Abraham went on the job market and was invited to interview at leading universities, Turner's ally Feldman contacted department heads and deans to warn them against hiring a scholar who had distorted and invented sources. Many people found Turner and Feldman's tactics objectionable—why not critique the author in a published review instead of going after him in private letters and calls?—but the campaign worked, as universities wary of courting

62. Richard J. Evans, *Lying about Hitler: History, the Holocaust, and the David Irving Trial* (New York: Basic Books, 2001).
63. My account of the Abraham affair is based on Novick, *That Noble Dream*, 612–21, and Wiener, *Historians in Trouble*, chapter 5.

scandal declined to offer Abraham a position. The unfolding saga of alleged scholarly fraud and nasty academic politics involving some of the nation's most prominent universities was widely reported in the national press.

The problem for Abraham was that, as he himself admitted, he had indeed been guilty of some rather egregious carelessness; a return visit to the archives in the wake of the critiques revealed that he had misdated at least one document, misidentified the author and recipient of a report, and, most seriously, on several occasions presented as direct quotes from the sources what were actually his paraphrases, restatements that happened to support his argument. He called his own errors "inexcusable" but denied that he had deliberately invented any documents, and offered to correct the mistakes in a future edition. Abraham's many defenders agreed that he had been sloppy in his research but maintained that his errors did not invalidate his overall argument; some made the point that no historian's footnotes would survive the sort of hostile scrutiny Abraham's had been subjected to, in his case apparently motivated by a combination of professional rivalry and ideological animus. In the end Abraham's foes prevailed: unable to find a position in history, he changed careers, eventually achieving success as a law professor. Causing considerable soul-searching and bitterness, the Abraham case brought up for historians a host of difficult issues: who should blow the whistle on what they deem to be unacceptable research, and how should they do it? How many mistakes does it take to invalidate a body of research? Above all, the case made all but the most dogmatic believers in the "sovereignty of the sources" ponder what happens in the process of selecting historical material to construct an original argument. Short of actual fraud, how can any historian know where and how to draw the line between interpretation and distortion? What counts as a legitimate, admirable feat of historical imagination, and at what point does a historian cross the line?

The most famous modern debate about historical imagination, invention, and their limits took place some twenty-five years ago around a book written by Natalie Davis, a much admired staple of the historical canon still widely read and frequently assigned in classes. *The Return of Martin Guerre* (1983) is Davis's account of a legal case that unfolded in deep rural France in the 1560s and has the potential to shed light on the lives of early modern peasants—in short, a classic microhistory. The story is of an imposture, a sixteenth-century identity theft that took place in the village of Artigat in southwestern France. Martin Guerre and Bertrande de Rols, the children of two prosperous peasant families, were married to each other in their early teens, though it took them eight years to consummate their union and produce a child. In his early twenties Martin stole money from his father and ran away. Eight years later, he reappeared in Artigat. His sisters greeted him warmly, his wife more reluctantly, but on the whole the community welcomed back a man who was in fact not Martin at all but an impostor named Arnaud du Tilh, eager to take up the marriage and property of the missing Martin Guerre. (The new Martin convinced people, including at least initially Bertrande, of his legitimacy by seeming to know all manner of specific details about everyone in the village.) Four years later, however, in the wake of a dispute over property, Martin's increasingly suspicious uncle became convinced that his alleged nephew was a fraud and had him arrested in Bertrande's name. Arnaud maintained that he was indeed Martin and two trials ensued, with villagers divided and the outcome hanging in the balance until, in a dramatic development, the real Martin Guerre, limping on a wooden leg, suddenly appeared in the courthouse. Arnaud was thus decisively exposed and sentenced to die by hanging; he was executed in the village after apologizing to everyone including Bertrande. The tale was many times retold over the centuries as a parable of the astonishing ways in which people's sense of what they know and see can be deceived by a clever manipulator.

The story is an excellent one, but direct sources are scant, consisting mainly in a couple of detailed accounts published after the fact by officials in the court cases, the trial records themselves having disappeared. Davis supplements these by combing through the village legal records for details about the families involved, and reconstructs much of the texture of life in Artigat—inheritance practices, customs, the details of daily life—laterally from her research on various villages in the region. She announces in the opening pages, "What I offer you here is in part my invention, but held tightly in check by the voices of the past."[64] The gracefully written book offers food for thought on many matters, but one of its central points is a reading of the behavior of Martin's wife Bertrande that grants her considerable agency. In contrast to previous accounts, which held that the young abandoned wife had been fooled along with everyone else, Davis posits that Betrande must have known that the man who came back was

64. Natalie Zemon Davis, *The Return of Martin Guerre* (Cambridge, MA: Harvard University Press, 1983), 5.

not Martin. Bertrande was no dupe, Davis proposes, but a shrewd woman with her own needs who understood the social advantages of reclaiming a spouse and probably came to love the clever and attractive man who took Martin's place.

Much of the book's enduring power comes from Davis's vividly rendered recreations of how the different actors in her story "must have" experienced things. Because his parents immigrated from the Basque country, "perhaps it was not so easy for the boy from Labourd to grow up in Artigat. There were languages to sort out . . . and surely he was teased because of his name, Martin." Struggling under the burden of a new child, the shame of his years of impotence, and his domineering father, Martin surely "dreamed of a life beyond the confines of fields of millet, of tileworks, properties, marriages." As for the very young Bertrande, right after her marriage to Martin, "she might not have put it in these words, but it seems clear that for a while she was relieved that they could not have intercourse." Years later, when she was older and a "new Martin" more to her liking had appeared in her life, she tacitly helped him to impersonate her husband. In the course of frequent conversations, "so one must surmise, they decided to make the invented marriage last."[65] All of these hypotheticals about motivation are predicated on contextual information, since no sources allow us direct contact with the minds of these illiterate peasants.

Davis's informed speculations did not sit well with another scholar in the field, Robert Finlay, who attacked her account in a high-profile article in the *American Historical Review*.[66] Finlay had no patience for Davis's "perhapses" and "may have beens," and he objected strongly to her rereading of the story in a way that, to his mind, takes unjustified liberties with the historical record. Central to his critique is Davis's portrayal of Bertrande as the impostor Arnaud's accomplice, motivated both by a growing affection for her new mate and a shrewd calculation that having a husband served her interests. (Davis also points to the inroads the Reformation was making in the area to propose that Bertrande and Arnaud may have dealt with the guilt over their knowing adultery by viewing their union as a nonsacramental Protestant marriage.) Finlay maintains that none of the sources state or imply a double game on Bertrande's part, and he accuses Davis of

65. Ibid., 19, 22, 44, 46.

66. Robert Finlay, "The Refashioning of Martin Guerre," *American Historical Review* 93 (June 1988): 553–71.

distorting the record to impose a feminist agenda on the story and tug it in the direction of a "historical romance." Her portrait of Bertrande, he writes, "seems to be far more a product of invention than of historical reconstruction."[67]

Finlay's piece was published as half of a forum, with Davis offering in the same issue of the journal a lengthy and spirited rebuttal, buttressed by far more documentary evidence for her arguments than in the original book.[68] Both *The Return of Martin Guerre* and the Finlay-Davis debate raise fascinating historical questions—how, for instance, could somebody's identity be ascertained after a lapse of years in a society without mirrors, photographs, and other trappings of modern selfhood? Would the impostor's sexual behavior have given the game away to Bertrande, as Davis believes, or as Finlay maintains, been irrelevant in an environment where people had sex mostly clothed, surreptitiously, in dark and freezing rooms? At the core of the matter, however, the dispute between Davis and Finlay comes down to their very different perspectives on the role of imagination in history. "In historical writing," asks Finlay, "where does reconstruction stop and invention begin?" In his view, none of Davis's central points about Bertrande's role and the nature of her relationship with Arnaud are in the records, and therefore she has crossed the line into writing fiction. Yes, he admits, historians often engage in "perhapses" and "may have beens" when the sources are missing, but in the end speculation "is supposed to give way before the sovereignty of the sources, the tribunal of the documents."[69] Davis retorts by describing Finlay's stance as narrow-minded traditionalism: the supposedly "sovereign" documents don't say just one thing, she insists. The main source about the case, the judge Jean de Coras's account of the trial, leaves plenty of room for different readings, and hers is but one way of putting together a complex, many-layered story. When she wrote that her version was "in part my invention," she explains, "I opened the gap between what I hope to accomplish and what the sources could yield with absolute certainty; by my last page, the reader has had ample encouragement to think about other ways of making sense of the evidence."[70] In sum, to Finlay,

67. Ibid., 556–57, 562–66, 570.
68. Natalie Zemon Davis, "On the Lame," *American Historical Review* 93 (June 1988): 572–603.
69. Finlay, "Refashioning," 569, 571.
70. Davis, "On the Lame," 599.

who accuses her of imposing her own preferred story on the sources, Davis replies that the documents are by nature ambiguous, allowing for an endless range of readings; hers is but one of the many stories the sources can tell. One historian's lapse into "fiction" is another one's act of sympathetic and responsible imagination.

The controversies surrounding postmodernism have all but disappeared today in the historical profession. On the one hand, the innovative perspectives and methods of the 1980s and 1990s (cultural constructionism, attention to texts and narratives) have become second nature to most historians; on the other, few people nowadays want to expend time and energy fighting over unanswerable questions about whether "the past" can be proven to have happened. But where questions about objectivity, invention, and the representation of the past are concerned, the debates of the last few decades have changed the nature of the discipline. It is impossible to imagine going back to a time when historians imagined that their task involved bowing down before "the sovereignty of the sources."

Narrative and imagination are probably more central to history as a discipline than to any other field of inquiry since, as we have seen, "doing history" consists above all in the creation of compelling, fact-based stories. The business of researching and writing the past is a paradoxical one. On the one hand, historians base their professional identities on meticulous, exhaustive research into the facts of the past; on the other, the line between terrific history and superior historical fiction can often seem vanishingly thin. Garrett Mattingly's *The Armada*, first published in 1959, and considered a classic of historical writing, contains many a passage, devoid of footnotes, such as the following: "When her dwarf cried out from the window that the duke of Guise was approaching, the queen told him he was mad to say so, and when her own eyes identified the affable man on horseback in the midst of his delirious admirers, her lips were drained of color and her voice choked and trembled."[71] How, one may wonder, is this different from the acclaimed novels of Hilary Mantel, set at the court of Henry VIII? In one scene from Mantel's *Bring Up the Bodies*, a messenger gives Jane Seymour a love letter and a bag of money from the married king who is wooing her; Jane returns both to the king's emissary, kissing the letter but leaving it unopened. Mantel, who takes pride in her

71. Garrett Mattingly, *The Armada* (Boston: Houghton Mifflin, 1959), 227.

scrupulous research, drew the scene from a contemporary ambassador's correspondence.[72] As William Cronon has argued, the distinction between history and scrupulously documented historical fiction (Mantel never, she says, includes historical fabrications in her novels) is not that one is true and the other untrue, or that historical novelists do not have to follow any rules. The biggest difference is that writers of historical fiction have license to recreate areas of the past inaccessible to historians, most typically the inner lives of characters and the informal conversations of everyday life. As historians, writes Cronon, "our rules of evidence build a high wall between us and the inner emotional lives of the human beings about whom we write."[73]

But like novelists, historians are constantly making choices that dictate the nature of their stories. The history of the American Great Plains in the nineteenth century has been told as a tale of progress, tragedy, or triumph over adversity. It has featured pioneers, New Deal federal planners, and nature itself as heroes, and Native Americans, the state, and capitalism as villains. Time frames—where one chooses to begin and end—have dictated narrative shape and tone. Where the descendants of European pioneers chronicle feats of courage and endurance that opened up an expansive future, a Crow Indian chief, Plenty Coups, ended his 1930 autobiography, set in the same place and time, with these words: "When the buffalo went away the hearts of my people fell to the ground, and they could not lift them up again. After this nothing happened."[74] History is always someone's story, layered over and likely at odds with someone else's: to recognize this does not make our chronicles of the past less reliable, but more varied, deeper, and more truthful.

72. Larissa MacFarquhar, "The Dead Are Real: Hilary Mantel's Imagination," *New Yorker*, October 12, 2012; http://www.newyorker.com/magazine/2012/10/15/the-dead-are-real (accessed February 2, 2016).

73. William Cronon, "Storytelling," *American Historical Review* 118, no. 1 (February 2013): 11.

74. William Cronon, "A Place for Stories: Nature, History, and Narrative," *Journal of American History* 78, no. 4 (March 1992): 1347–76, quote p. 1366.

CONCLUSION

In the United States the single most frequently quoted line about history's value is the Spanish-American writer George Santayana's "Those who cannot remember the past are condemned to repeat it," a superficially appealing but infinitely problematic aphorism. As we saw at the outset, remembering the past and applying its teachings to the present has often had catastrophic consequences. The French found this out in 1940 after their terrible experiences in 1914–1918 led them to prepare for a new round of sedentary trench warfare by erecting the massive defense system known as the Maginot Line along their eastern border, only to be quickly outflanked by fast-moving German tanks and troops surging north of the line: "lessons" from the previous war led to a rapid and humiliating defeat.

In many situations, to be sure, those who actively seek to forget the past are condemned not to repeat it but to create brand new forms of mayhem and terror, as has been the case every time a modern revolution, from France to Russia to China, has repudiated the old days and old ways at the cost of thousands or millions of lives. But reverence for the past can be just as dangerous: think of the masses of people slaughtered by religious zealots nostalgic for the One True Church, by racists yearning for the gallant South of old, by Nazis bent on restoring the glory of the German Reich. Those who choose to remember an idealized, one-sided version of the past can do as much damage as revolutionaries who try to stamp it out.

Throughout the chapters of this book, I have taken the position, held by most historians today, that the study of history does not teach "lessons" in the form of neatly packaged axioms applicable to present and future circumstances. Not only does no historical situation entirely replicate any previous one, but in many instances it is unclear which lesson best applies: during America's Vietnam war, conservatives drew on the example of Europe in the 1930s to make the case for standing up militarily to the North Vietnamese dictatorship while liberals argued for withdrawal by pointing out that French imperialists had been routed and driven out of Vietnam in the 1950s by Communist insurgents.[1] But while we may have rational doubts about the concept of historical lessons, many of us instinctively seek them out, especially in the case of more recent and highly traumatic events. In no instance is this more true than for the Nazis' mass murders: a Google search for "lessons of the Holocaust" yields hundreds of thousands of hits. This should not surprise us: when faced with man-made horror on such a scale, we feel a need to find some useful or redemptive "take-away" as protection against nihilistic despair.[2] Most historians who study the Holocaust professionally, however, are as skeptical as their colleagues in other fields that the past can provide us with neat templates for the future: "never again" may be an effective call to arms when populations are threatened with persecution, but in actuality the same thing never happens twice. Awareness of the Holocaust and other large-scale historical crimes certainly sharpens our ethical sensibility and puts us on alert for similar happenings, but no future situation will ever be like Germany's in the 1930s. Commemoration is crucially important, of course but, as a leading Holocaust historian concludes, so is keeping the past alive by constantly reframing and rewriting history: "This means disputation and disagreement, but also research, new questions, and new ways of looking at old problems."[3]

In order for the past to serve its best purpose we must not freeze it in place, we must argue about it. Accordingly, the chapters of this book are framed as questions, a choice that no doubt reflect the author's skeptical temperament, but even more so her conviction that "history" becomes useless or boring at best, and dangerous at worst, when it jells into consensual orthodoxy of any sort. For the same reason, the material in this book is not presented as a progression of approaches, from Homer and Herodotus to today's latest trend: history writing does not get better and better but shifts and changes in response to the needs and curiosities of the present day. Innovations and new perspectives keep the study of the past fresh and interesting, but that does not mean that we should jettison certain areas or approaches as old-fashioned or irrelevant. As Lynn Hunt has pointed out, no field of history should be cast aside just because it is no longer "hot," since we cannot know how and when neglected aspects of the past may re-

1. Michael R. Marrus, *Lessons of the Holocaust* (Toronto: University of Toronto Press, 2016), 37–38.

2. Ibid., 7–9.

3. Ibid., 171.

gain importance. A century or so ago the history of ancient Rome was seen as a crucial guide to political understanding; it no longer is, but who can tell when it might become useful again?[4] Few people would have predicted three or four decades ago the currently central place of Islamic history and culture in the concerns of Western nations; meanwhile, the Russian past is a less urgent concern to Americans than it was forty years ago, though it may well become crucial again. While it is easy enough to identify current trends in academic history—many people would name global, transnational, and environmental history as making up today's cutting edge—it is anyone's guess how long these will shape the discipline or what might succeed them.

But if the future of the discipline is unknowable, its enduring importance is not in dispute. Why study history? The simplest response is that history answers questions that other disciplines cannot. Why, for instance, are African-Americans in the United States today so shockingly disadvantaged in every possible respect, from income to education, health, life expectancy, and rates of incarceration, when the last vestiges of formal discrimination were done away with half a century ago? Unless one subscribes to racist beliefs, the only way to answer that question is historically, via the long and painful narrative that goes from transportation and slavery to today via Reconstruction, Jim Crow laws, and an accumulation, over decades, of inequities in urban policies, electoral access, and the judicial system. Any number of other inequalities that persist in modern, democratic, industrialized societies—between men and women, rich and poor individuals, groups and nations—can only be explained historically. Social scientists can diagnose today's problems and offer policy prescriptions, but only historians can explain such issues in depth by showing how they came about. Historians cannot give you answers, but looking at problems over time can teach you how to ask the right questions.

Temporal perspective matters because more than any other discipline, history plays out in public life. Another central aim of this book has been to emphasize the many ways in which history is a hybrid field: highly specialized and unspecialized; factual and imaginative; academic and popular. Recreating and interpreting the past takes place in scholarly monographs and specialized journals, but also in best-selling popular books, television documentaries, and historical museums, with many individuals bridging

4. Interview with Lynn Hunt, "The Future of History," https://www.youtube.com/watch?v=amkZ5TkxwY8 (accessed November 5, 2016).

those two worlds. This book has tried to suggest why history enjoys such broad appeal outside of the academy: not only because the past matters deeply to individuals, communities and nations, but also because the discipline privileges the vivid realities of specific times and places over theoretical abstraction. The field's strength can also be its weakness, however, as historical writing sometimes turns too descriptive and empirical, devoted to information for its own sake. Academic and popular controversies over the past serve an important role in reminding historians who love the minutiae of their archives too much of what is really at stake.

This book has emphasized, in sum, the two forces that keep history alive as a discipline: its role as a bridge between the academy and the public world, and the controversies it generates within history departments, schools, museums, and even governing institutions. Doomsayers are always predicting a decline of interest in history, but there is little to suggest that any such thing is taking place. There will be no grand pronouncements, therefore, at the end of this book about the Lessons, Laws, Crisis, or Future of History. This volume will have served its purpose if the questions and controversies covered in the preceding chapters sharpen readers' appetite and skills for learning and arguing about the past in all its forms.

ACKNOWLEDGMENTS

If this book is evidence of a crime, my colleagues' fingerprints are all over it, with some of the most egregious culprits mentioned by name below. Over several decades teaching in the Northwestern University History Department, I have had the good fortune to interact daily with a slowly revolving cast of remarkable scholars from whom I have learned most of what I know about history. This work reflects years of lively, at times contentious, always productive exchanges about the discipline we share: sometimes it does take a village to write a book. The blessings of my work environment were enhanced a few years ago when I became the director of Northwestern's Nicholas D. Chabraja Center for Historical Studies. In that capacity I have been exposed to the work (and good company) of some of the best historians working today. Careful sleuths will notice a suspicious overlap between many of the authors cited in my chapters and the center's recent roster of distinguished speakers. Thanks are therefore due to those who made the Chabraja Center come into existence and run smoothly: Nick and Eleanor Chabraja, Tim Breen, and Elzbieta Foeller-Pituch.

In the initial stages of sorting out the book's structure, many people read and reacted helpfully to various drafts of my outline, including Barbara Bloom-Genevaz, Dina Copelman, Susan Herbst, Yohanan Petrovsky-Shtern, Mike Sherry, Sean Shesgreen, Debora Silverman, faculty at Vassar College and Queen Mary University London, and several anonymous readers for the University of Chicago Press. Nearly every time I started a new chapter or section I found myself begging for help from people who actually knew something about the subject. Among the many colleagues who kindly guided me around their fields are Ken Alder, Lina Britto, Vincent Brown, Gerry Cadava, Peter Hayes, Donna Harsch, Chris Hodson, Forrest Hylton, Joel Mokyr, Susan Pearson, Dylan Penningroth, Indira Raman, Mike Sherry, and Scott Sowerby. Naturally, they bear no responsibility for the ways in which I have bowdlerized their various specialties. I am very grateful to those who responded generously to requests for readings of various chapters. Peter Gordon and Keith Woodhouse gave me advice on chapter 3, and Amy Stanley graciously read a big chunk of the work in progress to try to help me mitigate some of its Eurocentrism. My deepest thanks go to four readers who reviewed the whole manuscript toward the end of the process and gave me the benefit of careful and incisive readings: my colleagues Deborah Cohen, Jon Glassman, and Daniel Immerwahr, and an outstanding history major, Christopher Burrows.

Since this book is intended mostly for the classroom, the contributions of students to whom I've been fortunate to present my outline and ideas have been especially valuable. Graham Horn gave me a useful early response to the project and helped with some initial research. Graduate students at Northwestern shared their reactions to the outline in the context of a Teagle Seminar led by Daniel Immerwahr; their counterparts at Queen Mary University London did the same in a session organized by Miri Rubin; and, thanks to an invitation from Mita Choudhury and Lydia Murdoch, a class of impressively articulate history majors at Vassar College prodded me to, among other things, rethink the title and content of chapter 4.

It had been a pleasure to work with my editor, Karen Merikangas Darling, who took a chance on the project when it came to her over the transom and has been ideally flexible and supportive at every stage of the way. Joel Score edited the manuscript with consummate skill and care. Sean Shesgreen encouraged me as always to trust my instincts, provided a one-man cheering section, and read and edited the manuscript from first to last page on the day I finished it. Expressions of thanks to him are inadequate, as they are to Juliette for her love and infectious energy. The book is dedicated to the many graduate students at Northwestern who have taken my seminar on cultural history. Their smart, pointed reactions forced me year after year to clarify my thoughts in order to keep up with them. This volume is the result.

INDEX

Abensour, Léon, 34
Abraham, David, 228–29
Abramitzky, Ram, 19
academic fraud, 226n59
academic history, 125–26, 155–57, 237
Adams, Henry, 122
Adams, John, 130
Afghanistan, 50
Africa, 8–9, 46, 53–54, 73, 77–81, 99–100, 113, 152–53, 169n21, 207; naturalizing of, as unit, 48; and Santería, 58–59; and Voodoo, 58–59
African Americans, 44, 166, 191, 204–5, 217, 237; black culture, 64; and dozens, 32
agency, 33, 67; and identity, 53; and women, 34
Age of Homespun, The (Ulrich), 105
Air Force Association, 135
Akan people, 121
Alexander II, 165
Alexander the Great, 10, 54
Alexandra (empress), 161
Algeria, 46
Algonquian, 105
Álvares, Domingos, 62–63, 180–81
"America Made Easy" (Wilentz), 130
American Historical Association, 21, 60, 66, 123–24, 124n12, 132, 200, 203
American Historical Review (journal), 122, 157, 228, 231

American Revolution, 12–13, 47, 104, 121
Amnesty International, 50
Anderson, Benedict, 51–52, 81, 108
Anglo-Saxonism, 123
Angola, 46
Ankersmit, Frank, 223n54
Annales of Economic and Social History (journal), 168–69
Annales School, 26, 168, 169n21, 171, 187, 194; big history, tendency toward, 170; cultural studies, 170; total history, ideal of, 169
Annals, The (Tacitus), 120
anthropology, 169–70, 185, 202. *See also* cultural anthropology; structural anthropology
anti-Semitism, 140–42
Antony, Marc, 171–72
Appleby, Joyce, 224–25
archaeology, 101
Archaeology of Knowledge, The (Foucault), 190
Arendt, Hannah, and "banality of evil," 138–40
Argentina, 114
Aristotle, 13, 86, 92n16, 94
Armada, The (Mattingly), 233
Arming America (Bellesiles), 226
Asia, 8–9, 53–54, 73, 75–76, 78–79, 81, 99–100
Athenian empire, 159
Atlantic history, 60–61; as individual biography, 62–63

changing, 6–7; consumer goods, 104–5; as controversial, 7–9; curricula, battles over, 5–6; discipline of, 1; eclecticism of, 2, 6; elitism of, 123; empiricism of, 4; Eurasian societies, dominance of, 112–13; as Eurocentric, 81–82, 84, 174, 208; Eurocentrism, challenges to, 116, 177; evocative writing, 4; fact and fiction, 199; fictional nature of, 214; fights over, 5; of food, 106; formal training, 2; "great men" of, 10–11; as heritage industry, 130–31; historical fiction, distinction from, 234; historical imagination, 229, 233; historical objectivity, 201; history departments, minorities in, 205n12; history departments, women in, 204n10; human identity, 83; as hybrid field, 4, 237; individual "genius," 12; and induction, 162; interpretation and distortion, line between, 229–32; and invention, 7; laws of, 161; as less theory-driven, 3; makers of, 10; male elites, as default setting, 83–85, 116; mass-market authors of, 125; meaning versus causality, 158; meaning, creation of, 83; memory, study of, 53–54; men of letters, 119; military heroics, 54; narrative, commitment to, 4; narrative and imagination, as central to, 233; national focus for, 45–50, 65; nationhood, denaturalizing of, 51; nonhuman agency in, 114; objective truth, pursuit of, 123; and objectivity, 7; and objects, 106; objects and nature, 108; oral history, 154, 156; ordinary people, 15–17; and politics, 12–13, 15; popular following of, 118; in public arena, 138; public

controversy in, 6; public forms of, 155; public sphere, conspicuousness of in, 4–5; regional history, 49; of religion, 116–17; research process, learning of, 2–3; skills, requirement of, 4; as social science, 17; social temporality, theory of, 4; and sources, 146–49, 153–54, 233; sources, manipulation of, 227; stadial history, 160; structural dysfunction, 175; structures and events, 175–77; technical requirements of, 2; temporality and casualty, 4; as university-based, 121–23; and war, 11; Western academics, asymmetrical ignorance of, 78; Western culture, 75, 77; what of, 83–84, 111; where of, 45, 81–82, 116; who of, 82–84, 116

History Channel, 137
History of England from the Accession of James the Second (Macaulay), 14–15, 47
History of the English-Speaking Peoples (Churchill), 120
History of the French Revolution (Michelet), 47
History of the United States (Bancroft), 47
Hitchcock, Alfred, 30
Hitler, Adolf, 10, 12, 69, 71, 146; and Jews, 70
Hitler's Willing Executioners (Goldhagen), 138, 140, 142, 142n50
Hobbes, Thomas, 87–89, 97; absolute rule, defense of, 96
Hobsbawm, Eric, 22
Ho Chi Minh, 13
Hochschild, Adam, 118, 127–28, 136
Holland, 58, 102. *See also* Netherlands
Holmes, H. H., 126
Holmes, Oliver Wendell, 202

transnational history, 82, 177–78,
237
Trapp, Wilhelm, 139
Trevelyan, George Macaulay, 14–15,
15n7, 17, 22, 26
Trojan Wars, 158–59
Trouillot, Michel-Rolph, 149–52
Truman, Harry S, 130
Tubman, Harriet, 5
Tuchman, Barbara, 124
Turner, Frederick Jackson, 66–67, 69,
109
Turner, Henry, 228–29

Ukraine, 69–70
Ulrich, Laurel Thatcher, 105–6, 147–
48, 150, 181
Unbroken (Hillenbrand), 126
Unfree Labor (Kolchin), 165
United Nations, 50, 145
United States, 8, 10, 17, 19, 22, 27,
33, 43, 46, 48–50, 52, 54–55, 58,
61, 63, 73, 75, 77–78, 86, 98, 104,
106, 110, 122–23, 134–35, 137,
142, 145, 157, 163–66, 186, 191,
200–202, 205–6, 217–19, 228,
235, 237; American exceptionalism, 66; black cultural traditions
in, 64; borderlands in, 66; cultural
core of, 66; frontier in, 66; gun
culture in, 226; nature, conquest
of, 109; westward expansion, 66
University of Berlin, 121
urbanization, 79

Vega, Garcilaso de la, 207
Vico, Giambattista, 160, 207
Victoria (queen), 52, 126
Vietnam, 50
Vietnam War, 55, 203, 235–36
Vietnam War Memorial, 55

Vikings, 113
Virginia, 61, 71
Voltaire, 90, 119–22, 143–44

Wales, Rebecca riots in, 29. *See also*
Great Britain
Walkowitz, Judith, 189–90, 212–13
Wallerstein, Immanuel, 74–75, 77
War and Peace (Tolstoy), 169
Washington, George, 5, 125
WASPs, 201
Watergate scandal, 203
Wealth and Poverty of Nations, The
(Landes), 75
Webb, Beatrice, 22
Webb, Sidney, 22
Weber, Eugen, 65
Weber, Max, 1, 186n62
Wedgwood, Josiah, 103
West, The (film), 129
West Africa, 20, 121
Westfall, Richard, 99
What Is History? (Carr), 157–58,
171
White, Hayden, 214–15, 215n33, 216,
221
White, Richard, 67–69
whiteness, 218–19
Wiener, Jon, 226n59, 227n61
Wilentz, Sean, 130
William of Orange, 15
Williams, George Washington, 127
Wilson, Woodrow, 55
Winnicott, J. D., 204
Wollstonecraft, Mary, 91
women's history, 34, 41, 44, 102, 116,
216; big events, challenging of, 36–
37; gender history, 39; and "her-
story," 36; invisibility of, 37–38;
as scholarly ghetto, 35. *See also*
gender history